CHAMPIONS
OF THE
OCTAGON

Praise for Fiaz Rafiq

"An impressive collection of first-hand testimony from friends, rivals, contemporaries, scribes and his closest family illuminate Ali for a new generation while rekindling the memories for those that have always known he was The Greatest."
—*New York Daily News* (for *Muhammad Ali: The Life of a Legend*)

"Few can deliver the details and perspective that Fiaz Rafiq achieves in his exhaustive oral history covering all aspects of Schwarzenegger's epic life and career. This is the hard work of a dogged professional journalist."
—Alex Ben Block, former editor of the *Hollywood Reporter*
(for *Arnold Schwarzenneger: The Life of a Legend*)

"Yet despite the sheer volume of Ali books, Rahaman Ali (and Fiaz Rafiq) succeeds in telling us things we didn't already know about his brother, a man the *Guinness Book of World Records* decided in 1980 had surpassed Lincoln, Napoleon and Jesus Christ to become the most written-about figure in human history."
—*USA Today* (for *My Brother, Muhammad Ali: The Definitive Biography*)

"There have been hundreds of books on Bruce Lee since his shocking death in 1973, including my own. However, Fiaz Rafiq's oral history still punches and kicks into new territory."
—Alex Ben Block, former editor of the *Hollywood Reporter*
(for *Bruce Lee: The Life of a Legend*)

"An inspiring story of a kid who discovered his path in life—and success—through his passion for Bruce Lee and the martial arts. Highly recommended."
—Matthew Polly, *New York Times* bestselling author
(for *To the Top*, a.k.a. *Fighting Against the Odds*)

CHAMPIONS
OF THE
OCTAGON

One-on-One with
MMA and UFC Greats

FIAZ RAFIQ

**Forewords by Royce Gracie
and Michael Bisping**

SPORTS
PUBLISHING

Copyright © 2022 by Fiaz Rafiq

All rights reserved. No part of this book may be reproduced in any manner without the express written consent of the publisher, except in the case of brief excerpts in critical reviews or articles. All inquiries should be addressed to Sports Publishing, 307 West 36th Street, 11th Floor, New York, NY 10018.

Sports Publishing books may be purchased in bulk at special discounts for sales promotion, corporate gifts, fund-raising, or educational purposes. Special editions can also be created to specifications. For details, contact the Special Sales Department, Sports Publishing, 307 West 36th Street, 11th Floor, New York, NY 10018 or sportspubbooks@skyhorsepublishing.com.

Sports Publishing® is a registered trademark of Skyhorse Publishing, Inc.®, a Delaware corporation.

Visit our website at www.sportspubbooks.com.

10 9 8 7 6 5 4 3 2 1

Library of Congress Cataloging-in-Publication Data is available on file.

Jacket design by David Ter-Avanesyan
Jacket photographs: Getty Images

Print ISBN: 978-1-68358-442-1
Ebook ISBN: 978-1-68358-443-8

Printed in the United States of America

Dedicated to Rorion Gracie, the creator of the UFC.
If it was not for Rorion, the sport of MMA and the stars and champions
the UFC has created would not exist. Now it's a worldwide phenomenon,
and one of the most fascinating sports in the world.

CONTENTS

FOREWORD

MY BROTHER BROUGHT the UFC concept from Brazil to the United States. My father had been fighting in no-holds-barred competitions for a long time in Brazil. People in America, and all over the world, have always been curious to see who the best fighter in the world is. There was no such thing as an MMA fighter—this did not exist. It all started when the UFC was introduced. From the beginning it was one man representing his martial arts style against another. Today, everybody is an all-round fighter. You see strikers practicing grappling and the grapplers implementing striking into their game. The sport of MMA has come a long way to get to where it is today. It's not something that suddenly cropped up yesterday. The sport is, no doubt, going to grow even further.

This book is a great concept. Fiaz has compiled a good book for anybody interested in knowing "who's who" in the sport, which includes both the early fighters and the new generation of fighters.

—Royce Gracie, three-time UFC champion and MMA legend

FOREWORD

OVER THE YEARS the sport of mixed martial arts (MMA)—in particular the Ultimate Fighting Championship (UFC)—has exploded from a cult following sport to a mainstream phenomenon, with all major forms of media covering the sport from newspapers, magazines, ESPN, TV, and the internet. This is the fastest growing sport in the world. The sport has helped transform martial artists and fighters from regular hardworking fighters in the martial arts to bona-fide celebrities and household names.

In the early years people didn't give the sport and the fighters the respect they deserved, often disregarding them as thugs. Common misconceptions were UFC fighters being perceived as someone straight from a barstool into a fight. Thankfully these days with the right exposure the sport has received, the world realizes these fighters are highly trained athletes and experts in several different styles of martial arts disciplines, and world-class athletes in their own rights. From my own personal experiences from being a normal working guy having worked average working-class jobs, *The Ultimate Fighter* series and the UFC has completely transformed mine and my family's life.

In *Champions of the Octagon*, you will get to experience a one-on-one conversation with the baddest fighters on the planet. Find out what makes the fighters tick. Find out some of the secrets from their careers. Hear the fighters discuss the highs and the lows of their careers, and find out what it takes to be an ultimate fighter. This book is compiled in a unique way and is definitely a first. In my opinion, for any combat sport or MMA fan this book is a must have. It gives you a true insight into the minds of your favorite fighters.

—Michael Bisping, former UFC middleweight champion

INTRODUCTION

WHEN THE FIRST UFC debuted on November 12, 1993, many people and critics were incensed to see two combatants pitted against each other in a cage like the gladiators of the past. There were no rules, protection, weight divisions or time limits. Not surprisingly this led to accusations of brutality, many comparing it to human cockfighting. This was when modern no-holds-barred emerged in popular culture in the West, which had been made famous by the Gracie family in Brazil decades earlier. After many years of struggle in USA, Rorion Gracie—the eldest of the famed Gracie brothers—rose from obscurity and managed to stage the first ever UFC tournament. It was an instant success. His younger sibling Royce would showcase the extremely effective Brazilian jiu-jitsu skills in the Octagon, beating bigger and stronger adversaries, in the process forever changing the way the world perceived fighting. This planted a seed, the beginning of the sport of MMA, which would take the world by storm and propel Gracie's creation to an elevated level for years to come.

It was inevitable the UFC organization would have to reform itself—it had no choice but to adapt to stricter rules. Indeed, athletic commission sanctioned rules. This was imperative for the brutal fight sport to survive and prosper in a civilized society. As a result of overall evolution, professional training camps, improved cutting-edge training methods and a better comprehension of the hybrid disciplines, the participants became well rounded. UFC went from a novelty spectacle to a worldwide phenomenon, ultimately surpassing boxing in America, becoming the most popular combat sport breaking the pay-per-view sport industry's all-time records. It created superstars who are idolized by their legions of fans. Today, the fighters are treated like royalty beyond the confines of the MMA sphere.

Greg Jackson, of Jackson's MMA camp in the state of New Mexico, is one of the most prominent coaches who have trained some of the elite UFC fighters. I spoke to him at length in the hope that he could debunk some of the myths surrounding the sport. He explained why fighters are, more or less, considered intellectuals, as well as being the toughest athletes in the world. "Absolutely, we are the hardest-working athletes," Jackson told me. "First and foremost, the important thing is there is an art in every single part of our game. You have to know the art of boxing, the art of kickboxing, wrestling, jiu-jitsu, ground and pound—which is an art in itself. There are so many different disciplines you have to be aware of, and you have to be an intellectual person to compete in this sport." To the casual observer, it might not always look that way, but once you come to understand and appreciate all the diverse pieces of the puzzle, the more beautiful it becomes. Indeed, physically an MMA fighter has to get in there and fight full-contact, that's an extremely tough environment to put your body into.

Can a street fighter, who has no formal MMA training, get into the Octagon and prevail? Can an untrained fighter survive against the athletes who have pushed their bodies to the limits, honed their skills and competed at the highest levels? "You can't play tennis three or four times as a kid and expect to play at Wimbledon—it doesn't work that way," Jackson proceeded to explain. "So, street fighters don't really mean anything because an MMA fighter would be fighting people who have not got a lot of experience. Like any sport, you can play soccer as a kid but it doesn't mean you're going to win the World Cup." It's a long process where dedication is a pre-requisite and you have to pay a lot of dues. As an untrained fighter, even if you get towards the top, eventually you'll be exposed to a lack of skills. Essentially, you can't just hop into a professional MMA arena; like every other sport you have to possess skills. "You know, soccer players run a lot, tennis players are explosive, but they're not getting someone punching them in the face for 15 minutes,"

Jackson added. "You have to have that physical and mental toughness that other sports don't."

On the other end of the ricketier scale, in the past it wasn't unusual to hear people make blunt comments comparing UFC fighters to some untrained bar brawlers. This, by and large, would be perceived as an extremely ignorant comment now. Those who are cognizant enough have sufficient cultural experience of martial arts, which involves a huge amount of discipline and artistry. Still, certain people find it difficult to align a trained skilled athlete to what they see as a brutal sport where you're striking an opponent on the ground, although it's a sentiment shared by very few now.

The UFC is professional in the way the organizers have put their brand forward. And Dana White, an ardent exponent and president of the UFC which is now worth over $7 billion—has done a tremendous job in his quest to make the UFC a household name beyond the confines of North America. If you watched some of the other promotions—mainly the smaller ones—when MMA was a novelty sport, you would quite easily be thinking it resembled human cockfighting. I'm not referring to the fighters themselves, but essentially about the way MMA was being represented by certain people. Still, it was few and far between. MMA fighters are very honorable—their behavior and respecting the opponent. It's a combination of chemical powers, courage combined with almost a code of honor and behavior of the competitors. Today, UFC fighters are seen as role models for kids.

There has been greater exposure with TV and pay-per-view ever since *The Ultimate Fighter* reality TV series—initially produced by Fox Sports and UFC—aired in January 2005. Major sponsors like Budweiser and Harley Davidson were conducive to MMA's growth. That being said, I think you had a lot of characters in the early days paying a meager amount of money to the fighters. Before some fighters at the lower end were training for months and they were living in somewhat poverty—some had a second job. Eventually, as time went by, with proper management, the monetary rewards grew and distributed more accurately in MMA. Today, UFC fighters are very protective about what they do and very cautious. I think the sky's the limit. The boxers, without a doubt, are compensated to a much higher degree. But the whole pay structure in boxing is much different compared to MMA. Still, more recently Max Kellerman, a highly respected boxing analyst and host on ESPN, said that the moniker "Baddest Man on the Planet" belongs to UFC heavyweight champion, not boxing. "The rise of UFC and MMA means that the [boxing] heavyweight champion is no longer the baddest man on the planet," Kellerman said, "because in an actual fight, he'd lose to whoever is the best mixed martial artist because it's a closer approximation to a real fight." With the emergence of Conor McGregor, the whole MMA phenomenon has exploded even further as he spearheaded the boom. The Notorious has become one of the biggest superstars in sport boasting 40 million Instagram followers.

I wanted to compile a book in a way which has never really been done before as far as UFC and the sport of MMA is concerned. With the sport being made available to a bigger, broader audience, evidently more and more people are interested in the champions of the Octagon. Within the pages of this book, you will discover exclusive colorful tapestry of conversations with many top and most decorated UFC champions and Hall of Fame members ever to grace the Octagon from radically diverse backgrounds.

From the early legendary pioneers to the current stars who have climbed celestial heights, they give us, in their own words, rare personal insights into their lives and careers. Fighters pull no punches as they recount their journeys from the streets to stardom, offering vivid accounts of impoverished childhoods and epic battles in the sold-out arenas they fought some of their fiercest foes. This is also an oral history. From UFC's first ever champion, Royce Gracie—who introduced a generation to Brazilian jiu-jitsu in its inaugural tournament, and is widely considered to be the most influential figure in the founding of the sport—and fellow pioneer, Ken Shamrock, offer revelations pertaining to the early days when the sport was a spectacle. To the legends, Randy Couture, Chuck Liddell, and Georges St-Pierre—titans responsible for propelling MMA to a wider mainstream audience—offer rare anecdotes when they were at the peak of their careers. And modern-day champions and household names from Holly Holm, Jan Blachowicz, and Daniel Cormier shed light on some of their high-profile, pay-per-view record-breaking fights, with rare and behind-the-scenes tales. For those who want to get an insight into the life of a UFC champion, you won't be disappointed. You will discover many untold truths.

I think it's a great concept to have a plethora of top UFC names in a single tome in their own words tell their riveting stories with no third-party tampering. It can be argued there are a number of other names that belong on the list. Nevertheless, all the fighters that I spoke to that are featured in this book are no ordinary fighters—every single one of these thirty-six men and women has held the prestigious UFC championship belt. *Champions of the Octagon* gives an incredible glimpse into what it takes to survive in the world's most brutal arena, and what motivates these warriors and the challenges and hurdles they had to surmount to make a name in the Octagon.

CHAPTER ONE:
PIONEERS AND CHAMPIONS

Royce Gracie
Three-time UFC Champion/Hall of Famer

Question: Royce, tell me about your father, a man of diminutive stature weighing 135 pounds, who revolutionized no-holds-barred fighting in Brazil.

Royce Gracie: He based his style on leverage and positioning. It's about reality self-defense where you learn about defense and how to win a fight. You have to commit to not losing, and once you don't lose, the question is: how are you going to win the fight? He beat everybody. He fought in open-weight divisions. He was only 135 pounds and was beating guys double his weight, beating everybody up and sending them to the hospital. He challenged the heavyweight boxing champion, Joe Louis— we have a letter from Joe Louis declining. He said that he would fight anybody but wouldn't fight an MMA fight. My father would punch and beat his opponents up pretty hard. I asked him, "How come you beat your opponents up so much?" And he said because he would tell them to get off him, but they wouldn't get off him, so he had to beat them up. I said, "OK, I understand that."

Q: Tell me about when you arrived in the US to help spread the word in promoting Gracie Jiu-Jitsu with your brother, Rorion.

Gracie: I grew up in Brazil until I was seventeen years old. And I came to America to live with Rorion. I went to school in Brazil and trained in jiu-jitsu. When I arrived in America, I didn't know how to speak English; the only words I knew were "stop" and "like that." I would teach a class using those two words. I would say, "Stop." And then I would show the move and say, "Like that." I started teaching classes and that's how I pretty much started learning English. We had Chuck Norris, who took classes with us, [*Enter the Dragon* costar] Jim Kelly; professional baseball and football players would come and take our classes. They realized that this was something real and understood what we were talking about. So, a friend or a student of theirs would bring a professional athlete, try out and take the first class and fall in love with our art.

Q: Let's talk about the famous Gracie open-door challenge, which took place at the academy and the garage.
Gracie: The Gracie challenge is where we had an open challenge, but some people misunderstand the concept thinking it's just about: if you can beat me, I'll pay you money. It's not that way—most of the times there was no money involved, but if someone wanted to make a personal bet with money, that's OK. Whatever you put on the table we'll match it. Back in the garage days, even after that at the academy, the students got so hooked on Gracie Jiu-Jitsu they'd go out and tell their friends, who may have been a karate instructor, and say, "I've got a guy from Brazil, they'll fight anybody." So the instructor or fighter would want to see what they could do. They'd come into the academy or garage and we would tell them our style's the most complete self-defense system—you can kick or punch, but if I get in a clinch and take you down, you don't know what to do. Oh, man. The thing we started. The opponent would say, "You'll never take me to the ground because all my life I've never been taken to the floor before." So we would say, "Let's do it." So the whole challenge thing started.

If a student or a friend of a friend, or a karate instructor wanted to check it out, we had a challenge right there. I fought this kung fu exponent who had read about us Gracies, and we were willing to prove our style is the best. So he phoned the academy and said he wanted to try us out and came in. He'd been training in kung fu all his life and he wanted to prove his style against ours. We said, "Sure." So we made an appointment and he came in and I embarrassed him.

Q: Tell me about the first iteration of the UFC.

Gracie: The first UFC was exciting, it made history. That was a phase in history what people thought could not be done—putting two guys in a cage on live TV. Rorion pulled that off, man. The whole idea of building the UFC was to prove that Gracie Jiu-Jitsu was the best martial arts and fighting style. So, by training all my life I was ready to battle against different styles and show that Gracie Jiu-Jitsu was the best style out there. Knowing what I'm doing and what Gracie Jiu-Jitsu is all about, I had enough confidence in myself and technique. I knew I was prepared to fight against a boxer, kick-boxer or a wrestler. Gracie Jiu-Jitsu was a complete art. It was karate versus kung fu; Gracie Jiu-Jitsu against a kick-boxer; sumo guy versus a savate fighter. When they went to the ground, they didn't know what to do. And other arts like judo and wrestling didn't know what I know. That's the main difference.

In today's fighting, everybody knows Gracie Jiu-Jitsu. So everybody knows how to kick and punch and wrestle now—before they didn't. Today they are athletes and fight to see who's the best—everybody trains standup and grappling. It's not one style versus another style; it's more related to the person who can deliver his game. After the UFCs, I didn't change much. I'm still the same man. Still today I know where I came from. I'm the same person as I was back then. Of course, we got more students, even after my last fight a lot of Brazilian jiu-jitsu schools gained students, which is good.

Q: Do you feel you proved to the world that a smaller guy could beat a much heavier and stronger opponent when you beat Ken Shamrock at UFC 1 (November 1993), who weighed 240 pounds and looked ripped?

Gracie: Not just that, but his art wasn't a complete art. He admitted he got caught, and later said, "I got caught by surprise. I didn't expect this skinny guy from Brazil to know more grappling than me." He was out-grappled. His size was OK. He's big but the elephant isn't the king of the jungle. The first fight I had with him Shamrock came to fight me and I beat him in less than a minute—56 seconds. I choked him. As soon as he tapped, I let go of the choke and then he said he did not give up—he's a liar. So I looked at the referee and said let it continue, we are going to continue. I said to Shamrock, "Are you ready? Let's go, keep going!" I was ready to make a move and choke him out for good. But then he was like, "You're right. I quit. I quit."

In the second fight, the rematch, we fought again. He's 240 pounds; I was about 180 at the time. He took me down. I pull the guard. He got on top of me. All he did in the fight was hold me for 30 minutes. I was trying to go for chokes and arm locks. Even his father, who was in his corner, kept saying, "Stop hugging him, beat him!" His own father was saying this because he wasn't doing a thing. He hit me once with a punch. He was just holding me down. That's a shame somebody who is 240 pounds and a lot heavier. When the fight was over, it was declared a draw because nobody quit. And he's saying to everybody because he hit me once that he's the winner. Shame, the guy is more than 50 pounds heavier than me. If I'm fighting at 180 pounds fighting somebody 50 pounds lighter than me and I can't finish that person, then that person won. If you fight someone 50, 60 pounds lighter and it's a draw, I'll give it to the lightweight guy. I don't know where he got the idea that he won the fight, but he's not living on this world. When I fought Dan Severn, he did not know how to finish me. He could pin me down but he was wrestler. A lot of in judo and wrestling everybody cross trains now, learning how to take down, clinch and submit. You have to do the standup and the boxing.

Q: What do you think of the concept of judges' decisions? And why was it necessary to implement rules and regulations in the UFC after you left the company in 1995?
Gracie: Sometimes the judges' decision, one judge goes one way and the other one the other way. It's very common. I prefer the fighters to decide the fight instead of the judges deciding. It depends on what background you come from. If you are a standup fighter you're going to punch more. The gloves are there to protect the fighter's hands, not the opponent's face. So without the gloves you may break your hand and not be able to punch again for a while. A lot of people break their hands even with the gloves, but the boxing gloves protect the hands; not the opponent's face.

When I was fighting in the UFC there were no gloves, no rules, and no time limits. So the new owners got together with the boxing commission. And the only way to make the whole thing legal was they had to have gloves and some rules. It was either that or the boxing commission banning the UFC because it was too brutal.

Q: In terms of preparation, how do you stay focused before a fight?
Gracie: I don't get overwhelmed by the crowds or the size of the crowds, or crowds cheering me or booing me. I'm pretty much in a neutral phase. It doesn't matter whether I'm in another place or location, or the crowds are for or against me. I just connect to myself and I'm on my own stage. In Japan they have a lot of fans over there. People think all Japanese do martial arts, but there are a lot more fans and they appreciate the fights and the finer technique that is demonstrated in the MMA fights.

Q: You have battled opponents weighing as much as 490 pounds. When you face someone as big as that, who looks mean and can bench press 500 pounds, what keeps you so cool and calm?
Gracie: I know what I train for and what I'm capable of doing, how far I can go. If I showed you pictures of the training camp, I did exactly what happened in the fight when I trained that way in my training camp. The way I train at the training camp, that is what happens in the fight. My toughest fight was with [Kazushi] Sakuraba in Japan, which lasted one hour 45 minutes. Again, this fight made history. He's a very tough opponent. It's good to be strong but it's not what is going to win the fight, man. If you don't have the technique and don't know what you're doing, you have no business in the ring. So you have to know what you're doing, once you do then strength can help. You can have the fastest car in town, but if you don't have gas you're not going anywhere.

Q: What motivates you to continue to fight in such a brutal sport?
Gracie: I know what I'm doing, that's the main thing. What motivates me to fight? To shut up the crowd who are talking trash and prove that I'm still here.

Q: You challenged Mike Tyson, and he was invited to fight in the UFC (in both 1993 and 1997). Can you tell me how this challenge came about?

Gracie: People think boxers are great athletes, that they're the toughest in the food chain. But they are not the best fighters; they are the best boxers. Mike Tyson, at the time, was the best boxer, but not the best fighter—there's a difference. When we invited him to fight in the UFC, our aim was to see who's the best fighter and we said to him to come into the no-rules game and let's see what happens. He declined. I have nothing against boxers. I train in boxing, too. They are great athletes, top of the food chain. The shape you get doing the boxing workout is unreal. But they are not the best in fighting.

Q: How do you feel that Brazilian jiu-jitsu—the style you and your family started—has now become such phenomenon?

Gracie: It's getting there. People always are interested in seeing who is the best fighter. People like that, it's in the human nature. It's going to grow. Before grapplers were not considered martial artists, but this changed after the UFC.

Q: Tell me about some of the celebrities you have taught over the years, such as Nicolas Cage and Guy Ritchie, who seem to have embraced the artistic elements of your art?

Gracie: Yes, they are big fans of the sport. They want to know how to protect themselves—not to become professional fighters, but for knowledge. Not to use it in the movies or anything like that, but gain knowledge as a person and for self-defense if someone picks a fight. That's why everyone looks for Gracie Jiu-Jitsu. It's to learn how to defend yourself.

Q: Were you supposed to train Brock Lesnar? And which fighters have impressed you the most over the years?

Gracie: Brock Lesnar was so far away that it just didn't work out. He's in a different state, and it wasn't convenient for him to fly over to LA. Maybe he didn't need it. Some of the fighters I'm impressed by are

Anderson Silva, Lyoto Machida, Antonio Nougueira, Wanderlei Silva. I like the Brazilians—they're sharp.

Q: You look like the typical average guy on the street. You don't look like a fighter, but are one of the most dangerous fighters on the planet. How would you respond to this?
Gracie: One time, my brother said to me, "In a perfect world, you wouldn't be a fighter." And I looked at him thinking, *After all I've done?* I went home and after a week I called him back and said, "You're right, in a perfect world I probably wouldn't be a fighter." I never had a fight in the street. I'm not a mean person. All my fights are won in a kind of a nice way where I'm not pounding my opponent's face inside out. I don't have to. So, yes, in a perfect world I wouldn't be a fighter but the world isn't perfect. If I want to be a fighter, I might as well be the best. I fight because I know what I'm doing.

Q: Lastly, Royce, tell me about your traveling and training schedules. How do you fit everything in?
Gracie: I spend about six months each year on the road traveling and conducting seminars. The sport is growing all over the world, not just the USA. Everybody in the world wants to learn MMA. I get to travel around the world and do what I like. It's a great job. I've been on vacation for six weeks and I'm just getting back to work. When I've got a fight coming up, I stop traveling and just concentrate on training. I implement standup and a lot of grappling, check my opponent's weaknesses and strengths, and set up a strategy. I'm living my future, life's good.

Ken Shamrock

UFC Super-Fight Champion/Hall of Famer

Question: Ken, can you shed some light on your childhood?
Ken Shamrock: I grew up in Georgia and then moved out to California. I got into trouble when I was about ten years old, and I got shipped off to different group and juvenile homes. I ended up in a place called the Shamrock Boys Home with Bob Shamrock, after I had stayed at several different places. I was thirteen-and-a-half years old. This was a time when I started learning how to change my ways. I graduated from school and went onto college. After junior college I went into the Marine Corps. From that point on, I got interested in professional wrestling and got involved. Then I had an opportunity to go to Japan to fight. So, that's when I actually got my first taste of MMA in Japan. It was called the UWF. My first fight was against a guy who I beat. And from that point I never looked back and went from fighting in Japan to the United States in the UFC to where I'm at now. Once I got into MMA fighting I never looked back—this was what I was made to do.

Q: When you were growing up, did you get into trouble a lot?
Shamrock: Well, I grew up in group homes so you were always fighting all the time. And I would fight for my territory and my space. I mean, I had to fight for my own respect. So, it's something I did at a really young age when I was ten years old. I was fighting all the time. Fighting to me was just kind of who I was, and what I was all about and where I grew up. I had to fight in order to keep anything I had and any respect

I had. Then when I got into MMA and started fighting professionally, that was fun.

Q: Let's talk about your pro wrestling career before we go into the UFC.

Shamrock: I got into pro wrestling in North Carolina, where Gene Anderton and Nelson Royal had a group there. I did very well for a year and a half and it was from here I got the opportunity to go to Japan to fight in MMA over there.

Q: How did you hear about the UFC, and what steps did you take to get involved?

Shamrock: I was actually doing MMA in Japan, which was different than the UFC. When I first heard about the UFC, I realized it was in a cage, it was closed fists and fights took place with no gloves. I remember thinking, *I want to do that!* It was just another step up from what I was doing in Japan, where it was open-hand strikes and submissions on the ground. When I got involved, there was this guy named Royce Gracie that everybody was talking about. I, of course, just blew him off thinking he's just a karate guy wearing a gi, thinking I was the only one that knew any submissions. I really didn't do much study on it and went in there thinking, *I'm the best fighter out there and that I'll beat everybody.* So, I flew from Japan after having a fight with Funakai—who I'd beaten in a minute and 40 seconds—to the US three days prior to the UFC event into Denver, Colorado and fought.

I had my first fight with Patrick Smith who I submitted with a heel hook. Then I fought Royce whom I thought was a striker who didn't know much grappling—and he wasn't that big either. I had no idea what the gi was used for. And they took my shoes away, which I had done grappling with forever. They wouldn't allow me to wear shoes, but allowed him to wear a gi. So, I went in and I thought I had him in a submission hold, but he wrapped his gi around my arm. Then when I went for a leg lock, he pulled himself on me and wrapped his gi around my neck and choked me. From that point on I was like, *OK, these guys know how to cheat, so I'm going to learn how to defend myself from this cheating.*

Q: What did you think of Royce Gracie? On the surface he doesn't look like a fighter.

Shamrock: He's very deceptive, just like a normal guy who doesn't look like a tough guy, doesn't look very athletic. But put him in a gi and a ring and he's phenomenal. He's a wise guy and very good at what he does. And he proved it over the years that he was the "man" when it came to grappling. So no one can deny the credibility that he got through the UFC.

Q: When did you open the Lion's Den, which became one of the first MMA gyms?

Shamrock: When I first started fighting over in Japan, there was nothing over here in the United States where I could actually train both standup and ground fighting. There was no such thing as the UFC at the time and no gyms around that actually did that type of training. You either grappled or you were a striker. So you had to go to different gyms to do specific training. I decided to develop a gym that would do both—train striking and grappling. While I was over in Japan, I trained at the dojo. I put together my training facility where I would get a house and I would go out and find fighters. And I would have a try out and once they made it in the team, I would have them at the house where we would do the training. So I had a house full of fighters and all we did was train. That's how we developed the Lion's Den Team. One day when I was watching a show on TV called *Animal Kingdom* they were showing and talking about how the lion was the king of the jungle. A lion would attack a running animal, dig its claws into his back and neck, and it would pull it down in to the body. While the lion was on his back, he would pull the prey down to his chest and bite its neck and kill it. I thought, *What a great name "King of the Jungle,"* where you actually attacked the prey similar to grappling! So I thought Lion's Den would be a good name. So I named the gym "The Lion's Den" and started training fighters. We housed fighters and our guys would go out fighting, and the Lion's Den had a reputation for having the toughest fighters out there and the only team in MMA that was fighting all the time. As you see now with *The Ultimate Fighter* show, which is turned into a reality show which is what

Lion's Den did way before the *TUF* reality show came out. They took that and turned it into a reality show.

Q: On to your super-fight with Royce Gracie at UFC 5 (April 1995), which was declared a draw. Do you think, had there been no time limits, it would have been a different outcome?
Shamrock: There's no question about it. Royce Gracie was hurt and carried out of the ring. He was the beat-up fighter, there's no question about it. I was fresh and could have gone on a lot longer, but he was hanging on for the time to run out. He had so much damage to him, broken ribs, his eye was busted and his conditioning was low. He was pretty much saved by the bell. I think anybody who watched that fight knows that man got lucky because there was a time limit in that particular fight. So the question of, "Would it have been different?" He would have lost. He lost that fight, anyway—if you watch the fight, anybody would say he got beat.

Q: In your opinion, how important is conditioning?
Shamrock: No matter how good you are, you can't win a fight unless you go in there and fight. So you have to be able to do that. Conditioning is number one.

Q: Were you ever influenced by Bruce Lee?
Shamrock: I watched a movie called *Enter the Dragon*, and in the very first scene he's fighting some big dude and he gets the guy on the ground and jumps into an arm bar. That's when I first saw an actual submission mixed in with the standup fighting. Bruce Lee did it! Bruce Lee was actually one of the first guys who ever did the cross training where two combatants would fight on the ground and also standing up. Back in those karate days, people didn't go to the ground and fight, but Bruce Lee knew this was an important part of being a complete fighter.

Q: After you and Royce became the face of the UFC, did you want to go back to Japan and fight in Pride?
Shamrock: I went to a bunch of different places to fight. I fought in Pride for a while and had good success there. I went from Pride to the

UFC. And at the time UFC was doing 40,000 (pay-per-view) buys. And when I came back to fight Tito, it did about 140,000 buys. With Kimo, we did 150, or 160,000 buys. And then with the second Tito fight it was huge numbers. Ever since I came back in the UFC, they skyrocketed in the pay-per-views.

Q: You fought Tito Ortiz at UFC 40 (November 2002). Do you feel that, no matter how good a fighter is, a lot of the time just comes down to who the better fighter is on fight day?
Shamrock: That's true too, but a lot of people don't understand that at the time I had torn something. But because the fight was big and there was so much hype about it and so much anticipation on it, I couldn't back out. So I had to do the fight and did it anyway. So after that fight was over, I went into surgery and had my knee replaced. There are a lot of things that happened when I fought Tito. And even the second time I fought Tito. I blew my shoulder out and, again, I still had to do the fight because it was too close to the fight to back out and too much hype for the fight for me to step down. I had a lot of bad luck when it came to fighting Tito as I seemed to be always injured. You know what, that's not to take anything away from Tito. You do what you need to do and he won the fight and that's that.

Q: You and Tito Ortiz seem to have had heated words at the press conferences before your fights. Why did you both seem to have problem with each other?
Shamrock: I think Tito and I know how the sport works. I mean, it's not just two guys getting in there and fighting. That's a big part of it, of course, but people that understand the sport want to know why we're fighting and want something for you to fight about. I give people a reason for wanting me to fight and my opponent something to fight about. I find something in every one of my opponent that I don't like, and I will pull it out and make it public why I don't like this guy. And people tend to want to buy the fight and want to watch it more. It's not fake it's real. The aim is real, the reasons are real. I just tend to find those things and I bring them out. I don't ignore them.

Q: You and Tito were on the *The Ultimate Fighter* as coaches. Are there any interesting stories about that experience worth sharing?

Shamrock: The pool thing, where he thought he was such a good player, is one of them. The whole time when they mentioned that we were going to play pool and the coaches would be competing against each other. And there would be $10,000 for the coach that won. I, basically, kind of looked disappointed because I couldn't really play pool. And Tito jumped out of the seat like he played pool all the time, like he's a hustler. Then I went in and basically cleared the table and he couldn't recover after that. He was just completely taken out of his element because he was jumping up and down with his team players like he was going to win it, but I smoked him.

Q: After the UFC, you went back into WWE. Why go back to entertainment fighting after fighting for real?

Shamrock: The thing is the UFC at that time was having a lot of problems. They were in court all the time and getting banned from all these different places, therefore the money was going down. So I couldn't even support my family through fighting, so I started looking for other avenues. Someone in Canada had approached me several times about me coming in and doing stuff with the WWE. And so once the UFC started having problems, I decided I had to make money elsewhere because I couldn't support my family at the time. So, the guy talked to me and we got together with Vince McMahon and started working out some deals. So I got involved with them and had a very good experience with the WWE. It was a great time when I was there and making money to support my family.

Q: What do you think of some of the professional wrestlers making the transition into the UFC . . . someone like Brock Lesnar, for instance?

Shamrock: I think it's very difficult for these guys to make a transition. The sport's evolved so much that the UFC fighters are all cross-training and have been for several years. They all have had a lot of amateur fights. It's not like in the early UFC days when guys were just starting to learn grappling, striking, and getting their conditioning up. They were just starting out. A lot of guys can just jump in and do it. Fortunately for me I was already doing it over in Japan, so I had knowledge of submission and knowledge of striking. So I was able to go from the pro wrestling world into the UFC, and vice versa. I had already experience in both, which made my transition very much easier. But for guys who are doing it now, it's not going to be that easy, it's going to be very difficult making the transition.

Q: You had bad experiences with your management at one point. How important is it to have a good manager in the sport of MMA?
Shamrock: Oh, it's really important because you travel a lot and you're training all the time. You're always on the road. You don't know what you're being charged or where the money is all going. The sooner you find out things weren't going where they are supposed to go, you owe taxes here and there. It's very important that you have somebody managing your financial arrangements that you really trust because it's really easy for money to disappear and you not know about it for a long period of time. Then there's nothing you can do about it because the way it is being done is legal. So you just really have to make sure someone you can trust and make sure you are watching where things are going.

Q: How do you feel now that the UFC has been embraced more openly by the media and the general public, whereas in the early days it was promoted as no-holds-barred?
Shamrock: I think it had a lot to do with the athletic commission who got involved and the rules came in. Everybody has rules which are followed. And the fighters have their physicals before the fights. Sanctioning the sport and providing rules was a big thing for them to get in there and do this, and without them it probably wouldn't be at the stage it is today. It was good finding a way for the sport to survive and for the fans to be able to watch without the fighters going in there and getting seriously hurt.

Q: You fought Dan Severn in two super-fights. Am I right in saying both of you never got along? What was the reason behind this?

Shamrock: Well, I mean, again trying to build fights, trying to have animosity towards my opponent because I didn't like him. So I kind of picked upon things that Dan Severn said. We had a rules meeting. He seemed cocky, which he was, and all fighters are to a point before a fight. So, he was talking about certain things and he kind of over-stepped his boundaries, where he was the challenger and I was the champion. He was getting a little ignored as I was getting more media attention and questions. He kind of got upset that he wasn't getting asked any questions and, therefore, we got into a confrontation in the last meeting. And I told him, "Don't worry about it because I'm going to kill you anyway." And he got up and walked out of the meeting. I went into the ring where I proceeded to kick the crap out of him.

Q: You did a lot of media by appearing on some top talk shows in America. Was this the transition of bringing MMA to the attention of the mainstream public?

Shamrock: I think I was the first one to actually do the crossover to mainstream media. I don't know, but I guess my character really kind of appealed to a lot of people and was able to cross over and get the MMA to audiences that maybe wouldn't have been able to be reached otherwise. Then when I crossed over to pro wrestling fighting in the WWE, I was on mainstream TV and people were wondering where I came from. So, they knew about this MMA fighter and they started to ask the question, "What's MMA?" Then they started doing research on my background and people started watching MMA and started telling other fans. Then I went back from WWE into MMA and brought a lot of fans from that mainstream audience into the MMA world. For instance when the UFC was only hitting 40,000 pay-per-view buys, and then I went back in the UFC we did 150,000 buys. This had a lot to do with the fact that I had brought a lot of the fans from the WWE world.

Q: Has the UFC knocked boxing off the top spot in the US as the most popular spectator combat sport?

Shamrock: Absolutely. I think we were new and it was definitely a sport that was talked about. Any boxer, wrestler or karate guy could get into the MMA and fight an MMA fighter and lose because he's not well rounded. This thing about who is the toughest guy was proven, in fact, without talking, but through actual fighting. And MMA always won because boxing is one dimensional, just as is wrestling and karate. On the other hand MMA is multiple disciplines all into one. So, therefore, it was proven, *Hey, you know what, this is the real deal. These are the real fighters.* People want to watch things that are real, that are the best. It was proven over and over with different disciplines coming into the UFC and finding out. You cannot be one dimensional; you had to know all disciplines. So boxing has now taken a back seat, but boxing is a very good event—those guys are very skilled but UFC is hot right now. But like everything in life, what goes up must come down, nobody stays on top forever, everybody takes a turn. UFC and MMA will also go down again. And boxing will pull back up again and probably be on top for a while, and MMA will come back on top again and everybody will have its time and its place. It always does that—there's shifts and changes and it will always be that way in the world. Nothing stays the same, and it can't stay the same, otherwise we would cease to exist. It's always the way the cycle of life works. So, therefore, we are on top right now, MMA is doing very well.

Q: Am I right in saying you had some contentious issues with the UFC in terms of your contract? Did they release you before it actually expired?

Shamrock: It's something we have got to decide in the court of law. I don't want to get into it. For one, we're going to leave it to the attorneys. I've figured this thing out and I want to settle it in the court of law. So I can't really talk much about that. But everybody knows the kind of person I am. I don't get into situations like this, but when I am in a situation like this, it's usually because I'm provoked. So, I just want to let the attorneys figure it out and hopefully we can get this figured out without it getting too nasty.

Q: Dana White turned the UFC around. There are fighters, such as Tito Ortiz and Randy Couture, who believe there should be a lot more money for the fighters. Do you agree with their sentiment?

Shamrock: There needs to be a fighter's union so these guys have someone they can go to when they feel they have been wronged. Right now I think the UFC wants to keep that out because they don't want us in there because this way they can keep all the money. Fighters are not getting paid the way they need to be paid. I think everybody knows that. But how do you get them paid? The only way you can make it fair is to have a union, somewhere the fighters can go direct to but right now they don't have that. So, therefore they don't have anybody fighting for them. The sport is young and it will take some time to have this in place. It will have to otherwise it will cease to exist.

Q: You're currently forty-four years old. What motivates people like yourself and Randy Couture to keep fighting? Would you consider taking other avenues, such as coaching?

Shamrock: There's no question about it. I want to get involved in other areas, which I'm doing right now actually. I'll probably fight one more time, just so I can go out on my own terms and say goodbye to all my fans in the ring. But they'll be seeing me doing other things such as promoting fights, opening gyms, training fighters and I'll definitely be involved in this sport but in a different way.

Q: Your son is fighting in MMA now. Do you feel he'll go a long way? Does he have a future in this sport?

Shamrock: Yes, he's a very tough kid. He fought in England, which was his second fight. And he broke his hand and still continued to finish the round. He knocked the guy down with his broken hand and took him down twice. In my opinion he won the first round, but at the end of the round his trainer looked at his hand and he had a bone sticking out of his hand. It wasn't a fracture but a break, so he couldn't continue in the next round, but the toughness and the skill he showed being such a young fighter was there. He's still inexperienced, but he still managed to win the round, breaking his hand 36 seconds into the fight. He's still healing the hand, but once it does he'll be back in the ring and I think people will enjoy his fights. I've got a nephew fighting this week in San Jose in Strike Force. He's eighteen years old and is a phenomenal fighter, too. So I've got two of my Shamrock boys going into MMA fighting. And in probably three years' time, I'll have all of them in fighting.

Q: Will we see another Ken vs. Royce fight?
Shamrock: We're hoping that will happen. I don't know if Royce will do it, but if he does I'll be happy to punch him in the head again.

Dan Severn

UFC 5 Tournament Champion/UFC Super-Fight Champion/Hall of Famer

Question: Dan, you have an impressive wrestling background. Tell me about it.

Dan Severn: I started in amateur wrestling back in 1969 in junior high school in the seventh grade. I was in the high school wrestling team and good enough to end up getting a full athletic scholarship to go to Arizona State University. I'm from Michigan, but I lived in Arizona for ten years between going to college and wrestling and also coaching at the university. Job opportunities brought me back to the state of Michigan. During my high school years, I started doing freestyle and Greco-Roman wrestling. By my freshman college, I ended up doing sambo and judo. From then I just started competing in various types of events and going to National and State championships in amateur wrestling. I ended up doing my first main contest in the early nineties as of the 1992 Olympics.

I started doing professional wrestling after being approached by several companies in the early eighties. I thought this was my chance to live the lifestyle of a professional athlete. I used my real name and my amateur credentials. There was a gentleman there from Tennessee who asked me if my record was legit. And I told him that it was. He said I ought to be in Japan competing in a thing called a "shoot-fight," or "shoot-fighting," which I hadn't heard of before. So I gave him my business card and he gave one to me. Three days later I got a phone call. One week later I had trials. And a month after that, I was in Tokyo getting ready to take part in my first shoot fighting match. Into the fight I didn't know what I was doing, but my Japanese opponent kicked me about four or five times really hard. I grabbed him, threw him all over the place and went crazy. The guy who brought me over said, "Dan Severn, you will become a superstar in Japan." Then, in 1994, it was the beginning of my no-holds-barred MMA career in the Ultimate Fighting Championship. I've had a dual career ever since.

Q: You were the first world-class Olympic-style wrestler to enter the UFC. How did you actually get involved?
Severn: I lived in a rather rural community—and still do—but it was so rural at the time that they didn't have the pay-per-view capabilities. A friend of mine out of Detroit had watched the first couple of UFCs. And he brought them to me and showed them to me. He said, "Hey, you ought to think about doing this!" It was people getting stomped in the face. I told him, "These aren't exactly skills I possess." He said, "Look at this skinny little guy doing jiu-jitsu." Of course, he was referring to Royce Gracie. So, here I am I'm watching the tapes and I said to him that it kind of looks like wrestling. And I thought if someone is close enough to kick or punch me, I can either step out of the range or step in, close them down where they can't really get much velocity in the strike. That's when I kind of thought I'd do OK in a competition like this.

So I sent in an application but no one ever called me back. I was told that the UFC were receiving between two and three hundred applications on a daily basis. So a few more calls were made to the matchmaker Art Davie. I happen to be going to Los Angeles on a professional wrestling card. So, Art came down and watched me in my professional wrestling match, and then conducted his personal interview with me. The first thing he said to me was, "You do realize what we do is real, don't you?" And I said I knew. He asked me what my professional wrestling record was, and I told him I didn't have one. So he asked what my amateur record was. I said I didn't have one of those either. So he asked me what my skills were. I said I was an amateur wrestler for twenty-six years. He said, "Well, amateur wrestling has rules and regulations." I told him that was not necessarily true. I asked him if he ever had been to a foreign soil with a foreign referee, you'd be surprised what you can do. He asked me what I meant by that. I said to him, "Let me reiterate my very first international experience ever at seventeen years of age."

I was part of the US All-Star team and at sixteen to eighteen years old we went to the country of Turkey. We were supposed to be wrestling Turkish wrestlers, who were between the ages of fifteen and eighteen. My first opponent was a thirty-five-year-old military man, who was muscular, with his meanness and ugliness. And he's walking back and forth like a caged animal. And here I am a seventeen year old slender-built wrestler. I had all my hair back then in the early '70s. The match started and he grabbed back of my hair. And he head butted me splitting my eyebrow open. Then he tears a lot of hair out and slings it on the ground. My hand is up on the side of his head and blood is stripping down my face. I look at the referee to see if the match is over, thinking my opponent is going to be disqualified for non-sportsmanship conduct. All the referee did was simply step in between us and kicked the hair on the ground out of the way—and he cautions me for passivity.

This happened to be in the first 15 seconds of the match. Matches at the time were three minutes 30 seconds long with a one-minute break in between rounds. You didn't even stop for blood because it was normal—you got bloody noses all the time. They did not stop the matches. If you had a bloody nose or split lip you reached in, you wiped it and kept going—there were no timeouts for that kind of stuff. So, the guy split my head. And now I'm mad and angry and I channel my anger through my technique. I go for a hard double-leg takedown and we hit the ground. In wrestling you don't want to be on your back, so he turns around. There's a technique called the cross-face where you get the bridge of your arm across the soft tissue.

Now I had anger running through my body and I broke his nose, and his blood is pouring out of his nose all over my arm. I've got pain shooting up my arm because he's biting into my forearm trying to take a chunk of meat out of me. So at that point I decided to hurt him really bad. I reached up and grabbed my own arm and I was trying to jam it into his nose and skull—basically I was trying to kill him. Just because he inflicted injury to me, in return I was trying to inflict even more injury to him. Referee blows the whistle and pulls my arm off his nose, and he penalizes me for an illegal maneuver. I show him the teeth marks on my arm and he penalizes the Turkish opponent for an illegal maneuver. At the end of the first three-minute round, the referee sends me back to my corner and sends my opponent back to his. We were both a bloody mess. His coach was so angry that a little weeny-looking American is ahead of him in points that he pulled out a stick thickness of a broom handle, and proceeded to beat his athlete. I've had people saying, "No, you're kidding me." But I have lived that experience.

Q: Can you talk me through your epic battle with Royce Gracie at UFC 4 (December 1994) final. Did he surprise you, as you are yourself a grappler?

Severn: I don't know if he surprised me. Before entering the UFC, I only had two UFC video tapes to watch and he was in both of those. So I kind of knew what he was all about. The thing is I'm not going to make any excuse. At the time, I was told I was going to be in the upcoming UFC. It was kind of a last minute fill-in. I only trained for five days, an hour and a half each day and that was it. So, I walked into not only his world, but the world of no-holds-barred and held my own not knowing a single strike or a single submission, not even practicing a single submission or strike. I had a training camp with three professional wrestlers. We went inside the professional wrestling ring with an old pair of boxing gloves, and the name of the game was "Try to punch Dan and Dan doesn't like to be hit." So I was parrying the punches and getting into upper body clinches, or takedowns and slapping on an amateur wrestling move and turning it a little illegal. That was my training camp. So it was almost a joke in itself.

I didn't throw any strikes in my first two matches. I did after several minutes had passed in the match with Royce Gracie himself. Then I had to think about it because I had fought for twenty-six years under rules and regulations. I was struggling more with my conscious than I ever had with an opponent against Royce Gracie. I don't mean to say that in a derogatory sense, but that is how it was. Had I simply cut loose, it might have been a different outcome of the match, but I'll live with my decision, which was to do what I did at the time.

Q: After your experience at UFC 4, did you reevaluate your training approach?

Severn: I actually went back to train as I had time now. By contract they could not get rid of me as long as I finished in the top two. So I was automatically invited back. I like to think that I was the monkey, which hit the system because a lot of people don't realize the company was half owned by the Gracie family and half owned by Art Davie. So I really questioned if it was a real competition. I mean, they were real fights, but I think people may have been hand selected.

Q: Any behind-the-scenes UFC stories you'd like to share?

Severn: The funny part was that one of the guys who traveled with me, Al Snow, was a professional wrestler. Al Snow was wearing the typical muscle t-shirt and I was wearing a suit and a tie. Whenever we were walking around, everybody thought I was his manager and he was the fighter. Then at the day of the press conference, where it was going to be announced who was going to fight who, Al Snow was sitting in the crowd while I was sitting up onstage with the other seven men.

Q: Would you agree that Olympic wrestling is one the most physically demanding and hardest sports, and Olympic wrestlers now have a great platform to earn a lucrative living by becoming MMA athletes?

Severn: Yes, they have because there's no true professional outlet for them. If there was a real professional outlet for Olympic wrestlers then they would pursue that. But there isn't one. There's no real money that can be gained in amateur wrestling. Football players go play professional football; basketball players can turn professional; golfers and gymnastics can do the same. But real wrestlers, other than professional wrestling, which if you get into it, is basically entertainment and you're an actor and a stuntman. There are a lot of amateur wrestlers that look down on professional wrestling. I think with the MMA, it is a benefit to the wrestlers and the assets they bring into it teaches you a lot of body mechanics and body control. It doesn't teach you striking or submissions, but I have had a lot of jiu-jitsu practitioners and Muay Thai practitioners who come to learn wrestling from me. So, now they can incorporate it into their martial arts.

When you look at most jiu-jitsu practitioners, they're terrible at takedowns. Any jiu-jitsu practitioner that is any good at takedowns somewhere along the way worked with a wrestler because the mechanics wrestling teaches you are good for takedowns. But jiu-jitsu is good once you hit the ground, though.

Q: Let's talk about your controversial super-fight against Ken Shamrock at UFC 6 (July 1995).
Severn: He basically beat me on my first outing, but at the same token there should never have been a first outing. I come from the world of amateur wrestling, so if there's going to be a super-fight, basically it has to be between two people who've actually won things. At that point in time, Ken Shamrock hadn't won anything. The closest he had been was, I think, a runner up. To me, a runner up in wrestling never made it to super bouts, and they never made it to championship bouts—they are still a runner up. Only the top people make it to championship bouts. I beat him the second time.

Q: Some MMA athletes use steroids. Do you think Ken was on some kind of substance at the time he fought you?
Severn: I don't think it's a lot of steroids they are using now, but a lot of them are prone to human growth hormones because there are no tests for human growth hormone, but there are for steroids. So, more athletes are moving over to human growth hormone. I have to say Ken was on something because he has faced Tito Ortiz at 205 pounds, Ken has been as high as 245 or 250-pound range when he faced me. How do you put on that muscle mass in that short period of time? I only know one way, and that's through chemistry. The thing about me is I'm a lifetime chemical free. And there are not too many heavyweights that can

actually claim life-time chemical-free status. If you only knew how little I trained in all of these years and still came away with the results I have . . . I'm a freak of nature.

Q: What would you consider, in terms of style, to be your "toughest fight?"
Severn: The hardest fight would have been with another wrestler because the skills I bring in, and if he had the kind of wrestling skills to match then that would have neutralized each other's skills and bring into play then secondary skills. By secondary skills, I mean striking ability, whether it's your hands or feet, would determine the fight.

Q: You are an educated man and have a college degree. Why did it take the public so long to realize that UFC is not about two thugs fighting?
Severn: I would disagree with the way you stated that. I think the general population loved it [the UFC]. I just think it was the politicians and Athletic commissioners that had the misconceptions. [Arizona] Senator John McCain was one of the biggest detractors of the sport, yet he knew nothing about it. I was conducting two of my training camps held in Arizona at the North Phoenix Baptist Church, which he is a member of. Right in the basement of his own church, they have a youth program called "Rosy Cheeks." They had five-year old kids who were doing open-glove shots to each other's faces. That's why they came up with the name "Rosy Cheeks." This was in his own church and he didn't even know about it.

Q: In your opinion, how has the UFC evolved as of 2008?
Severn: UFC is just one company—it's the most recognized company—but you've got Elite XC that is doing some great things. Then you've got Showtime. HBO is getting to work with some promotion, too. CBS just aired the Kimbo Slice against James Thompson fight. I'm happy with that because UFC needs competition. As more competition arises the athletes will be compensated better. When you look at what boxers are making, one big super bout they're making millions of dollars. The

very top UFC guys, by the time they get a piece of the pay-per-view, it's a little over than a million dollars for either one individual or a pair. I think it's going to grow and you are going to see more changes which will start to occur. There might even be more rules along the way. Still, corporate America has not embraced it yet. There's a lot of growth yet to come and financial purses will grow as well.

Q: Is there any particular fighter you would have liked to have fought? If so, who would it have been?
Severn: It would have been Royce Gracie. Had I known just a little bit about the politics—I have nothing against Royce Gracie or his family and I'm not trying to attack anybody—but had I known a little bit more what that company represented and how it was being run, I would have done some different things in my match. And it might have been a different outcome. It might have been. I can't guarantee that. But I would have had a different mindset, let's put it that way.

Q: What was the public's reaction when you first made the transition back to WWE from MMA?
Severn: I was a professional wrestler first in 1992 before embarking on my MMA career. Then in 1994 the Ultimate Fighting Championship started out, and later I ended up with working with WWF—now known as WWE. I had always been a professional wrestler first. A lot of people in the fight world think I was a sellout to the fight world when I went to professional wrestling, but the reality is: I was a professional wrestler first. They shouldn't be mad at me, but the only people who should be mad at me are the professional wrestlers because I sold out and became a cage fighter.

When I tell people now they think that's fine. Now it's become a Catch-22 kind of a thing for me. I didn't go to the WWF for the money; I went for the exposure. The UFC was a very small niche market in the beginning when it was known as no-holds-barred because you had Senator John McCain and other politicians and athletic commissioners trying to eliminate no-holds-barred fighting altogether. It had to change in order to survive. I am the only triple-crowned champion from the no-holds-barred era that will be marked in the history books because no-holds-barred fighting doesn't exist anymore. This is a title I will hold forever.

Q: Who is your favorite UFC or MMA fighter?
Severn: I couldn't even say. I just don't watch it enough to render an opinion. I very rarely watch it.

Q: What has been the proudest moment in your MMA career?
Severn: I would say a couple of things: being the only triple-crown champion in the UFC history in no-holds-barred era—that's one aspect. Then it's the Hall of Fame, which to me is a very political type of thing because we have new ownership. To me, it's like, *Who is voting in for these athletes? Who voted Randy Couture or Mark Coleman, who voted me in? Who is on the selection committee?* Because I don't know if some people who have been inducted into the Hall of Fame is because there were some political reasons behind that. I don't know. I mean, I look at it from a couple of different ways, but it's an honor to be recognized. But just because you have third ownership of the UFC, is it Dana White and a few of the people in his office that decide who gets to go in the Hall of Fame?

Q: You were one of the many UFC fighters to cross over to Japan and fight in Pride. What are your thoughts on fighting in Japan?
Severn: It's different fighting in a ring opposed to a cage. I don't like the fact that if you get tangled up in the ropes in a ring, they stop you trying to pull you out in the center and restart you. That's kind of a tough thing to do because if you were in a bad position, you're going to go for a better position—that's human nature. That's the thing I didn't really like about it. I rather know if I'm in a cage I can use that cage to my advantage against my opponent. I'm one of the best guys using the cage as part of my tactics.

Q: Any advice for anyone wanting to get into MMA?
Severn: I'd say train hard, do not give up your day job and hopefully your day job have health benefits.

Q: We hear some WWE wrestlers wanting to fight in the UFC. Kurt Angle has showed interest. How do you see them ever performing in the Octagon?

Severn: Kurt Angle has been talking about that for the last three or four years, but I don't think we'll see him jump in the Ultimate Fighting Championship. He might go into a smaller MMA company, but I can't see him walking into the UFC. On the other hand, Brock Lesnar is younger and would have more of a future. Other Professional wrestlers like Kurt Angle and Brock Lesnar, who were both amateur wrestlers and were very good amateur wrestlers, could.

If you take an athlete who has a certain mindset with a work ethic, he would do just fine in other sport endeavors because the work ethic is strong. They know they have got to work hard and have this mental mindset. I think Brock would do just fine in his upcoming matches. He was little bit young to be put against Frank Mir, but at the same token had it been me training Brock Lesnar, the match wouldn't have gone to the ground in the first place in the first round. I would have taught him to keep hitting Frank out of his reach, bludgeoning him, bludgeoning him, and bludgeoning him. I can't see Frank going to take Brock Lesnar down. Maybe stand for the first round and second round and then go on the ground finish him off. Brock is a very powerful individual and most wrestlers can win with takedowns and ground-and-pound. Mir is good enough in submissions and early on he can catch a leg or arm and he'll finish it.

Q: What are you involved in presently?

Severn: I'm sitting here in my office inside of a 10,000-foot training facility in Coldwater, Michigan. It's called Michigan Sports Camp Training Facility. We teach amateur wrestling, which still is my first teaching because I've been doing that for longer than anything else. We also teach professional wrestling. And we have athletes going onto WWE and TNA and a lot of the independent circuits. Once a month we run pro shows inside of our training facility. We also teach MMA. I have several other instructors teaching boxing, kickboxing, Muay Thai, jiu-jitsu. I've been working with law enforcements for over six years and developed defensive tactics. They've had several states come up to our facilities because of our effective methods, which are very functional for what they need to do. I continue to do a lot of MMA seminars, speaking engagements, appearances, and last year I fought in ten matches and three matches already this year. I still have a few more matches to do this year, but the reality is I turn fifty years old as of tomorrow. I'm not the young man I once was, but I started my UFC career just before I was thirty-seven years old.

My MMA company is called Danger Zone. We run a show every couple of months. We've ran thirty-six total shows so far and have had people like "Rampage" Jackson—who competed earlier in his career—also Forrest Griffin, Sean Sherk, Ric Clementi to name a few. I also helped Rashad Evans' amateur and pro career and helped him get his video out to *The Ultimate Fighter*. He's a high-profile athlete in UFC now. I have a degree from Arizona State, a teacher's certificate. And right now I'm probably teaching a few times each month, as my schedule permits. I engage students and make them think for the first time in their lives. That's what the administration loves about what I do. So, you might have a fighter with a ring name "The Beast," but I'm probably the furthest thing from it. This ring name was given to me by Jim Brown, the legendary football player. He said, "You're like Dr. Jekyll and Mr. Hyde. You're the nicest guy in the world outside of the cage, you wear suits and ties which make you look like an insurance agent. And when you step inside the cage, you bring a whole different image!"

He couldn't believe how I was able to do that transition. I got kind of giddy there. Jim Brown, who is one of the top one hundred athletes ever, and for that man to give me my ring name, that is another one of those honors. The world record was seven title belts when I started. I had eighteen title belts. I started MMA at the age of thirty-seven. I'll probably pick up at least one more before I retire. I will probably retire in a year and a half or two years because I have some other interests that I want to pursue. I don't want to do injustice. I feel like I've been doing some injustice to my MMA career, which has lasted more than ten years. Anyway, I've had some losses, which I ended up with which should have never occurred. Because the lack of training and preparation, I ended up going into the matches and losing them otherwise I could've done otherwise. I do MMA seminars and if people want to learn some good mechanics when it comes to MMA, then I'm the man.

Mark Coleman

UFC Heavyweight Champion/Hall of Famer

Question: Let's talk about your childhood and your freestyle wrestling career.
Mark Coleman: When I was a five-year-old kid, I wanted to play all sports. American football was very popular and so was baseball. And wrestling was in between these two sports. I loved one-on-one competition. My father was a wrestler. I wanted to be the best at everything I did sports-wise. Sport is the only thing that mattered to me. I wanted to be the best in all three of these sports. That's how I got started as a very young boy. That's all I did—athletics. In school maybe I didn't try so hard with education. I wish I would have, but I did just enough to stay eligible and to be able to compete. As a young boy, my goals were to be an Olympic champion or an NFL football star or Major League baseball player. This is what I dreamed of when I was a little boy.

Q: Did you ever try out for the Olympics?
Coleman: I became a State champion in high school and went on to college and became a national champion for Ohio State University. After I graduated from college, I became a coach and began my preparation for trying to win a world championship and Olympic gold medal. In 1990, I became the Pan-American games gold medalist—this is when I became a national freestyle champion. So I was ranked the number one in America in the freestyle division. In 1991, I made the world team and finished second, losing to the Russians which made me the second

ranked in the world that year. Now I had one more year to prepare for my ultimate goal, which was to become an Olympic gold medalist. I made the Olympic team, which was one of the biggest highlights of my life up till then. I finished in seventh at the Olympic Games, which was very disappointing for me at the time because I was planning on winning the gold medal of course.

Q: When did you first hear about the UFC, and what was your initial reaction?
Coleman: After the 1992 Olympics, when I finished seventh place, it was the turning point of my career. In America amateur wrestling is only important to me; it means nothing to rest of America, because it's very hard to make a living and there's no money in the sport of amateur wrestling. And it's not very popular compared to the other sports. So I retired from wrestling and I started seeing ultimate fighting on TV in 1993. I immediately knew this is what I wanted to do, but you have to get the opportunity. So, in order to get a chance I started wrestling again in 1995. I met Kurt Angle, who was the world champion in America that year, and I beat him in a wrestling match. He made the American team and, again, in 1996 I tried for the Olympic team but lost in the semi-finals. At this point I'm thirty-one years old and my wrestling career is basically finished at this stage. So now I need to find a way to get into the UFC. Fortunately a manager was at the Olympic trials when I lost. He had heard about me and he knew I was interested in fighting. He approached me with a contract and asked me if I wanted to fight in the UFC in about 30 day time. So basically I signed a contract with this manager and I went from the Olympic trials wrestling match and walked into a cage 30 days later.

Q: When you first walked into the Octagon, did you only have Olympic wrestling experience and some street fighting experience?
Coleman: The manager knew I wanted in and some rumors that were circulating were I had street fighting experience before. I would admit to doing a little bit of street fighting. I won all my street fights, of course. I never wanted to lose a street fight and never wanted to lose a wrestling

match. To me wrestling and fighting went hand in hand. I just didn't like to lose.

Q: Being a grappler yourself, what did you think of small guys— such as Royce Gracie—beating much bigger, heavier, and stronger guys in the UFC?

Coleman: Early on, just like everybody else in America, we call it "being dumb" or "naive." I did not care about jiu-jitsu or standup fighting because I knew I was going to nullify the standup game very easily. And as for the jiu-jitsu, I never had much respect for it at the time. All we wrestlers in America always felt that in a street fight or in a cage, we were the best. In the beginning every athlete was representing their sport. I was representing wrestling and I believed the wrestlers were the toughest and the best. I had 30 days during that time and I did study the very basics of jiu-jitsu. Back in the early days, what made jiu-jitsu ineffective was that head butts were legal—you can't go for an arm bar or a submission hold when somebody is able to head butt you or punch you with their left or right hand. My game plan was very simple, that's why I came up with the phrase "I'm gonna ground and pound him." Now everybody uses this term and it's a very famous term now. I was the very first to say this. It was very effective, but I must admit I was also a little lucky in the beginning because I did not face anyone who had really good submission skills. This was very helpful in the beginning because maybe I would have got into trouble. The head butt is the equalizer as it nullified most submission attempts.

Q: In the beginning, grapplers were dominating the UFC. Later strikers started to do well. Is it imperative to be a complete fighter?

Coleman: In the beginning some guys were much less talented than others, for sure. Obviously, nowadays fighters are well rounded. That's what I said in the beginning: the strikers will have to learn how to grapple to stand a chance in the Octagon. And this is what happened. The grapplers learned how to strike as well as learning submissions. Nowadays you have to be black belt level in every area to be the champion. In the beginning, I was fortunate that my style was effective enough to win me the title, but if you only know one style now you don't have a chance in a fight these days. The athletes now are incredibly well rounded in all areas. Now you have fighters who started out when they were ten years old who now are twenty-five years old. That means they've been doing it for fifteen years—obviously, they're excellent in all areas. I consider them the best athletes in the world

Q: You became the first UFC heavyweight champion after beating another legendary fighter, Dan Severn. Was this your ultimate goal, to become the UFC heavyweight champion?

Coleman: With this fight, people had their own conception of what was going to happen. When I took my gloves off, they assumed it was going to be more of a wrestling match and that I was going to try to take him down and choke him. But my game plan for this fight was different. When I took my gloves off, I knew I'd do more damage when I hit him. I wanted to stand up and trade with Dan Severn. He decided to take me down, which at the time in our careers I thought I was a much better wrestler and striker than him. But when he decided to take me down, he was unsuccessful and from that point on people say that I was maybe kind to Dan Severn because he was a fellow wrestler. But I'll tell you this is just not true. Because once I'm in the cage it doesn't matter. I've been in the cage up against many friends before, whether they're a friend or not they're not a friend in the cage. The reason I didn't punch Dan Severn by ground and pounding him like I did to many other fighters, is because I had to take what he gave me. And what he gave me was a side headlock choke. I don't care how I win the fight—I just finish the fight any way I can. He gave me the side headlock choke and I took it and finished him off early and quickly. For me, this fight was incredibly great and one of the highlights of my career.

Q: Any behind-the-scenes UFC stories you would like to share?

Coleman: All the fighters seem to be a lot like [each other]. Obviously we have a lot of differences, but before a fight and after a fight it's completely a different atmosphere. After a fight we like to drink a couple of bears and enjoy the moment, and are happy that the whole things over.

Win or lose, you live to see another day. I definitely had some incredible times in the last ten years of my life and I've traveled and seen the whole world. To me, it's been an amazing experience and I met some great people in the process and had a lot of fun. Actually, I've not been to the UK, but I really look forward to going there. The dollar's not worth shit, so someone will have to lend me a few pounds over there. The sport has grown and the UK has accepted it. About five years ago, I was supposed to fight James Thompson, but the fight got cancelled a day before we were supposed to fight. I respect how far he's come along and he's a big name here right now. He's obviously paid his dues. Maybe we can have that fight one day in England. I hope it works out, for sure.

Q: How did your career blossom in Japan?
Coleman: My history over in Japan was a great experience and I had a good time. I had some real high moments with the Pride Grand Prix in which I competed in. There were some big wins for me. I became a professional wrestler in Japan with Hustle Hustle and a couple of other companies over there. So, I got to work as a pro wrestler which was another great experience. The fans in Japan are second to nobody because they really love the sport of MMA and treat the fighters really well. It was unfortunate how everything had to end for Pride, but there are a couple of other companies who have started up to fill the void. You get 50,000 people waiting to see the fights in the stadiums in Japan. Someone needs to put the shows on because the fans want to watch these. I miss Japan as well. At the same time, I'm very happy to be back fighting in the UFC, which was my goal all along. UFC was the first, and now it's the biggest and the strongest organization in the world. I'm very happy they have given me the opportunity to fight again. They are the NFL of MMA and I look forward to the challenge of coming back and showing the Americans I am still fighting and I'm proud of it.

Q: Did you really stomp on Wanderlei Silva's throat after your fight at Pride 31 (February 2006)?
Coleman: No, I did not stomp on his throat. I visualized winning the fight against [Mauricio] "Shogun" [Rua]. But after the fight I thought

there might be a problem with the Chute Boxe corner. Even prior to the fight I and the Chute Boxe team had a very good relationship. I knew if I win the fight this relationship might become sour. When I did win the fight, sure enough they jumped into the ring and it was no longer a fight in the ring or cage where there is a referee; now it became a street fight. Like I said, sometimes I do my best fighting when there's no clock and no referee. The fewer rules for me, the better. All I had in my corner was Phil Baroni and my father, and on their side I don't know who walked in because it happened so fast. I had a lot of people coming at me all at once so I had to move. I threw a couple of punches and finally, before he [Silva] got to me he tripped up. So he started to get my leg and we scrambled a lot and took a couple of punches.

Near the ropes, Phil Baroni and Wanderlei Silva were fighting on the ground with each other. The next thing, I was stuck up on the ropes and looked down and made eye contact with none other than Wanderlei Silva, who was down below me in a very bad position. He was looking at me. And, yes, I did have the opportunity to stomp on his face if I wanted to. But this is not my style. I am a fighter not a killer. So, instead of stomping on his face, I did put my foot on his throat just to let him know that. This pissed him off, so he started squirming really hard, and he got up back on his feet. I thought it was going to be round two but somehow they kept matters calm. I'd seen him coming and I didn't appreciate him attacking me like he did. If he didn't trip when he was coming for me, he would have hit me as hard as he could in the side of the head without me looking with a sucker punch. If he had the opportunity he would have hit me. That was the end of the evening. I was very happy because that was a very critical fight in my career because it was the last fight on my contract and I needed that win really bad. I really prepared hard for it and was very confident. The adrenaline afterwards, the whole thing about the Wanderlei incident looking back at it, is just another story to tell. It was scary and dangerous but a lot of fun. After the fight it was more fun than doing the actual fight. I felt for sure they were going to create some controversy with me and the Chute Boxe team. That would have been a nice little rivalry between the Hammer House versus the Chute Boxe teams.

Q: Another one of your controversial fights was against Don Frye at UFC 10 (July 1996). Was a man named Hamilton responsible for this mess?

Coleman: I don't talk much about Hamilton because in the beginning our relationship started out good. He approached me for the Olympic trials and gave me the UFC contract. Even though the contract was very unfair, I had to pay him a lot of my money—but I didn't care about that. I signed the contract. He was also looking at Mark Kerr and Tom Erickson—all three of us—and offered us all a contract saying in 30 days we could be in the UFC. I asked him where I needed to sign. He said, "Don't you want to read it"? I didn't care, it wasn't important to read it. I just needed the opportunity to get into this UFC tournament. I didn't want him to give it to anybody else like Mark Kerr or Tom Erickson. I don't want to call him "Mr. Hamilton," his name's Rich Hamilton . . . whatever his name is . . . that's not even his real name. Rich Hamilton is not even his real name.

Anyway, he went to Tom Erickson and Mark Kerr and both of them told him that they wanted to think about it and would get back to him. I asked Rich Hamilton where I needed to sign and asked him who else he was looking at. He said Mark Kerr and Tom Erickson. I said, "Listen, I'm the man for the job. I'll beat Mark Kerr or Tom Erickson's ass. I'll tell you what. I'll win UFC 10. I guarantee you." He said, "You have to be in Alabama in two days." I told him I'd be there. I packed up some shit and I flew over. I had to listen to this guy trying to teach me in the ring. In the beginning I wasn't open to learning stuff from other people. In wrestling I always mostly taught myself to wrestle. I was considered not very coachable. In wrestling I was called the 'Black sheep' because when most of the coaches in training sessions told me to do one thing, I would go over there and do something which was best for me instead. Maybe in hindsight I should've listened more, but I did things my way.

Now, in fighting I already had my game plan in how to I was going to win this tournament, but now I had to listen to Richard Hamilton who was trying to teach me. I didn't really want to listen to him very much because I had my own plan. He told me Don Frye was a very bad guy—he had trained him for UFC 9 (May 1996), but Don Frye left him. Everybody left Richard Hamilton for a reason. We all left him for a reason; we didn't like him. I don't want to get into that but it just didn't work out. Anyway, when Don Frye left him, he told me many bad things about Don Frye to get to hate him. He told me Don had hurt people and couple of his students on purpose in practice. He told me he broke this guy's knee, messed up the other guy's ankle. And these guys actually came in clutches and then told me that Don Frye was a bad guy. So it made the fight personal. During the fight, my girlfriend and Don Frye's wife were made to sit next to each other—during the whole fight. I could hear them both screaming the whole time.

The fight went just how I planned it to go. I was a bigger, stronger wrestler than Don Frye and I was very talented. I was going to take him down and there was nothing he was going to do about it. What I didn't count on was just how much balls he had. I couldn't believe the punishment and damage he was taking. Back in those UFCs, the referee wasn't allowed to stop the fight. It was getting pretty ugly now. At one point the referee did break us up. I didn't understand why he did this because there were no stoppages back then at all. They just cleaned Don Frye up. I think the promoters wanted Don Frye to possibly win this fight because sometimes the promoters have their favorites, of course. So they re-started the fight and the same thing happened. I took him down and I was ground and pounding him. Finally at the 11-minute mark they stopped the fight. Honestly, I was so tired myself. A lot of my friends came into the ring and crowded me. I remember it was so hot I almost passed out because I couldn't breathe. Don Frye has the biggest balls and heart in the business. We have since fought in Japan as well, but it's very hard to talk about the first fight. It was a classic. We have since had respect for each other and he is considered a very good friend of mine. Richard Hamilton is a friend of neither one.

Q: What do you think of the steroids controversy in the MMA world? Would I be right in saying your friend, Mark Kerr, went through some of this?
Coleman: Mark Kerr was more addicted to pain killers. If you watch the documentary he was doing pain killers. As far as steroids in MMA,

I think they've done a great job with the drug testing. I don't see it as being a problem because if you cheat you are going to get caught.

Q: The UFC has now spread into the mainstream, while you were fighting when the sport was still being blacklisted. What are your feelings now that you are back?

Coleman: It's obviously grown into the mainstream, just look at the buy rates and the ratings on the TV. They are on the charts doing a million buys. It's grown into an incredible phenomenon in America. You have fans everywhere and I'm happy to be part of it still. The UFC announced my comeback and inducted me into the Hall of Fame, which was an awesome great experience. If I just got into the Hall of Fame, that would've been OK but the UFC has also signed me to a contract, and this is what I always wanted. Now I realize how big this thing has become. The fans have treated me very well. America is the UFC country and in America they love UFC and MMA. There are all these other companies competing with the UFC, but the competition is needed. And in my mind UFC is the NFL right now.

Q: What is in store for Mark Coleman?

Coleman: Having restarted with the UFC, I recently signed a four-fight deal. I was scheduled to fight Brock Lesnar on August 9, 2008. I was looking forward to this fight. This was my chance to really make an impact back in America. A lot of people were looking forward to this fight. I was training and everything was going very well. I was training hard. At the same time, in this sport any day can be your last day. During sparring I tore my ligament and basically it's going to take six weeks to heal up. The only good thing about it is there's no surgery. The fight's been cancelled and I'm healing my leg right now and I'm doing what I can. And when I'm 100 percent, I'll continue my training and we'll see what the UFC has in mind for me. Hopefully a rematch with Brock Lesnar or I'll fight either in the heavyweight division or drop down to 205-pounds division and maybe fight Michael Bisping.

CHAPTER TWO:
LEGENDS AND CHAMPIONS

Frank Shamrock

UFC Light-Heavyweight Champion

Question: You grew up in a rough environment where it was all about survival. You later were adopted by the Shamrock family, and took their name. Can you elaborate on that experience?

Frank Shamrock: I first left home when I was twelve years old, and that put me in the juvenile system. I went from one home to another home, about five different group homes. I ended up at the Shamrock Boys Home—that's where I met Ken and Bob Shamrock. That's where my life changed from a street kid to a martial arts guy. It was really hard growing up. I felt I was alone a lot because I never had my regular family. It was more about survival for me. I didn't really know any different. I came from a broken home with a lot of brothers and sisters. I always kind of felt I was really alone and always kind of looking for my family and reconnect to a community or something. So, I remember being lonely and confused when I was growing up.

Q: When did you start training in martial arts, and what system did you initially take up?

Shamrock: I started when I was twenty-one years old. The first system I trained in was submission wrestling, which is Pancrase-based martial arts style.

Q: Did you ever take up wrestling or boxing prior to this as a kid?

Shamrock: No. I was completely the opposite in that I never did any martial arts or any sports. I never really did any of these until I walked into the gym one day and started the whole wrestling thing. I started weight training when I was about fourteen. And I did that consistently for about ten years.

Q: When did you first hear about and see the UFC?
Shamrock: Actually, I started training in submission wrestling before I ever saw the UFC. I watched my first UFC after about four or five months of training. I came from a weird situation because I didn't want to keep going to community college, but I wanted to live at home with my dad—my adopted dad—who was an avid sports person. He suggested I go down and try wrestling, submission wrestling, the thing my brother was doing at the time. I walked into the gym and into the martial arts not really knowing rules or anything. So, it was a pretty much an eye opener my first experience.

Q: What did you think of the earlier UFC, before you pursued it?
Shamrock: It was amazing—the whole art itself. I didn't really know much or studied UFC at the time; my study was submission wrestling and Pancrase, which was from Japan. I understood the dynamics of submission. I thought the UFC was really crazy and barbaric at the time. I thought it was more of a street fight than actual martial arts. But I was always impressed with the submission ability and thought the submissions were kind of the key to winning fights.

Q: When did you first start training for the UFC?
Shamrock: For me it was just an evolution of technique. I won the King of Pancrase championship and after that it was just like, *Where do you go next?* So the next big show was the UFC. I began training in MMA in 1997 and won the UFC title about six or seven months later. My first match was for the middleweight title, just after gloves became mandatory and just before weight classes. I remember the fight vividly. I fought Kevin Jackson for the middleweight title and I ended up beating him in 14 seconds. What I remember most about the match was the size of the cage, which was very different than a ring, and inside the cage the dynamics were very different. I had done big competitions in

the Pancrase organization and I had fought pretty big matches in front of large crowds before. So I didn't feel nervous in that way, but I felt nervous that I could get hurt and this worried me.

Q: What was it like fighting in Japan before and after your UFC career?
Shamrock: My most memorable fights were with Bas Rutten. He was a mad man. He was there to fight to the death and he had a different mentality than everybody else. I had the kind of a sportsman's mentality, whereas he had the kind of street fighter mentality. Different feeling made all the matches tough and really memorable.

Q: Can you talk to me about your UFC battles with Tito Ortiz?
Shamrock: It was a huge turning point for me in my career. I beat everybody so fast and dominated the whole sport for a long time. He was the new generation of fighters, big strong guys who knew how to wrestle and it was a big test for me physically to go out and do battle with him. I took serious damage but I learned a lot about leverage, technique, conditioning, and was a big match for me.

Q: What is your "on-season" training conditioning regime?
Shamrock: I do a lot of stuff for conditioning a month before I go out to the camp. So, maybe two or three months out I do a lot of bodyweight muscular conditioning like squats and pushups. Then, nearer to the fight, the conditioning becomes more explosive. So, I do kettlebell training, plyometrics, jump training to condition muscles that are going to explode. My core is the key to all punching power and kicking power, and wrestling conditioning as part of my muscular conditioning. Then I train with weights. I love lifting weights—it's good for your bones and body. This I do a couple of times a week. Then two weeks before my fight, I drop all my conditioning and relax and work techniques. Pad work, I separate it into two sections where I do a boxing workout and a kickboxing workout. On my boxing workout, I always work five-minute rounds and usually work myself up to five or six rounds—so 25 or 30 minutes of constant pad work. For my kickboxing workout, I lean

towards more technique than anything because the technique will also aid in building up the conditioning and balance. I do this for five or six rounds as well. And, probably one or two days, I kick really hard working on my power kicks, and those are all done on Thai pads. I used to do about four rounds of power kicks.

Grappling is something I do every day. I think the difference between the grappling style that I do is that the positioning doesn't really matter as much in our style. Movement and fluidity of movement and transition and submissions are the most important things. So most of my grappling workouts consist of mat drills, partner drills or technical or wrestling where we just change position quickly looking for holds. I do this 30 or 40 minutes a day. Then I do 50 to 60 percent working the technique where I'm just doing technical drilling.

Q: You're an advocate of weight training, conditioning, and fitness. What weight training routine do you implement into your workouts to keep in top physical condition?

Shamrock: I've got a real simple method: I always do three sets and three exercises for each large muscle group. For small muscle groups, such as biceps and triceps, I work them once or twice a week and I do two sets and two exercises each part. For biceps I like the barbell curl and the preacher curl. For triceps my two favorites are seated triceps exercises. Shoulders are in between the small and medium muscle groups. I usually train them as a small muscle group "twos and twos." I like the in-front of the face shoulder press, and side lateral dumbbell raises. For upper-back my favorite exercise are the seated row and anything pulling down like a seated pull-down. In addition to these two exercises, my other two favorites are upward row with a barbell and one-arm pull-ups with a dumbbell. I tend to train lower back, abs, and neck every day. I do a set of 100 reps. I'll do 100 crunches, the next day 100 leg raises, and the next day 100 side bends. For lower back I do 100 hyperextensions or any other lower back exercise I can add in.

My legs are broken into two parts—the front and the back part. I train these every week. Actually, I do legs twice a week if you look at it. I do three exercises and three sets with eight to ten reps. My favorite ones are 45-degrees leg press, the hack squat and the dumbbell lunge. For the hamstrings and the calves I do stiff dead lifts—also on the machine cable hamstring curls—and I work on the stability ball and do hamstring curls on the ball. I don't really focus on calves as a specific part because I box every day. I spend about 30 or 40 minutes on the balls of my feet. I think MMA fighters should be training with weights two or three days a week, preferably three days a week. The sessions should be an hour or hour and a half of high intensity. The goal should be, in my opinion, to strengthen and condition the body above and beyond, the muscle mass each muscle group being conditioned so the entire machine is strong.

Q: How important is nutrition to you as a professional MMA athlete?
Shamrock: First of all, food and nutrition is your fuel which runs your machine. For me, it's all about eating small meals—five or six small meals a day. Each meal I try to consume about 20 percent protein, 20 percent carbohydrates. I always like to eat green, orange vegetables. I also add a protein drink after training. I also drink Electrolex in between my training and I drink lots of water.

Q: You coach a lot of fighters now. What are your key coaching principles?
Shamrock: I think the biggest thing that I teach is, physically and mentally, you can do whatever you want. And you can do anything as long as you prepare yourself for it—conditioning, technique, whatever you want to accomplish. I'm a believer in meditation, focusing and creating the technique or the game plan you want to create, and the secret is of course hard work. My biggest success has always been being in the gym and training hard. And I teach my guys if you train hard and you focus and have a good plan, then you can succeed.

Q: You are close to former UFC heavyweight champion Maurice Smith, who was one of the first strikers to be crowned UFC champion. Am I right in saying that you both trained together, exchanging ideas and methods?
Shamrock: I made a deal years ago where he would train me in striking and I would train him in grappling. So we've been doing that for about

twelve years now. He's one of the best boxing and kickboxing striking coaches you can get because he really understands the game. He's also always being a student learning new techniques and upgrades his methods. When you're always studying and always getting better, you're always getting more efficient and effective. He's one of those students of the arts that keep me on my toes competing with you at anything, which makes you stay on edge and focused.

Q: How do you think a professional boxer would do in MMA?
Shamrock: I think there's no doubt that punching people in the head causes the most deaths. There's no doubt about that. The problem is, when you mix the kicking, and the grappling, throwing and the submission holds, then all these have strength of value. So, a straight boxer is never going to be as powerful as an all-round MMA fighter. I definitely think boxers are not the best fighters in the world, but they are definitely the best punchers in the world. Punching is just one part of the game. Every athlete would be good at MMA if they trained at it, because boxing is a very fine art which takes a long time to get good at, a lot of repetitions and training is required. MMA or even grappling is much more organic and natural styles your body knows how to move and wrestle. It's very foreign to punch stuff you have to train your body to do it. Anybody with that kind of dedication and training would be good at MMA. Any boxer would be good at MMA if they trained MMA. If they didn't then they'd fall prey to technique just as someone who didn't know how to punch would fall prey to punching.

Q: MMA and UFC has broken into the mainstream. How do you feel about this?
Shamrock: It feels great! Being one of the leaders of the sport I knew the sport from the beginning will be as popular as it is today. It's an amazing art form, and when you get the right combination of social environment, like now the sporting organizations right now, it realizes its true potential. It's fantastic to be in the game right now.

Q: What do you say to people who have misunderstood the sport of MMA? It feels as though they need to be educated and look beneath the surface before making comments.

Shamrock: Again, you hit it on the head—it's a lack of education. I say, "You know what? Watch the show and meet some of the fighters because you can't make a decision on what you hear or even by seeing one fight." I don't go around judging religious words and commenting on them because I don't know anything about it and why they are doing it. This is a good example.

Q: Did you coach BJ Penn at one time?

Shamrock: Actually, he was a young guy who trained with me at the Shamrock camp at one point. I was impressed with his natural ability, amazing flexibility, and his amazing balance. I think when he's focused and in shape he could beat everybody in the world.

Q: How has UFC evolved since you exited?

Shamrock: The sport in the marketing aspects has definitely evolved. The techniques have evolved, but only slightly. The marketing, selling of the sport and promotion side of things have really evolved. The technical side has done so too, but a lot slower than I would have wanted it to. Because truthfully a lot of the information was still available seven or eight years ago, just now the athletes are getting masters in the way they look at us. Before it was martial artists mixing styles to get better, that's the game; now these people are truly training in all styles all the time. Much like Bruce Lee did with jeet kune do, most people are just throwing away the stuff that doesn't work at all and not really worrying about it, just training the core techniques of MMA.

Q: You mentioned Bruce Lee. Were you influenced by him?

Shamrock: When I was a kid he's the guy who really sparked my interest in martial arts. It was like being in school: there was always some lesson to be learned or some story from his films. That was the first feed of martial arts I latched onto. When I got older, in my late teens, I started reading about him and his philosophies. He was the first person who was, in my opinion, looking at this very old art form in a very spiritual way. And that just made a real sense to me, especially the life I lived, some kind of way to live your life, having a goal or path.

Q: You got injured in your fight against Chung Le at Strikeforce (2008). What happened?
Shamrock: I got kicked in my forearm and it displaced my bone. Actually it got broken. And to repair it they cut it open and put a plate in it and screws and had to bolt it back together. I would like to fight him again. During the fight I didn't feel like I was in any danger, even with the broken arm I felt I could beat him.

Q: You were one of the first UFC fighters to get involved in TV and film work. What was it like working with Chuck Norris?
Shamrock: I worked with Chuck Norris which was really amazing. I met him socially a few times and he invited me to be on his show. He is a very respectful and a professional guy. I worked for eleven days on one of his episodes of *Walker Texas Ranger* and it was absolutely amazing. It was some of the hardest days of work of my life, but some of the most gratifying as well. We did a show about a prison where the guards were running the inmates prison fights and putting them on the internet. Chuck and I starred in it and it was just a wonderful experience. Also, I did a Burger King commercial. When I first started fighting in 1999, I went into acting and entertainment and I got a lot of offers for films and TV shows. And when the sport started growing again, I got out of that and back in the sport to fighting more. I also did a couple of more films between now and then, one called *No Rules*. I do a movie a year and a couple of commercials.

Q: You are one of the pioneers of the sport of MMA. What does the future hold for you?
Shamrock: Pioneers of the sport are people like Royce Gracie, Ken Shamrock, Mark Coleman, and Maurice Smith. They all made a huge impact on the sport when it was very young and really misunderstood. Some of them were artists and others were artists in their own way.

Some guys were there trying to adapt and made a huge impact. I think there are a lot of guys who made the sport what it is today. One of my focuses recently has been to spread the martial arts word, and this is something which is important because martial arts is what made me who I am today. And for me to be able to share that with other people, it's huge for me. I plan on fighting more. I love fighting and feel I've got ten more years left in me. I love being a martial artist professionally, so I want to keep doing that as long as possible from the teaching, training, and fighting. I think it's the greatest life any one can ask for.

Jens Pulver

UFC Lightweight Champion

Question: Jens, you had an extremely tough childhood, where you went through hell when you were growing up. Could you tell me more about this?

Jens Pulver: Yeah, when I was growing up it was tough. I was the eldest. I had two brothers and a sister, who is eight years younger than me who was a little too young to be in the middle of it all. My parents were young—twenty years old when I was born—and it was really hard with the abuse, drugs, and alcohol around us. My entire life growing up was one of those things when I was a kid I went out and I used to think to myself when I come home my mother might be dead. Anywhere I stayed, at my friend's house, a lot of the times I could hear her screaming my name when I was five or six years old. She was kind of taking a beating with her. At least when he [my father] was beating me he wasn't beating the others. This has kind of been my rule, a family theme where I didn't want anyone else to get beat. Soon as he moved past you moved out of the way, and he did what he did.

Q: Is it true that your father went as far as to actually placing a gun in your mouth when you were as young as seven?

Pulver: It's true. My mom actually told the story later on. It was one of those things when I was younger. What I remember more than anything was being lined up and being scared. I knew it was a gun, but more than anything I'd seen because I was too young. I remember him going out saying he was going to kill himself. And later coming back and talking with my mom. She explained everything. So, I guess at some point my body just kind of went elsewhere—it froze. When my mom brought that story alive in a book, I pretty much remember exactly what had happened. I never sat back and really delved back on it as I was growing up. But I do remember him few times going out telling us he was going to kill himself, and then coming back and beating my mother up. So, yes, that story is true.

Q: You graduated from Boise State University in criminal justice. Did your rough childhood have any impact on your education?
Pulver: I went toward the direction I wanted. I really wanted to do wrestling. The truth was that in school I was never a serious student, but you had to make grades Bs and Cs in order to do well in school. That's what kept me going. I always wanted to be able to wrestle, which I did in junior high school and college. When my wrestling career ended, I went for the college degree. I went to college and graduated and then went into MMA. So, it wasn't one of those things coming out of high school and finishing. I went to college and got my masters, but I never expected to be a fighter for the rest of my life.

Q: Why did you start fighting in unsanctioned underground MMA fights?
Pulver: Well, they weren't sanctioned because no-holds-barred was not legally sanctioned as a sport. UFC was on pay-per-view and cable and everybody was watching it. I fought with the intention of making a video tape. In high school gyms we got in the boxing ring or a wrestling ring, we weren't sanctioned because nobody really knew what to call it. It wasn't even considered a sport. I just fought wherever I could fight. So that I could get a video tape made more than anything else. So I can send the tape in and try to get in shows like *Extreme Challenge*, which I had read about over time when I first started MMA. This was one of the big shows out there at the time.

Again, if you are not getting paid for fighting, it goes under amateur rules—so there is no sanctioning body. We didn't have the gloves that you see in the UFC today, but they looked like them. I think they were called Boxer-genics. The first time I ever fought in an MMA fight, I just took my t-shirt off and went out into the arena and got the guy down and was able to get him in a rare naked choke. It was different.

Q: Do you remember watching the early UFCs, when Royce Gracie was beating bigger guys? Did this inspire you in any way?

Pulver: Yes, it inspired me. He was winning his fights, but I've always believed in wrestling and I had the street fighting mentality to go with it. I was always in great shape. How many people on the street are in that kind of good shape? I mean, I can wrestle for two hours and go all day long and outlast the other guy. And when the ground fighting was brought to our attention, that's what gave me hope. I always wanted to be a boxer, but the reality is when I'd seen MMA, I said to myself, *You know what? This is it.*

I thought it's good to do boxing and I was wrestling growing up and thought if we had something like punches and grappling put together, it'll be a different outcome in a fight. When MMA came about that's what made the whole fighting thing great. And when I saw Royce Gracie out there doing what he was doing, I was all excited about it. Then fighters like Pat Miletich and Randy Couture started to get into it all, and all the wrestlers I grew up watching came out and started competing too. That was the direction I wanted to go.

Q: You started training with Pat Miletich, and later Monte Cox took you under his wing. Is it true you packed your bags and flew out to Iowa with only $200 in your pocket?

Pulver: I didn't have $200; I had a bunch of change. I had two bags with me when I came to stay with Monte. I had my wrestling and training attire in one and my personal clothing in the other bag. I got my first UFC fight before I even went out there. So, I went out there to test my skills and it ended up with a draw. But I knew then that I was hooked. I had met Monte and Pat on the plane when we were flying out to one of the UFCs. This is when I knew what I wanted to do in my life. At the time, I was talking to Bob Shamrock a lot and he called Monte Cox.

And he said, "I've got this guy you really should take him in." Monte remembered who I was from the UFC and said he would absolutely. So I was extremely excited. I had no idea how cold it was going to be when I arrived in Monte's town. My mom packed me a big pack of lunch and I rationed it for two-and-a-half days. I wrote down all the goals that I wanted to accomplish and achieve when I got over here. I gave up everything. I still don't know where all that stuff is—it's gone. It's kind of like I had to say goodbye to that in order to live the last ten years of my life of MMA.

Q: You became the first UFC lightweight champion after you beat John Lewis at UFC 28 (November 2000). Can you tell me more about this?
Pulver: What happened was, John Lewis had stepped onto the scene. John Peretti, who was the match maker at the UFC, was the referee at the Bas Rutten Invitational event. And it was here where I had a bunch of fights. Peretti noticed me and decided to give me a title shot. He always had this goal which was to start a lighter weight division in the UFC. People used to say to me that if I wanted to get into the UFC, I had to get up to 170 pounds. I said, "No, I'll just keep knocking people out and beating them up."

I believe we both weighed in at 150 pounds, but still under the 170 division. And this kind of started the talk for the weight thing. Then they kind of started making it more official. When John Lewis fought me, he had two guests with him on the day—it was Dana White and Lorenzo Ferrita. I went out there and knocked John Lewis out in 14 seconds. And when they took over the UFC they went out and got Caol Uno. And they wanted the number-one guy and got me to fight for the belt. This was the first ever lightweight title.

Q: Your fight with BJ Penn is considered one of the highlights of your career. As I understand, you both had disdain for each other?
Pulver: The first fight I had with BJ Penn, I remember at the time I had already defended my belt twice. And at the time, Frank Shamrock was talking BJ this and BJ that, and how BJ is the greatest thing. So that's

really what got that rivalry going. I was the champion, but then when I watched him fight I thought to myself, *Oh, my God.* He knocked out Caol Ono in the head in 12 seconds, and he beat Joe Gilbert and Din Thomas, too. I was like, *Good God, look at this!* So for the first fight against BJ at UFC 35 (January 2002), I was a big underdog—six to one underdog going into that fight. That had me fired up and motivated because although I was the champion I was the underdog, so it was a big fight. Going into the fight, it was close. In the second round he almost had that arm bar on me, but I didn't tap and the time was up. I just never gave him that opportunity to be on top because I knew he could be extremely dangerous.

Then five years passed and people would always ask when the re-match was going to be. And I know BJ was up to 200 pounds. Then I came back and they wanted to put the fight on, which would be in the lightweight division in *The Ultimate Fighter* series. So BJ and I would be the coaches. There was bad blood between us and it changed to a brawling theme. We were on the show for seven-and-a-half weeks, and we were really mad at each other at that point. Then going into the fight, BJ did a good job. I got out of the first round, he got on top and again I made it tough, scored shots and takedowns. I spent the second half on top. I knew, and the corner knew, that he's going for a takedown. This time he didn't go for a submission which I was hoping for. He kept his position and kept throwing punches, that's when I knew I was in trouble. And he got that rare naked choke on me and that's when I had to tap.

Q: You began competing in pro boxing and won all four of your fights. Why did you decide to make this transition?
Pulver: After I left the UFC, the first time I gave up the belt, I thought MMA wasn't that big like we see it today. So I made the decision to leave. I had this time on hand now, so I thought I might as well use this time to really better all my skills. So, what better than sparring guys every day or I can go and start boxing. Whether or not it was for $600 when you first start off boxing, I put myself in that scenario where you have that atmosphere and crowd and the thrill of fighting somebody

you don't know. I never expected my pro debut to be on ESPN. Sure enough, I was on ESPN on *Tuesday Night Fight*. It was just a way to keep me going and really work on my other skills. People can work on them all day long, talking to the coach and working the pads, but you're just not going to get the same kind of effect unless when you are going up against someone you don't know, and get that atmosphere. That's really why I took this direction, to stay active. I even did a couple of grappling matches.

Q: Now that you've boxed professionally, what are your opinions on heavyweight boxing champions who were previously labeled as the world's toughest guys?

Pulver: Well, I always say this: boxing and MMA are two different things. I know Muay Thai fighters and MMA guys who can sit back and break the boxer down. But what I learned from boxing is, like any sport or in a domain where you are only allowed to punch using one method, some people can do an amazing job mastering the craft. Look at Mayweather, the guy's a gift. And a guy like Ali or someone with the power of Mike Tyson. I look at it like this, OK: if the boxer does not train knees, clinches, takedowns, elbows, and punching is all he has in his arsenal then all he's going to concentrate on is punching his opponent. It's amazing what some people can do. I think hardcore MMA fans realize who focus on boxing that when you appreciate when you see a great boxer you have to stand back and go, *Good God*. It's a very good sport and to be that good, that's an amazing thing to do. There's no comparison on the two. Could a boxer beat this MMA fighter? No! If that boxer went and became an MMA fighter and he got really good as he was a boxer, then he'd be disgusting [lethal]—but if he is only a boxer, then no. But if you go in his world, now could an MMA fighter fight a boxer in a boxing match? Let's take Mayweather, for instance. Tell him to go over there and fight BJ Penn or someone. Mayweather may have some chance and BJ will obviously get him down and beat him, strike him, and submit him.

But now it's BJ's turn to go into the boxer's world. Now you have to go out there and go six rounds with him in boxing. That's going to be the worst day of your life. He's going to hurt you bad. So you have to have appreciation for what boxing is, it's an amazing art when it comes to just using your hands.

Q: You returned for UFC 63 (September 2006). What was it like to be back in the Octagon?

Pulver: I never thought after being gone for three-and-a-half years that I would ever be back. And that was just an amazing honor for me. I sat back and watched Robbie Lawler, Kendal Grove—Matt Hughes was on top level; he was destroying Georges St-Pierre. When I was going to get that chance to come back in the UFC, when the time came, the walk down in the ring says it all. I had a smile on my face and I'm laughing and waving to every single person in the crowd. It was just great being back. I was never caught up in the moment that I was fighting—the fight wasn't important to me. The fact that I made it back and I was fighting back in the UFC in the Octagon that was important to me—that fight was nothing.

Q: Do you believe hard work, effort, and suffering have to be endured to be successful in this world? What is your philosophy on life?

Pulver: As far as fighting goes, the biggest thing is always the conditioning, hard work is definitely there. When I'm watching and learning more than anything to get in shape is one thing, and to move with the sport and get good at your craft and all your weak areas is another. That's what's amazing about watching a guy like Georges St-Pierre and Anderson Silva, even BJ Penn in his last fight. This guy just hit him so deadly in every facet of the game, and at that point it will come back to conditioning. It's hard to be able to focus on your conditioning, which takes a lot of time and, at the same token, you have got to work on the elements that got you there, and develop some things that will help you progress and get better in fighting. Now you see people who are good at everything because they've been training long enough and the sport has been here for longer. Conditioning is still the biggest part. I don't care who you are. Bruce Lee or Muhammad Ali, if you're out of shape it doesn't matter after a minute you ain't that fast, you ain't that good. But after developing the conditioning, then what do you do? Can you evolve to be an exceptional fighter out there in the same process?

Q: To date, what has been the biggest battle in your life?
Pulver: For me the biggest battle, first of all I have to say that fighting and training has been the best part. Battling with myself and dealing with the pain of growing up and allowing myself to be happy, allowing myself to know it's OK and feeling positive. When something good is happening and you sit back and say to yourself, *Alright, when's the shoe going to drop? Who's going to die? Or somebody's going to get sick.*" Whenever I was happy we went and wrestled, but when we got home there would be nothing but the beatings and sadness. So that's been my biggest battle. I'm learning every day that you have got to be positive and how to be a lot calm, instead of with my hairs up on my back waiting for that shoe to drop. I'm always expecting bad things to happen and never really allowed myself to enjoy what I'm doing. So that's been my greatest battle. I've never been afraid to admitting it to anybody. The fighting part is a blessing. To fight in MMA and do what I love doing and to be able to meet the fans every day, this has been the greatest part ever.

But to go home afterwards and get stuck, fear and it's like paranoia, the damages that happened to me and not allowing myself to have fun and enjoy myself. I don't drink, or do drugs. I'm not a violent person, but I'm bad on myself because I beat myself up with constantly being having fear anxiety attacks and worry. Even Monte gets a kick out of it as he teases me sometimes. I just freak out for no reason as I sometimes think, *God, this is going to happen and I'm not going to make it.* I'm waiting for bad things to happen to me all the time.

Q: Some UFC fighters have had childhoods parallel to yours. On the other hand, a lot of them have college degrees and are educated people. How do you compare the two?
Pulver: Everybody thought you had to be a delinquent drunk punk, straight from the bar stool into the Octagon. And people used to think we had to be punks because it was like your everyday fighting in the

street. No, it's not. Now people have started to understand it's a sport. I don't fight in the street. I haven't been in a street fight for ten or eleven years. I have got no need. Like I said, I don't drink and I don't go in the bars. I went to college and got a degree. MMA is not about going out there and beating somebody up; this is my sport to test myself against another opponent. My opponent came into it freewill to the sport and he's going to work on his skills. This is what we do. Some people are good at books, some at math, some can fix cars. What I'm good at and love doing more than anything is working on skills—boxing, kicking, punching and being in shape and entertaining people. Now it's just a lot bigger world of fighters, and more fans and people are starting to understand now that this isn't human cockfighting. The fighters don't have to come from a prison background or abused lifestyle to want to do this as a sport. It's definitely turned a full circle in way the people viewed the UFC in the beginning.

Q: Cub Swanson accused you of faking an injury because he felt you didn't want to fight him at WEC3 (2007). What have you got to say on this subject?

Pulver: The injury happened a week and a half before we were supposed to fight. I was disappointed. I have the doctor's report and the X-rays. Then I get this guy tell me this, after all the wars I've lived through and everything I've been through, all the people I've fought who I said I'd always fight. I'd said I'd fight anybody they'd put in front of me. So he's got to be dumb enough not to remember who I am and tell me I'm going to pull out of the fight because I'm scared. The first thing that came into my mind was, *You know how much money I make? I'll tell you what, it's a hell lot more than you think if you think I can miss a fight!* I'm a 145-pounder. They don't make that kind of money. I'm not making Chuck Liddell or Randy Couture cash. I'm not making cash what heavyweights make, period. I haven't fought for six-figure sums ever in my life. So that had me mad and made me realize sitting here talking to my fiancée Konika, this guy's forgotten what I've done for the sport and he's exactly the person who's got to learn and he's going to learn quickly. So this is what really started that war and got me fired up, but also got me to back to where I needed to be, which is training and fighting.

Q: You have two books out, and it seems you have a really fascinating story to tell.
Pulver: The book *Little Evil: One Ultimate Fighter's Rise to the Top*, I have no idea about that book as far as where to get it from. I remember writing it a long time ago with a buddy of mine who co-wrote it with me. His name is Eric Krause. This was long time ago. I know they stopped printing copies about three years ago. I don't know where you can find the book. I've not seen a penny from it. I don't even know how to get a hold of these people [the publishers]. They won't give back the rights. God knows whatever. The book itself is a timeline. It goes through my childhood up to the BJ Penn fight. The other book, *Never*, which is written by a friend of mine, is the book I love. This book is more of the mental side of me whilst being in MMA and it's pretty cool. It's about the conflicts and religious groups. I would say the book isn't all about me but most chapters cover me. It talks about moments with Matt Hughes, Tim Sylvia, Pat Milletch, Monte Cox—these people who have been around me and in this group that's why I love the book *Never*. It's an amazing story.

Q: It's obvious that you love to compete. Where does this thirst of competing stem from?
Pulver: Well, wrestling really saved my life—literally saved my life. I wouldn't have a college degree, plus I didn't need a 2.7 [grade-point average] in order to wrestle. The will to compete kept me in school and kept me in on the right path. If people don't believe me then I'll tell you. I have my brother who is serving fifty-five years in prison. And he and I are only a year apart. He just went on a different road. The reality for me is also on the other side. Here is my dad beating us, beating me and telling me I'm a piece of shit. I'm never going to make it. I'm a bastard and a loser just like my mother, and so on and so forth. But here are all these coaches showing me that if you go out and put all the hard work and train your butt off and stay focused, then you'll be successful.

If people are going to be positive you're going to feel it. The amount of gratitude I got from that by hearing praises from coaches and other athletes, it was a big scale tipper. I mean, here I was in-between. I was on a fine line the whole time—my dad in a big city beating me up on one end and on the other hand the positivity and the amazing feelings I got from competing.

Really, this MMA is just adding punches in the world I've already known. I've been through one-on-one combat. I love the idea of one on one. I could be in a team of eleven people and I might go train hard. I might stay focused on the pads, but the other ten guys might be out drinking, screwing, whoring, or whatever they do, and then we go out and lose—that's what I love one-on-one competition. If I have a broken heart, if I go in there out of shape then that's going to show. If you go out that way then this will fall back on you and there's nobody to turn to but yourself. I loved it that way, that's what shaped me and training and being around the coaches. One day being able to be in a position that I'm moving towards now just turn around and help kids who were walking in my shoes before. Turn around and tell them, "This is what I did and this is what you can do." That is going to be my job when I'm ready to retire from the sport. I'm going to move in with the full circle become a coach as the coaches saved my life.

Q: We hear you're a big video games fan. Tell me more about your obsession with video games.
Pulver: Oh, I love games. I don't know where it comes from but, for me, I love the graphics and I love the styles of certain games. I'm not going to grab a gun or be in a war or jungle, or fighting and shooting other people—that's not going to happen in my life ever. But I can simulate and play on the video games and the feelings are there. I've always loved playing computer games.

Q: Can you tell me your final fight under the WEC banner before the organization merged with the UFC?
Pulver: I fought on June 1 for the world featherweight title and lost in a five-round decision. It was voted one of the Fights of the Year and the

organization was WEC, which is the same owner of UFC. We sold out the arena, broke records as far as how many tuned into view the fight. And that's great because the co-main event was 145-pound and 135-pound fights. That was an amazing event.

Q: Were you influenced by Bruce Lee?
Pulver: You know what, I was influenced by him. Because of his size, he's a little guy out there doing his thing and this gave me hope. I was in one of those positions where I was too big to be small. My parents were jockeys and I spent my whole life up till I was fifteen preparing to be a jockey. I was going to ride horses and that was what I was going to do as a career, but then I got too big and heavy but I was too small and not big enough to do anything else. Bruce Lee gave me hope because he was my size, his speed and flexibility alone, if I can have that alone, oh my God. Absolutely I was influenced by him. I wasn't a big practitioner of the martial arts, but I was a practitioner of his discipline and style of Bruce Lee. The way he thinks, the way he trained, the way he focused on it and the way he believed in himself and slept, ate, and drank his art. And that was very influential.

Q: Do you think Bruce Lee was one of the first martial artists who opened people's eyes to investigate and evolve the sport?
Pulver: I think he's one of the reasons why MMA came about, absolutely, because people had that question. This guy was fast, he'd kick you six times in the face before your eyes could see him do the first kick. How are you going to beat him? So that started really the question. Some of the people he competed against, he was comparing their style. What if I grab a hold of you, you've got to figure something out. I think that's what really started the revolution of that question. What if a guy on the ground grabs a hold of somebody, let's find out how to deal with it.

Q: UFC is beating boxing in certain respects and filtering into the mainstream. How do you feel about the enormous success of MMA?
Pulver: The reason it's beating boxing is because for one, a lot of those top fighters in boxing for a long time wouldn't fight each other. You

finally started seeing the 142, 146 pounders, such as Ricky Hatton, Sugar Ray Mosley, you started seeing big matches like that. Right now, MMA is the biggest thing because the guys who want to fight are not only good with their hands, but you don't have to be good with just with your hands; you can be good at grappling, wrestling, kicking. So, right now in this sport we always ask the question, "Have you seen Mike Tyson do his thing?" And then, "Have you seen this great wrestler do his thing?" and, "If those two met I wonder what would happen?" MMA came along and answered those questions, and this is the front runner for combative sports.

Q: When are you fighting next?
Pulver: There's no official news but I would like to fight as soon as possible. I'm waiting and sitting back just waiting for the official send out the agreement and I sign it. I want to fight as soon as possible. I want to get back on the horse again and I want another shot at Urijah Faber. I want to fight him again and go out there and take my fight and earn my rematch. I'm still under the same umbrella WEC owned by the UFC.

Q: What are your future plans?
Pulver: I have a daughter who I want to see grow up. My wife Konika is pregnant with our baby. Future for me personally is to have a family and be the opposite father that I had. Fighting-wise I want to fight as soon as possible. And I think I've shown people I'm not done yet. I'm not retiring and still ranked the number-four guy in the world. Really, right now, man, the future is wide open. God knows, I'm after this fight hopefully in December.

Tito Ortiz

UFC Light-Heavyweight Champion/Hall of Famer

Question: Tito, I understand your childhood was not the happiest time of your life. Can you tell me what obstacles you had to overcome in everyday life to survive?

Tito Ortiz: From the age of seven to thirteen, my parents were drug addicts, but I was never using drugs with them—ever. But it was a factor of them using them and me going along with the "ride." It was really tough moving house to house, motel to motel and college to college. We had it really tough. My mom left my father and got remarried. And I got a second chance of life, I think. We lived in peoples' garages and couches—it got really rough for us. It wasn't until one of the gangs I was in that one of my friends got shot and killed, that she came to realize that she better get me out of where we were living or I would be next. When I was in high school I mixed with that gang culture really bad. So when one of my friends got shot and killed, it was a chance for me to get out of all that from Santa Ana, a city here in Southern California, which is very gang populated. I was always fighting every weekend and then guns started coming out of the fights. My mom got me out of this and brought me back to Huntington Beach. I kind of got my nose cleaned by getting into wrestling.

Q: Can you tell me more about your involvement in wrestling?

Ortiz: I got interested in wrestling in my freshman year in high school. I walked into the wrestling room because I was always a big WWE wrestling fan. I always wanted to wrestle. So, I walked into the wrestling room and there was no ring. I asked where the ring was. I came to realize that collegiate wrestling was totally different to professional wrestling. But I got attracted to it because it was a one-on-one sport. The harder I trained, the better I became.

Q: What were you doing to make ends meet?
Ortiz: At that time, I was actually on working on a fishing boat here in California. It was day times in the summer and night times in the winter. It was a full-time job, but just enough to make ends meet. When I got out of high school, I really had to make ends meet because I was on my own. My mom gave me 800 bucks and said, "It's time for you to be a man, time for you to grow up." I went out and bought a car, rented a house and just started finding jobs. Then this fight game came along from the wrestling.

Q: Can you recall when you first saw the UFC?
Ortiz: I watched the very first UFC all the way up to the sixth one. I was nothing but a fan. And after the sixth UFC, when Tank Abbot fought, he trained where I was wrestling at. I was one of the better wrestlers in California so he brought me in as a training partner. Then from that point on, it was an evolution of the sport to what it is today and I was the front runner of all of it. After I competed for a year and a half in the UFC, I became a world champion. And after that one year after I defended my world title, I became one of the biggest stars in the sport today. As a fan watching it back in those days, I thought these guys were crazy and I never really thought to myself I'd be fighting in the UFC in the future. These guys were great athletes, like Royce Gracie who was choking the wrestlers out left and right. That was a turning point for me and I started learning jiu-jitsu. I've got to thank Royce Gracie for that.

Q: Was Gracie a big inspiration to you, as the early UFCs were seminal?
Ortiz: I think he was a huge inspiration to all of the athletes back then and even now. If it wasn't for Royce Gracie, no one would know what

jiu-jitsu was. Royce Gracie is an icon of MMA. He was the guy who brought the martial arts side to it, and then there's guys like me who brought the spectacle side to it and made it interesting for the fans—to fall in love with their favorite fighters, like myself.

Q: You and Chuck Liddell were both managed by Dana White in the early stages. Tell me about the early relationship.

Ortiz: The early relationship was always great. Dana White always had our best interests in everything we did. But as soon as he became the president of the UFC, it was the best interests of the UFC and not us, the fighters, who got him there. I look at it as disrespect. It just got worse and worse, where he cared more about the company and cared less about us. In the beginning he was fighting for us. He said his fighters need this amount from the pay-per-view and they need this amount of money, etc. And now I'm saying the same thing and Dana calls me a moron. I'm arguing for the same thing that he was arguing when he was my manager. Dana White is talking smack about me because I'm looking out for my best interests.

Q: You won the light-heavyweight belt at UFC 25 (April 2000) against Wanderlei Silva. What are your thoughts on achieving this milestone?

Ortiz: For one, I slept with my belt for the first month after receiving it. It was great glory for me. After only being in the sport for a year and a half, I beat one of the top light-heavyweights at the time, Wanderlei Silva, who only had a couple of losses on his record. He was just crushing through people. Prior to this fight I fought Frank Shamrock and lost to him at the end of the fourth round. It was pretty much because of exhaustion. Frank Shamrock never wanted a rematch, so they got the best light-heavyweight out there—probably one of the most dangerous guys—which was Wanderlei Silva. We fought for the vacant title belt and the best guy got his hand raised. Thank God that was me.

Q: One of the toughest fights of your career was against Randy Couture, who beat you at UFC 44 (September 2003). You once

related to me this was one of the saddest moments of your career, why was that?

Ortiz: Losing to Couture when you are on top of the hill and you're the champion and everybody wants a piece of you. No one says no to you. And all of a sudden you lose it and you look in your dressing room where in the beginning of the fight there were twenty people in there, and after your loss there's only three in your room. You kind of realize how people react to losers, I guess. It really hurt me because I didn't suffer a loss for almost four years and all of a sudden I lost and it felt like the world got ripped underneath me. I compare it to a loved one dying when I suffered that loss. Couture fought a great fight. I got injured about a month before the fight with my lower back disc. So I wasn't even able to wrestle, but boxed and did jiu-jitsu. And that's what it came down to in the fight—he dominated me by outwrestling me. He finally got a takedown and dominated me. He didn't hurt me seriously, but he fought a fight. It was one of my worst losses I ever had.

Q: At one point people thought UFC fighters resembled street thugs. Do you feel UFC fighters are the hardest training athletes in the world?

Ortiz: The competitors competing now are 100 percent athletes. They are well-rounded athletes not just in fighting, but marketing and interviewing. All these guys are educated and come from a college background. Like myself, Randy Couture went to Oklahoma State; Chuck Liddell went to Cal Poly here in California; [Quinton] Rampage [Jackson] went to college. All of us have got some sort of a college degree and a college career in wrestling. We thought we were going to be professional wrestlers. Now we are professional fighters and make the sport what it is today.

So, the athletes that compete now are nothing like any other combative sport. Just because the great athletes we are, we train six days a week, eight hours a day, and we treat it as a full-time job. We carry the whole business on our shoulders. Everybody is watching what we do. We're getting mainstream each and every day more and more and as people watch us and understand what we do, they see that we are human. We do make mistakes and there are a lot of guys who take this job very seriously. And it is a full-time job. We're not bar brawling morons trying to pick a fight; we are athletes that compete in a sport, which is growing each and every day.

Q: Let's talk about your rivalry with Ken Shamrock and his brother Frank.

Ortiz: With Shamrock it all started off when I fought one of the Lion's Den fighters at UFC 13 (May 1997). I fought Guy Mezger and I was kicking his ass. He got me in a choke and he won the fight. I felt like I had to get revenge. So next time I fought Jerry Bohlander, I put on a t-shirt—it was a sponsor shirt, a porno company—and it read on the back "I just fucked your ass." It wasn't meant personal towards Bohlander at all; it was strictly a sponsor shirt. And I made some money on it and I put the shirt on after the fight. Everybody assumed that I was talking about Jerry Bohlander, which I wasn't. And this was the beginning of my rivalry with the Lion's Den. Then I had a rematch with Guy Mezger and I put on a shirt after the fight, which read "Guy Mezger's my bitch," they didn't like it. I didn't have a Lion's Den backing me up. I was myself with a couple of my trainers, but they had a whole team who trained with him. I wasn't going to back down to him, it was automatic. Ken Shamrock and his team started talking smack about me.

A couple of years later, me and him had a chance to fight each other. The rivalry had already built up and we fought. I stopped him in three rounds and it got worst. He kept talking more and more smack and so we fought again. We did *The Ultimate Fighter* and built hostility on that and we fought again. I stopped him in a minute and 18 seconds. He said it was a premature stop, but I thought he was clearly knocked out. The UFC came to me and asked if I wanted to fight Ken Shamrock again. I told them I already beat him twice. But I said, "If the fans deserve to see it then let's do it!" I stopped him for the third and final time. We shook hands and let bygones be bygones. He's an acquaintance, no more than that. It's history now. We've gone on our own business ventures and we're separate people now.

Q: In one of the press conferences, Ken Shamrock lost his temper with you, but you seemed to stay cool and calm. How did you manage to do that?

Ortiz: I think this happened in three or four of the press conferences actually. I push the buttons. I do things that not many fighters can do to others. It's kind of like Ali and Frasier. Ali can talk as much smack as he can as long as he backs it up. I try to get into the guy's head, and that's what I do. Like I said there were a couple of press conferences which had these incidents. First fight, then when after he fought Kimo he talked some smack that he wasn't healthy and wanted to fight me again. And another opportunity came by at *TUF* where he tried to be a bully and try to push me around, which wasn't happening. But we solved our differences in the cage—that's for sure.

Q: How did you find the experience on *The Ultimate Fighter*?

Ortiz: The experience was great. I got to train with some really great guys. Michael Bisping came out on top—number one. He was leaps far above all the guys competing on the show. Bisping and I got a good relationship now. He's actually out here in California training. I worked out with him yesterday and most likely work out with him today. Kendal Grove and Matt Hamill were also on the show. A lot of normal fans got to see what kind of a coach I was. Coaching is one of my secrets. I'm a good coach. I did coaching in the collegiate wrestling for high school students and college students. I understand the team game and the personal game to be better fighters. I think I showed a lot when I did *TUF* and it helped me a lot. People used to say, "Tito Ortiz talks shit in the Octagon." Then they see that he gives back something and helps other fighters. In *TUF* they got to see this side of me.

Q: You fought Chuck Liddell at UFC 47 (April 2004). Is it true that he said you tried to avoid fighting him?

Ortiz: There was a lot of bullshit behind it because of the picture Dana White was painting. Chuck Liddell and I said we weren't going to fight each other unless we got paid big dollars. I tried to hold on as long as possible, but Chuck Liddell sold out to the company not really caring about it. All he wanted was the belt. For me, for a friend to fight a friend, I thought we should be paid a lot of money. For him money is more important than friendship. That's fine. It shows what type of a person he is. The fight happened and I lost. Shit happens. I made a few mistakes. I really think that blood is thicker than water, but he sold out. When you have a person staying at your house—and I was staying at his house—you think there's a friendship built there. But Dana White painted a picture like there was no friendship—it kind of sucks because we were good friends at that point.

Q: You are friends with another notorious fighter, Mike Tyson. Tell me about your friendship with the former heavyweight champion.
Ortiz: Actually, I met him when he fought Francois Botha. After that I gave him my Punishment gear and he walked out with a beanie hat when he fought in England. He always came to my fights. I love the intensity of Tyson and the fighting style he has. Since I was really young I've always been a huge supporter of Tyson. And he's been a huge supporter of me. So we have a great relationship.

Q: What are your personal views on a heavyweight boxing champion being labeled as the toughest guy in the world?
Ortiz: It's like comparing apples to oranges. With boxing, it's like checkers and MMA is like chess. We have to move so many directions to win a game; boxers go forward and backwards, that's it. But MMA is multiple disciplines—kickboxing, wrestling, jiu-jitsu, boxing, cardio and weight training. There are so many things you need to be a great athlete at. You can't just be good with your hands. There's so much stuff that relate to MMA. Boxing is simple using two hands. A boxer wouldn't last a minute—any heavyweight, lightweight, middleweight champions, they wouldn't last a minute with any of the champions in MMA. Now let me give you kind of an idea, so people say boxing is always better. If I went and participated in a boxing match, I may last a round or two because I have a little bit of boxing experience. It's two totally two separate games.

Q: MMA has now evolved into a mainstream sport. What are your feelings on this?

Ortiz: When I started fighting back in the no-rules and no-time limits era, there were only three weight classes—lightweight, middleweight and heavyweight—that's it. But as you see, the sport evolved and became what it is today. It's just amazing knowing that I was one of the ambassadors of the sport making it what it is today. The athletes competing today are so well rounded. There are not just jiu-jitsu guys or kick-boxers, a lot are really well trained in all areas. In the beginning they were so one dimensional, but now there's a lot to learn. That's why there's so many good fighters compared to the beginning. When I started fighting in the beginning, there were 1,500 people in the audience with maybe 10,000 pay-per-view buyers. Now there are 16,000 people in the arena and over a million pay-per-view buyers. So the sport has grown a great deal. If two guys get into the ring and fight, this is something the fans want to watch and pay the money. Like I said, we're pretty much the modern-day gladiators like back in the Roman days. That's why people are attracted to our sport.

Q: What are your views on Dana White and the UFC not paying enough money to fighters? Boxers get paid millions of dollars.

Ortiz: Exactly! What it really comes down to is that the fighters who are making them the money need to be taken care of. But they're not taken care of. They take advantage of them and solicit them and not pay them what they're worth. In boxing the fighters are making $10 million to $20 million per fight and we scratch up to get up to a million. They're making 30 or even 40 million an event. We'll bite them in the butt in the long run. And I'm a person to stand up and make a difference. Muhammad Ali did for the boxing. I'm going to do the same thing in MMA.

Q: You started speaking up about fighters deserving more money. Is it true that Dana White and his guys told you to be quiet and not to make noise, and if so they'd give you a little more money?

Ortiz: That's very true. I thought it was going to get better and I wasn't going to say anything. And all of a sudden Dana White started painting a picture that I'm a moron. And I'm afraid of Chuck Liddell and that I'm no longer a fighter and I want to be a movie star. He was just talking so much smack about me it was just non-stop hindering my image. It degrades me 100 percent. I couldn't handle it anymore. So I keep speaking out for what I'm really worth. These guys try to disrespect me, time and again, but I have great fans that are going to follow me no matter where I go. I'm really excited about what will happen in the future.

Q: You've said that Dana White seems to want to be a star. Do you still stand by that?
Ortiz: He was the guy on Spike-TV in a show showing Dana White flying in the jets, taking cars and doing the weigh ins. He's doing the pictures and autographs and after the events he's doing the after-parties. You tell me that is someone who doesn't want to be a superstar? He wants to be a star. He's doing all those things. Soon he'll be fighting in the UFC—that's the next step. Now that I see the Fertita's [UFC co-owners] came in and started to clean up some of the stuff Dana has done. It just shows his desire at wanting to be a superstar. Time again he wants to be at the forefront. The last fight between Forrest [Griffin] versus Rampage [Jackson] happened it was all about the main two event fighters *and* Dana White. Dana White hasn't even fought in the Octagon, but he's trying to be that champion and superstar. When you have a billion dollars behind you, like he does, you can make that happen—and Dana White's doing it.

Q: It seems he didn't want you to come to the press conference at your last fight. Did he indeed make every effort to keep you out?
Ortiz: He didn't want me speaking out. He didn't want me to say what was true, especially with all the fighters around him at the press conference. The authorities tried to hold me out of getting into the press conference, but this is the United States of America and we have the freedom of speech. I was stepping up and said what I believed in. I told them, "I'm staying here. You guys better get security to rip me out of here because that's the only way I'm leaving!"

Q: Why didn't the boxing charity bout between you and Dana go ahead?

Ortiz: In the beginning, it was supposed to be for charity. He was going to keep the money all to himself—he wasn't going to cut me into it. We had an agreement that we would go 50/50 on any revenue that grossed from this boxing event we had. Then, all of a sudden, when it didn't go down, I told him he tried to take advantage of me and use me to get himself to be a superstar. He said it was all for charity so Tito isn't going to get any money. Once again, he tried to make me look bad and I didn't know anything about that. I thought it was going to charity, and I said, "That's terrific. Let's do it. Then give all the money to the charity." But they dropped the ball on it because it wasn't going to happen.

Q: Would you honestly really like to beat up your former boss?

Ortiz: Yeah. I'd like to beat him up as a street thug. Me and him just don't get along. And if we did have a boxing match, he wouldn't last a round. He'd be lucky to last a round. The only way he would have lasted a round is if he ran around the cage the whole time. But if I got hold of him, I guarantee you I would have knocked his ass off. That's history now. I'm willing to move on in my career and think about all the good things I have in the future.

Q: Tell me about your appearance on the TV show *The Apprentice*.

Ortiz: My Punishment Athletics company started with $500 and has grown to a multi-million dollar company in the last eight years. We've done really well. Donald Trump knew I was a great fighter and they wanted to bring a sports guy in. And they knew I was a good businessman because of my clothing company. I had a conversation and they told me it was for charity. And all the money I would raise would go to my favorite charity, which is St Hughes Children's Hospital. I got to raise $70,000 and build the awareness of the charity, too. It was a good opportunity for me, too. The average fan who watches the UFC got to see Tito Ortiz the businessman, not just a fighter. I also filmed a reality show, *Anytown Beat Down*, where we have a couple of guys who have a beef with each other. Some stuff has happened between them when they were kids, or one guy had sex with his wife or something and they have hostility for each other. We teach them how to train for five days and they fight on the sixth day, solve the differences in the cage. It's similar kind of thing to *TUF*, but these are people off the street who have anger towards each other.

Q: Your last fight for the UFC was against Lyoto Machida in May 2008, where you nearly pulled off the win when you had him in a triangle choke. What happened?

Ortiz: I came to fight, man. I was in great shape and I came at him and he took me down in the first round, but I got overanxious try to grab hold of him. In the second round he ran a lot more. Then end of the third I tried to get hold of him, but all he would do was try to run when I engaged to fight. He would take a punch and move back and forth. He was running the whole time. Last time I saw an MMA match, we fight. We bring it on in the fight; we don't make it disinteresting for the fans. I've always been like that making a fight interesting for the fans. But he would run. I got over-extended, he dropped me, got a couple of punches and I pushed his arm through and triangle lock. Then he got out of it because I switched to an arm lock.

Believe me I kick myself every single day. No one is going to get out of my triangles ever again. I've been drilling them so much ever since this fight. It's just one of those things where I can catch somebody in that position, they are not getting away. Machida got lucky, which is fine, he's undefeated. But who wants to watch a boring fighter who runs away the whole time and doesn't fight? It just shows where his career is going to be going.

Q: You stated once that you would fight Chuck Liddell five or six times if you had to. Is that true?

Ortiz: That was some time ago. My business ventures have changed a whole bunch. I may even not be fighting in the UFC ever again. I might be going to Affliction or EliteXC. Next month, I'll know 100 percent where I will be going. As far as calling UFC home, as long as Dana White is president, I'll never call that home. I feel bad for the company and for all the fans who have watched me fight in the UFC, where I go they're going to follow and Dana White screwed that up. He wanted to be stingy with the millions, instead of paying us the fighters more money. He says, "All you are stupid fighters." There was another interview he did in *Rolling Stone* magazine, where he was calling us morons. Once we start to talk about money, we're all morons and we don't know what we are all talking about.

That is fine, I'm a businessman and they want to negotiate certain ways, but I'll be looking elsewhere. About fighting Chuck Liddell, well he's going to be retiring pretty soon. He's almost forty years old, so he is near to end of his career. I'm only thirty-three years old. I'm still a young guy. Randy Couture started his career at thirty-three. So my future is very bright and we're going to see where we go from there next.

Q: How do you see the sport of MMA growing? Do you think it has overtaken boxing in the US?

Ortiz: I think it has a lifetime left, in particular in the mainstream. In the next year, there are other companies coming about, finding other fighters. It's about the fighters, they are the ones that get into the cage and entertain the fans that watch. It's not the brand that's doing it. It's not the UFC, Affliction, or EliteXC; it's the fighters showcasing their skills for the fans to watch. So the next three years the sport is going to be huge. We're overtaken boxing and pro wrestling. We are the new brand sport now, we're true athletes. Like I said, modern-day gladiators who people used to watch this type of fighting for thousands of years. We're in the right place at the right time and it's going to grow bigger.

Q: Who would you say is the godfather of MMA out of all of the fighters who have stepped into the Octagon?

Ortiz: You've got to think about it and I believe Royce Gracie as being the godfather of MMA more than anybody. He got in the cage and fought. Royce Gracie is the really true pioneer and godfather of MMA. I say the real godfather out of all of them has to be Royce Gracie, without a doubt.

Q: Any final comments to add?

Ortiz: I just want to thank all of my fans for the support buying the pay-per-views. You know you're going to get an action-packed fight no matter who or where I fight. My clothing company Punishment Athletics. We'll see what happens in the future, where and whom I fight. I have some great business ventures which are going to happen.

Rashad Evans

UFC Light-Heavyweight Champion/Hall of Famer

Q: Rashad, you have a fairly extensive wrestling background. Can you please tell me about this?

Rashad Evans: My wrestling career started off in high school. I did pretty good. I placed fourth in the New York State tournament. After that I went to Michigan State Community College, where I placed fourth in the national tournament. And then I became the American champion the following year. I never actually trained with Dan Severn, but I went to his gym and trained there. But he was never there when I was training. So I never got a chance to train with him. He's the kind of a guy who would show up from time to time.

Q: You graduated from Michigan State with a degree in psychology. What are your thoughts on UFC fighters, as a large percentage of them are actually highly educated individuals?

Evans: I think because of the development of the sport, you can't just win with lacking technical excellence. In this sport you have to perfect things. In boxing you have to hone your skills, and you have to be a pretty good boxer by the time you get to twenty years old, otherwise you're not going to be a good fighter. But in MMA there are so many different avenues and ways to win a fight, and so many different ways you can be good at different skills—some of those backgrounds take years to get pretty good at. So, it's where you start off. You have a huge background than boxers. This gives you time to go and do other things and go to school. Most of us fighters in MMA have wrestled before, anyway.

Q: Do you feel the sport of MMA has become a lot more accepted nowadays?
Evans: It's getting there, to the point where it's not seen as violence. There are some pretty devastating knockouts that occur in some of the fights, but for the most part, the fans have learned a lot about MMA. They can understand and appreciate more technique. What I think is going to happen is that the fans are going to be more educated about the fight. It'll get to a point when a fight hits the ground people aren't booing—that's what happens now sometimes.

The crowd wants to see someone getting knocked out or somebody bleeding. The fans still need to get to the point to appreciate the technique. If you watch a fight in Japan, you'll see the fans are so quiet. They appreciate all the little technique along the way. But the fights in the US and other places, fans are booing if you're not throwing a punch or knocking someone out in a minute or two. There's still a long way to go before the fans really appreciate all the little things and factors that the sport has to offer.

Q: Your first exposure to the UFC was when you watched the earlier shows with your friend. Is it true you made a decision early on that you'd one day want to fight in the UFC?
Evans: Yes. My friend and I used to watch the UFC when we were baby-sitting his kids. In school we always had this question, "Who would win against if a boxer such as Mike Tyson fought Bruce Lee?" We were always wondering and trying to figure out which would be the best style that would beat everybody. When we saw the UFC for the first time, I was like, *Yo, man! I'm gonna' one day do that, man.* At the time, we were taking a martial arts style called tang so do, and we were like mimicking all the time.

Q: What did you think of Royce Gracie when you witnessed him in the early UFCs?
Evans: I love Royce Gracie. Royce Gracie to me is a huge inspiration. He's the man! Royce Gracie is the man! He gave me so much hope

because I was never the biggest guy; my brother was always bigger and everybody was bigger than me. I was always the little guy and I always hung out with my brother's friend, who was a lot bigger than me. But when I'd seen Royce grappling with guys twice his size and this and the other, it gave me hope. I realized it wasn't about being a bigger guy, but more about technique and what you know. So I didn't worry about being a little guy anymore. Royce is a big inspiration to me. He's excellent. He's the father of the sport.

Q: You love fighting. Is it true you once said to yourself, *Why fight on the street when you can get paid for it?* When did you make a decision to pursue your MMA dream?

Evans: It was pretty much about street fighting which changed my perception of fighting on the street. One day on the street, when I was in college I was drunk and acting like a fool, like fools do when they are drunk. One time I was not trying to fight, the fight actually came to me. I was actually trying to make peace with the person. And the guy sucker punched me, knocked me out cold. My head hit the concrete and I was knocked out cold, man. I was laid up for a couple of months and I couldn't even move my neck, totally messed up. That's when I thought to myself the fighting on the street is not worth it. Then from that point on, I realized I wasn't invincible and I could really get hurt, or do that to somebody else and even kill them. I thought to myself, *It's not worth it!*

Q: You participated in the second season of *The Ultimate Fighter*. Can you share your experience from the show?

Evans: I sent in a video tape. I got a call back and went and did the trials. They liked what they'd seen so it went from there. It was weird, man. It was like fake reality imposed on you. You have cameras on you and all these different circumstances happening—you're kind of like a guinea pig. It's weird because your whole reality is totally misconstrued just because you're in a house in a reality show. Once you get adjusted to the cameras, everything else is cool after that. But just being in a situation having to eat with people and then fighting them, this was very tough for me to deal with. I'm the kind of a person that I'm a friend for life, and I don't like to fight my friends. This was really hard for me to deal with. After I got over that it was business as usual.

Q: What was it like to finally step into the Octagon for the first time?
Evans: It was a dream come true—a big dream come true. It was just unreal. I couldn't believe this was happening and I'm the one that people are watching on the TV. It was just like, *Wow,* and truly amazing. I wanted to go home and watch the video. Then I was going through the motions of the whole thing and really had the chance to analyze everything. And I was like, *Damn, that's really me on there!* It was just a surreal moment.

Q: I understand your mom is actually a big Bruce Lee fan?
Evans: Yeah, my mom's a huge Bruce Lee fan. She always watched Bruce Lee films growing up. And I was watching them, too. She now tells me, "Rashad, you gotta get your kicks right like Bruce Lee." She's like the coach Cus D'Amato (Mike Tyson's former trainer). I'm like, "OK! OK!" Sometimes her predictions are right, man. My mom's a big fan and now she knows the moves and the sport. She would say, "Rashad, you gotta work on passing the guard like Joe Rogan said." I'm thinking, *Damn, Joe Rogan's getting me into trouble!*

Q: What are your own opinions on Bruce Lee?
Evans: I think Bruce Lee is a great inspiration, a great fighter and was ahead of his time. Now people are starting to realize what his message was. Was it not for MMA, people would just say, "Bruce Lee said this or whatnot." I think they would have appreciation for him but not like now. Now they understand just how truly great he was because he was there from the beginning experimenting with the MMA. He didn't believe one single style was the best; he was mixing all different styles to make a complete fighting style. He was saying it back then and people thought, *This dude's crazy.* He was preaching it in his days and now people can see MMA, they can see that you need to have all these elements to become a great fighter and flow quickly into all of them.

Q: At UFC 73 (July 2007), you fought Tito Ortiz to a draw. Can you shed some light on this fight?

Evans: I really got caught up in all the trash-talking before the fight. I got out there but I didn't go out and grab the "moment," as they say— but the moment took a hold of me. So that was the big problem. Instead of going out grabbing the moment, the moment got hold of me. Then before I knew it, I realize I'm in here about to fight Tito Ortiz who I had watched fighting as I was growing up. I'm like, *I'm about to fight this dude.* So I was kind of a little gun shy in the beginning of the fight, but then I opened up a little bit but it was too late. Tito is good for the sport because whether you like him or you hate him, you want to see him, you want to see him fight.

Q: At UFC 78 (November 2007), you fought and beat Michael Bisping, breaking his undefeated record as a pro. Do you have any comments on this fight?

Evans: I got this fight on a short notice, but Michael Bisping was coming in from a very controversial win. I had my mind set on fighting Tito Ortiz again, but that didn't happen. I went into the fight thinking, *I'll just go in there and get the fight over with.* Michael Bisping came out and he was ready to go. He was charged up and he was a tough fighter than I actually anticipated. This is one of the fights where you go into a fight and you don't have any sick days. If you wake up in the morning of your fight and you feel like crap, it's too bad because you have to go in there and fight anyway. That's what I was going through. Not taking away anything from Michael Bisping because it would have been a tough fight, anyway. I really wasn't feeling 100 percent—it was one of those days. But luckily I prevailed and pulled off the fight and a win.

Q: You have a clean record in the UFC, as you are still undefeated. Do you feel any pressure at all?

Evans: I try not to think about my record too much because that's when you fight from a mindset where you can't preserve something. When you have something to lose, the person who has nothing to lose usually ends up putting you in a situation where you feel you may lose what you are trying to hold onto. What I recently started to do is to have a mindset where I'm thinking, *You know what, I don't care anymore. I don't care about my record or anything like that because the only thing that is important to me when I step into the cage is the fight right there. Anything else doesn't matter to me.* Once you know how to win, it's kind of a flow you always follow so you know what you need to do to win the fight.

You think, *If I do this or that, I can win the fight,* but that doesn't automatically happen. I need to take a little bit more chances, not being afraid of taking the chances because you're not afraid to lose. Confidence is the most important factor. You have to find the medium where you're not afraid, you're not afraid to lose and you're not afraid to go out there. Everybody has, I don't care who they are, one thing in common: once they step into the Octagon they're thinking, *Oh shit, this is going to be the day when I have to wake up in the locker room and have somebody tell me what happened because I just got knocked out.* Everybody has that feeling, but you have to go inside your mind and pass that, and say to yourself, *You know what? I don't give a damn. Today is the day because as long as I'm in there, this guy's going to wish he never ever has to fight me again. Even if he sees my name on a piece of paper he's going to get the chill. He's not going to have anything to do with me after the fight.* It's hard to get that through your mindset.

Q: Do you feel MMA is a good outlet for African Americans, who have traditionally been involved in boxing?
Evans: There will be more people getting involved, but it's a sport where the economics can make a difference. Because in order to get good to a level where you should be at, it's not something you can pick up on the street and do without too much instruction and get better yourself. You need proper instruction, you have to take jiu-jitsu classes, Muay Thai, boxing, etc., and you have to pay for it. Sometimes you're in a situation where you are not able to do this. I think if there are any programs which help out kids, who are athletes or any kids who are financially struggling then that would be great. When I have a gym I'm hoping I can help kids and put them on a kind of like a scholarship program, which will to help kids to get into the sport.

Q: What was your family's reaction when you started fighting in the Octagon?

Evans: My mom was kind of surprised. She didn't really know actually how big it [UFC] was, but people came to her and would talk to her about it. Then she really started to get more into it. But before she was just like, "Oh yes, you are going to fight." I was really a rough kid growing up and always trying to fight somebody and getting into mischievousness. She knew that's what I was good at. She wasn't really too surprised after I got into *TUF*. Now she's an expert at it, and she calls me and tells me what I need to work on in my training. Now she's a professional, like she's some great boxing coach like Cus D'Amato telling me what I need to do and work on. It's kind of funny.

Q: You said you wouldn't fight a friend in the Octagon. Why is that?

Evans: It's true. I love my friends, man. When I have a friend, he's a friend for life and I'd do anything for my friends. When you train with somebody you kind of give a piece of yourself because you want your training partner to be good, too. You want to be able to give something back to him. So, when you exchange that, all the blood and tears that come along with training, it's hard to go in the Octagon and fight somebody who is your friend and your training partner. To fight somebody, you have to treat them like your enemy in a way. You have to dislike a man to a point. Even though you don't dislike the person personally, you have to hate a man a little bit inside, even if it's just for that fight. For me, this is what I do.

Q: What did you think of facing Chuck Liddell in the Octagon, and were you surprised of knocking him out like you did?

Evans: I got a big opportunity to fight someone like Chuck Liddell, not only him but I want to fight the best. Sometime you kind of confuse yourself on which ones are your favorites to fight. Sometimes you're thinking Chuck Liddell is just another fighter like myself. Then you think, *It's Chuck Liddell, the legend! Oh man! He's the icon and the one guy who puts his heavy fist on somebody's chin!* Then you kind of focus on the fight. When I went out there, I made myself comfortable not getting caught up thinking too much about my opponent—like it's a big fight with a legend similar to how I felt against Tito Ortiz. It wasn't a fight where I felt comfortable right away and wasted a whole lot, and this ended up costing me. But this time I took the moment, at the same time not getting myself caught up with it. So I went out there and made myself feel comfortable and it was just a matter of performing my game plan.

I knew I was going to win, but I was just surprised on how it ended because of the very dramatic end. I trained really hard for this fight which showed. The one important shot knocking him out, you could see how quiet everybody was once I knocked him out. I mean, you could have heard a pin drop in the arena once I performed the knockout and everybody saw Chuck on the floor. Everybody was like, *Ohhh!* You could hear a huge silence around the arena.

Q: What has been your ultimate goal in the UFC? Is it winning the UFC belt?

Evans: Well, I definitely want to win the belt and that's something I'm going to achieve, but more than anything I want to be a UFC great. I want something the guys in the future can look back at, and looking at the knock downs and think, *He was the man.* I want to make my mark. As far as what it will feel like to be a champion, I think it'll be like when I became a junior college champion when I won the wrestling championship. After I won there was a second of a pause—the excitement and everything was so short time. The moment of jubilation and excitement just came to the peak and then it was gone. It was like, *OK, I won it.* And I was ready to move on. Not ready to move on from the sport, but it was a feeling parallel to now I've achieved the goal. I think it will be the same thing when I get the UFC belt.

You focus on getting the thing and then you finally get it. Even when you are the champion, the thing is in order to keep the belt you have to fight another champion. You have to stay hungry and fight like you're trying to get the championship. Then if you can't stay hungry, you have to graduate from being hungry and be greedy. You have to say, "I used to be hungry but now I'm greedy." You have to have that kind of a mindset. The way to keep that mindset is you have to fight everybody like a dog, it's like he's got something and you're trying to take it from him.

Q: What do you think of people criticizing fighters, and how do you take criticism?

Evans: I probably take more criticism than anybody, especially being undefeated. But it comes with the territory. I used to get upset about it. But one thing my mom always said is, "You can't make someone like you." I go out there and give it my best. My best fights in me are definitely still ahead of me. Criticism is just criticism. People who criticize are people who don't do anybody that *does* do—they criticize that person. It's a different game when you get in the Octagon. You're an entertainer and you put yourself out there, so you have to be able to take criticism because people are paying to see you. I accept criticism but I know the difference. I don't let criticism take over control my head, I don't like doing that. People that always impose certain things on you. For instance, if I feel bad about myself I'm going to say you suck, that you're not good and what you can't do because I believe that I can do it if I were you. People are going to impose weaknesses on you, so sometimes when someone criticizes you, most of the times they don't even believe in themselves.

Q: Who is your favorite UFC fighter?

Evans: My favorite fighter has to be Randy Couture because he's a great guy. I've trained with him and he's always been a straight-up dude. And besides that he's a great fighter. He's one of my all-time favorites. Also my good friend Georges St-Pierre because he brings it on each fight, sometimes very fearless. And I admire that.

Q: You were a hospital security guard—a job you enjoyed—before becoming a UFC fighter. What does it feel like now, that you are making a living in the fastest growing sport in the world?

Evans: It's a whirl-wind. Sometimes I sit back and think, *Is this really my life now? Is this really happening to me? Am I going to wake up one day and*

I don't have to put on my security uniform, is this really happening to me? Sometimes it feels like that because you have people coming up to you who are fans who you wouldn't have thought would be coming over to talking to you. I met a lady in the church who is sixty years old coming over to me talking to me about fighting. I couldn't believe it. I couldn't even believe she was even watching it. She was a big fan. It's amazing. My job working as a security guard was probably one of the best jobs I ever had, but this is far by ten times better.

Q: How many more years do you think will you be fighting professionally?
Evans: God willing, I don't know. In this game you are always one fight away from your last fight. Who knows how long I've got. I'm on God's time. He gave me the gift to fight and he's put it in my heart to be the fighter I am—and the fighter I'm going to be. And once that's over, when I'm done and I walk out of the door, I'll find something else what God has in line for me. Who knows what this is going to be. I definitely would like to give something back to the sport, open up a gym. The reason I don't have one right now is I can't be the coach I would like to be because I'm trying to learn a lot myself, and concentrating on the fighting and I won't be able to give back to my students.

Forrest Griffin

UFC Light-Heavyweight Champion/Hall of Famer

Question: You graduated with a bachelor's degree in political science from the University of Georgia. Can you tell me what your educational background is, and what interests you had growing up?
Forrest Griffin: Yes, I did. I went to college just like anybody else and got a degree. I really liked international affairs and stuff like that. I enjoyed the usual sports and I played basketball and football.

Q: Why did you pursue a career as a police officer?
Griffin: There are two answers to why I became a police officer. The first one, which is true, is because I liked the idea of driving around for eight or twelve hours and helping people out and getting paid to do this—kind of being a good Samaritan. To do stuff that you don't have any opportunity to do in another job and get paid to do that. And the second reason is that I like to drive fast and to carry a gun and wear the uniform. And on top of this, getting free coffee. These are the two reasons why I became a cop.

Q: Did you witness any major incidents that you want to talk about?
Griffin: You know what, it wasn't as dangerous as I perceived it. There were no pistol shoot outs. Actually, I shot only once and hit a deer, which was pretty horrible. But, yes, that's the only time I ever discharged my weapon. I didn't get to shoot that much back then. I don't think fighting is more dangerous than a cop's job—no one's died in the UFC.

Q: Is it true that when your defensive instructor at the police academy showed you a UFC tape, you thought it was boring?

Griffin: The first time I saw UFC was on a tape when I was actually in high school. I didn't really like it as I thought it was kind of boring and barbaric. Then when I was in the police academy, when I was twenty years old, the defensive tactics instructor had us do all the training stuff. I really liked the boxing and the wrestling and had fun with it. I loved it. He said, "You really love that UFC stuff." He knew I was doing some toughman contests at the time just for a laugh. I said the UFC looked kind of boring to me. So he gave me a UFC tape, which featured Randy Couture who fought Vitor Belfort for the first time. That whole event was pretty good and professional. There were weight classes. It looked like a real sport and not just a barbaric fight with no rules.

Q: How would you compare today's UFC to the earlier no-holds-barred era, when it first started?

Griffin: It's hard to compare that earlier era, which had a lack of official elements and the lack of refereeing, lack of sportsmanship that you had back then compared to what we have now. But it's not that much safer now than it was in the no gloves days because the athletes are better now—they hit harder and they do their submissions harder, they are just better.

Q: How did you get involved with *The Ultimate Fighter*?

Griffin: Yes, that was kind of my break. I had actually given up on making it to the UFC before I got a call to be on the show. I thought it was great and a real good medium for the transfer of viewership, targeting people who wouldn't otherwise buy pay-per-views or, in the beginning, most people weren't interested as it was hard to get people to watch fights. I know that for me, I always try to show people fights.

Q: At UFC 59 (April 2006), you fought one of the all-time greats, Tito Ortiz. What was that experience like?

Griffin: It was kind of my first experience on the big stage. I didn't do so well. There were a lot of factors that go into that fight, but the biggest thing is just to keep my head in place. I kind of got a little star struck.

Q: What happened to you after the Keith Jardine fight at UFC 66 (December 2006)? It seems you had an emotional breakdown.

Griffin: My thing has always been: if you never found something in your life that you were really passionate enough about to cry about—because you never felt that way towards something—and you had a goal that you believed in that greatly that you finally achieved it. I kind of felt sorry for myself. You haven't experienced what you in reality like to be, what you felt so passionate about something.

Q: Am I right in saying you wanted to fight Ken Shamrock?

Griffin: Yes. The situation behind that was Tito Ortiz had hurt his knee and might not have been able to fight Ken Shamrock. And the fighters out here knew I was in good shape. And I said I'd love to fight Ken Shamrock. But Tito Ortiz ended up being OK and ended up fighting after all.

Q: Tell me about your shoulder injury—and any other injuries you sustained—during your UFC career.

Griffin: I hurt my shoulder originally in 2001 in a fight in South Africa. It wasn't the same anymore and it hurt. And in the beginning of 2005, I kind of popped it out again where the shoulder joint actually came out. Then it really got painful to do basic stuff like brush my teeth. This went on for a year. The thing is I hadn't fought for a while, so I wanted to have at least one more fight before I did that shoulder surgery.

Q: Can you tell me about the cameo part you had in the popular TV series *Law & Order*?

Griffin: I got a bunch of crazy offers and that just seemed something like cool. I liked *Law & Order*. It's one of those shows that have been going on forever and you watch it growing up. I said I'll do it because I thought that would be cool. It was an easy part, something I can do without messing up too bad. So I did it. I played a fighter and a rapist with a small penis. So, I think it was tailor made for me.

Q: When you're battling against your opponents, what goes through your mind?

Griffin: I'm not sure. I mean, it's what I want to do and it's fun. It was super fun when I didn't care so much about results, when it wasn't my way of making a living, or the pressure of making a living where you want to send your kids to college. Now there's all that pressure, but it's still fun to go out and trying to beat the opponent and hit guys.

Q: You say mental preparation is unnecessary before you step into the Octagon. Is this true?

Griffin: It's not something that I do but I'm not saying it's unnecessary. It's just not something which I've ever done. I try to develop a game plan and try to work on my game plan.

Q: Do you have any heroes?

Griffin: Yes, a guy named Pat Tillman. He's one of my heroes. He played pro football in the NFL. And he actually quit playing football to become an Honorary Ranger. He was killed in Iraq. He turned down $3 million-a-year for $30,000 to go and be a hero. So I've always thought of him as a hero.

Q: What was it like promoting the UFC on the road?

Griffin: Doing different interviews. I don't do much of it and I'm not a real good traveler. What I want to do is fight people. And what I like to do is stay home and train.

Q: Is it true you knocked out Kimbo Slice in a sparring match?

Griffin: I didn't actually—that's just one of those sparring stories that just kind of got a life of its own. I've heard that story before but it never happened. I did spar with him but never knocked him out. Before I met him I thought he was kind of a lark. I really didn't respect him as a fighter and an athlete. But now that I've met him and trained with him, I know he does the same workouts as I do. And he wants it. He's making the best out of it. You really can't hit a guy who's trying to make the best out of him. He's thirty-four and still learning the ground game. He's a pretty athletic guy. Once you meet him, I think you'd wish him the best. He's not a bad guy.

Q: How was the Rampage Jackson fight put on at UFC 86 (July 2008)?

Griffin: Dana and Lorenzo came in and offered me a shot at the title, and I did what every guy would do: I jumped at it. Not only did Rampage have a good record but he had fought the best of the best. He's good at a lot of things. He's a good wrestler and a better striker. It's kind of funny that you see the guy all the time, when you're filming the *TUF*, and you know you are going to fight him in a couple of months' time. But it is what it is. The biggest thing in the fight was that I wanted to move with my feet—maybe if I can get him on his back or maybe surprised him a little with my wrestling. I don't think the fight was that controversial. I'm seeing a lot of good fighters at 205 pounds. I don't worry too much now that I have the belt, it doesn't really make a lot of sense by troubling yourself by worrying. Once you get the belt, I think anybody will tell you that, now it becomes, *I've got to win my next fight.* I've never done anything super impressive, so I'm looking to get the next win.

Q: What kind of activities do you take part in to relax and get away from all this fighting business?

Griffin: I actually don't watch fighting after I have my last fight if I can help it. I just relax and I don't have any fighting stuff in my house. I watch a lot of movies and TV. I read a fair amount. I get stressed out a lot—I don't know why. But I'm a very hyper guy. Sometimes I'm laid back, at other times you get hyper about stuff. I think obviously the UFC is making a lot of progress, they are doing the marketing and doing the work. You have to understand that I started fighting for the first time in 1999. When I saw the first UFC, I really couldn't understand why everybody was still watching other sports. I've been a lifelong basketball and football fan and I still follow the playoffs, but I felt this [MMA] is so much better than everything else. It just seems to be more natural sport than the traditional sport fighting. I couldn't understand why everybody didn't love it. The goal for me was to make more money in fighting than I could in my other job.

Tim Sylvia

UFC Heavyweight Champion

Q: Tim, you endured a horrendous abuse from your parents, who were both alcoholics. Can you talk me through just how hard it was for you growing up?
Tim Sylvia: I think everyone knows my parents were alcoholics when I was growing up, and my mother was very abusive, both mentally and physically. She decided that mentally would work better than physically. That's what I had to deal with my whole life, and even still today. Sometimes she would call and say, "You're a piece of shit you're not good enough." And if I lost a fight, she would call and she'd laugh and say, "Ha, ha, ha, you lost, you suck."

Q: You joined a karate school as a young kid, and also enjoyed playing basketball. Did you always want to pursue a career in sports?
Sylvia: No, not really. I was just doing it because it was fun. I liked martial arts and I was a big Bruce Lee fan obviously. He was definitely my hero.

Q: A lot of UFC fighters have been influenced by Bruce Lee. How do you think he would have fared in MMA?
Sylvia: I felt he was "the man" growing up. He was the badass fighter that we used to watch his movies and stuff like that. That's what worked for me and that's why I was doing karate. I wanted to be like Bruce Lee. Bruce Lee is an athlete and a mixed martial artist, therefore he'd

obviously know to train jiu-jitsu and wrestling. If he just had the mentality that his striking is the best and went out there and fought an MMA fighter, he'd get taken down and ground and pounded. But Bruce Lee, being the martial artist he is, he knows the way of MMA. I believe he would train properly for it and do very well.

Q: Your first no-holds-barred fight lasted a mere 17 seconds. Is it true that you had to pay a $50 dollar entry fee to compete?
Sylvia: Yes, I did. It was the Rhode Island Vale Tudo. I was scared as hell, very scared, and he was the first fighter I fought. I was bouncing on the town and playing semi-pro football at the time. And I'd been in a few street fights, but when you grapple a couple of times a week, you're learning. I wrestled in high school before that. So, I was boxing and grappling couple of times a week to prepare for the fight.

Q: You became a UFC fan right from the beginning. When did you see the UFC for the first time?
Sylvia: Yes, I did. I saw the first UFC when I was in high school, I think. I had buddies who said to me, "You have to go to Blockbuster movie store and see this Ultimate Fighting Championship." They said there was this little Brazilian guy, Royce something—who, of course, was Royce Gracie—who was beating everybody from the karate guys and other fighters, and he fights on the ground. It took me about two weeks to get the tape because everybody had heard about it and they were renting it. So, when I saw it I was like, *Oh my goodness, I love it.*

Q: When the UFC came to Atlantic City, did you really drive for eleven hours with your buddies to watch the show?
Sylvia: The guys that I trained with all had heard of the UFC. And we were fans for previous years six or seven years. The drive to Atlantic City was an eleven-hour drive and there were four of us. We rented a minivan and drove down there. When we got there, we started walking around and went the other way round and saw some people, including [Ken] Shamrock, Tito [Ortiz], and the Miletich crew. It was pretty cool. So, before the fights we went down the lobby to see if we could catch any

fighters going in, and get some pictures and autographs. As I'm walking with my buddies a security guard says, "Oh, it's you. Why don't
you come in?" Because of my size and with my friends, I'm assuming
they thought I was Gan McGee—who was fighting that night with Josh
Barnet. So we all walked in and there's Kevin Randleman warming up,
who was going to fight Randy Couture, and all the other fighters were
all hanging out there. This was UFC 28 (November 2000), where Jens
Pulver knocked out John Lewis.

Q: How did you get involved in the UFC?
Sylvia: I was fighting a little bit. And I met Pat Miletich that night, and
we just started talking about fighting. He was really outgoing. I told
him I had a hard time finding fights as I was 6-foot-8, 240 pounds. The
fights I had scheduled did not often materialize because when my opponents saw me, they were like, *I ain't fighting him.* And they'd leave. Pat
said, "Why don't you come to Iowa and train? Come down for a couple
weeks and if you like it then train with us." I took him up on the offer.

**Q: What did it feel like when you entered the Octagon for the first
time?**
Sylvia: It was crazy. I was fighting [Wesley] Cabbage Correira. He was
someone I wanted to fight. I was supposed fight him in a previous event
called Superbrawl, but he had faked an injury so he could fight in the
UFC. It was just awesome, the electricity and the crowd, me being in
the UFC, how big the cage was, it was pretty nerve racking.

**Q: You fought Randy Couture who is, no doubt, one of the greatest
UFC fighters ever. What do you remember from your battle against
him?**
Sylvia: It was a hard fight. I went into the fight injured. And him being
a good friend of ours, I probably just didn't take it like it was going to be
a "fight." I thought, *Oh, it's just Randy,* like I was just going for a sparring session. When he hit me with that overhand right, he knocked me
out. For the first 20 minutes I didn't know where I was. Then the fifth
round came, Pat is yelling at me, "You're gonna knock him out! You're

behind! You're behind on points!" And I'm like, "I'm going to knock him out in the second round." My corner is telling me, "No, this is the fifth round!" I'm like, "Oh, OK!" Randy is a great friend of mine.

Q: Would you say you are a natural fighter, or did you have to learn a lot to prepare for MMA fights?

Sylvia: I'm a natural fighter, definitely. I was born fighting. I've been fighting for my life since I've been born. But you have to train in MMA. I had to train in jiu-jitsu, Muay Thai and the boxing. I mean, I trained my ass off! Everything comes to me because of hard work.

Q: Tell me about the most disturbing sports injuries that you sustained when you fought Frank Mir at UFC 48 (June 2004).

Sylvia: Well, I went into that fight with a little a bit of anger because Frank was talking some shit. So I went into the fight angry and not really composed. I was like, "I'm just going to kill this guy." So I made a mistake. I took him down and I was just thought I'd be on the ground and I'm just going to ground and pound him. He went for the arm bar and my elbow popped out and I broke my arm. And I'm thinking, *He's just broke my arm. I'm just going to kill him.* After the injury, I never wanted to stop fighting. I just wanted to get better and fight Frank Mir again. Going into the Arlovski fight I was still a little timid. When he put a toe hold on me, I felt my ankle pop a few times and I reached out and tapped out. I think if my arm hadn't been broken in the fight with Mir, I might not have tapped prematurely and the fight might have ended differently. But maybe it's good I did tap because I'd rather have a broken arm than a broken leg or ankle. Because at least I can walk around and get around just fine, but with a broken ankle it's not good.

Q: What MMA shows did you compete in before fighting in the UFC?

Sylvia: I fought in Superbrawl and Extreme Challenge events. UFC is the big show and most fighters' goal is to be in the UFC eventually. That's where everyone strives to fight, and most fighters eventually want to take this avenue. It's the big show—it's the Super Bowl of MMA.

Q: You beat Andre Arlovski twice to regain the heavyweight belt. How do you rate him as a fighter?
Sylvia: I'm bigger and stronger and a better striker than he is. The second fight I had against him, I kind of mentally got to him and I knocked him out. That's really easy to get to someone mentally. When we had another fight, I said, "I'm going to knock him out again. He's got a weak chin and I'm going to knock him out again." And that he's easy to knockout. So I made him real timid. So when I hit him in the third fight, I rocked him and gave him wobbly legs. He didn't want to engage anymore. He played it safe and wanted to stop the fight. Sometimes you can do this to fighters and sometimes you can't, but he's one of those fighters that I can get into his head very easily.

Q: Before you are fighting somebody, do you first do research on your opponent?
Sylvia: I watch some of his fights along with my trainers. And establish a game plan and start training for that fight. We decide what we are going to do and how I'm going to oppose myself on my opponent.

Q: To this point, what has been the most difficult fight of your career?
Sylvia: My hardest fight was probably with Randy Couture. I just got my ass kicked. I wish I wasn't that stubborn going into the fight injured. I think it would have been a different fight. Randy was a great guy that day. He had a great game plan and he kicked my ass for five rounds. I think if it happens again, it'll be a different fight. I'm not saying I'm going to kick his ass, but if it happens it'll be different.

Q: Can you compare the early UFCs in the no-holds-barred era to the sanctioned sport we enjoy today?
Sylvia: It's just a little more safer now for the fighters and the sanctioning makes it a sport now. Back then it was basically the Gracies trying to prove that jiu-jitsu was the way of life and they could beat anybody. There weren't a lot of punches thrown back then because Gracie would take the opponent down, get in the full guard and submit his opponent. So there really wasn't a concern about the guys getting hurt and there

were no gloves. It's a sport now which has evolved. Fighters who have a wrestling background have become good strikers, and you see a lot more punches thrown now. Something had to be done because fighters were getting cutup on the knuckles. So the sanctioning bodies came in and made rounds and weight classes. This just made it better for the sport and make more money and grow to where it's an actual sport now.

Q: Do you feel MMA fighters are real athletes?
Sylvia: There's no question in my mind everybody in the UFC is an athlete. We are the hardest-training athletes in the world. Because it's not just like boxing, where all you worry about is your hands and your roadwork. In boxing you don't train your elbows knees, kicks, grappling and wrestling like we do. There are so many areas of training in our game that there's not enough hours in the week to get all the areas covered. It's difficult to because there is so many elements you have to cover in MMA.

Q: Were you ever influenced by any pro boxers? Boxers have been revered and widely thought to be the toughest men on the planet.
Sylvia: I grew up watching Sugar Ray [Leonard], Marvin Hagler, [Mike] Tyson, but I wasn't really a big boxing fan until I started fighting in MMA. Then I started watching more boxing and I enjoyed that small part that had to do with our sport. That's no longer true regarding boxers being the toughest guys on the planet. A boxer would never survive in the cage with us, or a ring, as long as it's MMA rules. I'm not saying everybody can compete, but I believe that I can beat any heavyweight boxer out there at his own game. I believe I can outbox any heavyweight boxer out there. I truly believe that my hands are that good. If they came into MMA then they wouldn't stand a chance.

Q: Was winning the UFC heavyweight belt the proudest moment of your career?
Sylvia: The first time I won the belt it was cool. It just kind of happened; it wasn't a lot of hard work. I worked hard coming through the ranks, but I fought one fight in the UFC and then they asked me if I

wanted to fight for the UFC title. So, it happened and I won. I was the heavyweight champ. Then having the belt and losing it and working my way back up to the rank—two losses in a row and Arlovski already beat me—going in there, getting knocked out and coming back and knocking him out, this really meant a lot to me the second time. It meant more to me the second time.

Q: What is your philosophy about fighting, and life in general?
Sylvia: You definitely have to surround yourself with good people, good trainers and training camps—someone you can trust who will be there for you. I have been with the Miletich camp for ten years now and they are with me when I'm on the top or bottom. All the same guys are with me there like my family now. Definitely you have to train hard, condition is important so you have to bust your ass in the gym to make sure you're in peak performance. Conditioning is the only area you can control; you can't control submissions, etc. But you can control your conditioning. So in the Miletich camp, we make sure we bust our ass to make sure we are in great shape.

Q: Do you train with separate coaches who specialize in certain areas?
Sylvia: We have everybody in the Miletich camp—we have got great wrestlers, great strikers, jiu-jitsu guys and boxers and so forth. I'm very fortunate in that I have some of the greatest heavyweights in the world in my gym. I bring in jiu-jitsu and boxing coaches to work with.

Q: You say you want to fight the best. How important is this to you?
Sylvia: I'm a fighter first. I want to fight the best and prove myself I'm one of the best out there. Therefore, I need to keep fighting the other best to prove that.

Q: Do you take part in any mental preparations before a fight?
Sylvia: There's a lot, especially weeks before the fight, sitting in the corner thinking what I'm going to do to the guy—warming up, shadow-boxing, a lot of visualization, etc. That's about it, nothing too serious.

Q: Do you feel the UFC and MMA will grow beyond our expectations in the near future?

Sylvia: We're taking over the world. MMA is going to take over the world. If you look at all these celebrities and pro athletes, such as football players, soccer players they're all coming to watch us. They know we are the next generation and the next big thing. These guys watch us and like us, it's cool when you get these people come watching an MMA event.

Q: What are your future plans?

Sylvia: I have four or five years left fighting as long as I stay injury free, just planning on being dedicated and working on my legacy. And when I'm done fighting, I'll be doing hunting full time. I love to hunt and I've got a hunting company. It definitely relaxes me and takes me away from the fighting when I'm out in the woods. Fighting doesn't even come in my mind. I go out there and enjoy the great outdoors. I just enjoy been in the outdoors. I want to thank all the fans still following me. I'm not in the UFC anymore, but with Affliction and Adrenalin MMA—thanks for all the support.

Matt Serra

UFC Welterweight Champion/Hall of Famer

Question: Matt, when did you get involved in martial arts?
Matt Serra: My father is a longtime martial artist. He started me off with the wing chun/kung fu system. There was a lot of pad work involved and we did combat drills as far as training goes. I started at an early age as a kid, till when I was in high school. But then I found out whenever I got into a real altercation, which happened often with me as a kid growing up, I ended up using what I had from my training and would wrestle the guy down and did a lot of ground stuff just because it was second nature I guess. It was just natural to me. Then my father showed me the tapes of the Gracies when I was a senior in high school. It was the *Gracies in Action* tapes, which had the Gracie family fighting all these other martial arts exponents. I was very intrigued by it. Then I saw the *In Action 2* tape, and I thought to myself, *I don't want my arm broken. I've got to learn this martial art.* So soon I hooked up with Renzo Gracie, moved to Manhattan, and took it right from there. He took me under his wing.

Q: Can you describe your training and experiences with Renzo?
Serra: Renzo is family to me. I was working in security and bouncing on the weekends just so I could train with Renzo in Manhattan, which was a 45 minute train ride from Long Island in New York where I'm from. He saw I was tired in class sometimes, not training to the best of my ability, so he told me to quit that night job and just work doing some

private lessons in the gym. He took me out of that situation and took me under his wing. Whenever he went to compete in Japan he'd ring me. He went to watch me in the Pan-American games where I got a gold medal. He was my mentor and a great instructor. I owe a lot to him. So, no matter how far I get or go, I never surpass my instructor because Renzo Gracie really changed my life.

Q: Speaking of the Gracies, what did you think of Royce? Was he an inspiration in any way?
Serra: Obviously I was just about fascinated like everybody else watching Royce fighting in the UFC. I was a fan before I became a participant in the UFC. Watching him beat those much larger guys using jiu-jitsu techniques, I was totally blown away by this jiu-jitsu. I had to learn that system and thought this was just phenomenal—this art was something we've not seen before.

Q: How did you eventually get involved in UFC?
Serra: I made a name for myself on the grappling circuit. I won the Pan-American games in purple belt in Miami. I also got a gold medal the same year in the brown belt division in the Mundials in Brazil. I also went to Abu Dhabi in the Middle East and competed in some high-profile grappling matches, beating some big names in the MMA and grappling world. With that along with my team mate Ricardo Almeida, the UFC stopped by Renzo's academy in Manhattan and they wanted Ricardo and me to fight in the UFC. I'm like, "I'll do it." In my first UFC fight I fought Shonie Carter and lost this fight, but it gained me some experience and taught me something. That's how I got involved in it, man.

Q: Let's talk about your victory over none other than Georges St-Pierre, when you won the belt in April 2008. How did that feel?
Serra: That was great. Before that fight, I got a little more respect for my power as far as my punching power and striking ability goes. Before that I was pretty much known as a jiu-jitsu guy. People knew me as a guy who trains with the Gracies. And I was a name in grappling. So people

kind of avoided going to the floor with me. No one really gave thought to my standup game. So I knew I had the elements of surprise going in, and sure enough I got the right sparring partner Ray Longo—who is my striking and conditioning coach—and we had a great game plan. We worked the body and to the head. It's always like just another day of sparring. It actually worked out to be a little easier, but that's great. It was an indescribable moment when I won the title. It was just such a great feeling. It was almost surreal. I was thinking, *Look at me now*. It was unbelievable and a dream come true, which may sound very clichéd but it was really a dream come true.

Q: How did you get involved in *The Ultimate Fighter*?
Serra: I had lost to Karo Parisyan. I had a knee injury after that loss and I had to rest a little bit. I got a call, maybe eleven months after that, but I figured I'd be back in the UFC anyway because me and Karo had put on an exciting fight. The UFC called me up and said they were doing something called *The Combat Show*. I'm like, "Man, where do I sign up?" I went to an audition and next thing I'm on season four on *TUF*, along with another veteran including "Mr. Flashy" Shonie Carter.

Q: Let's talk about Matt Hughes, behind the scenes on *TUF*.
Serra: In the beginning he tried to be really nice, but not nice like a nice guy type, almost like an asshole/kind of condescending type. Later on behind the scenes I figured, *He's just a dweeb I can't stand the guy. The guy is really not a good person. I can't wait to fight the guy because I think he's a total ass.* If some people win enough fights their real personality comes out. In his case, he's arrogant—or some people such as him, just don't think. He's just a stuck up jock. He's the type of guy that bullies people in high school. He's that guy. We pretty much ignored each other. As a fighter he's very dangerous and good at what he does. If he gets you down he's very good on the top. He is a very good fighter and deserves to be in the Hall of Fame, but that doesn't mean he's a good person, or I can't exploit the holes in his game. I feel I'm a complete fighter than him. I proved to him I'm a better coach. He can't say his guy won the whole thing because that guy had thirty fights going in there. I took

guys who had a few fights and took them further. I feel like I'm a way better coach than he is. I want to fight him to show him I'm a better fighter. It's not just about being big and broad. There's something called "technique."

Q: If the fight finally happens, how would you prepare yourself?
Serra: I have to be in phenomenal shape. I told the UFC I need three months, no less. There will be no secrets. I will be looking for his chin. On the floor, I'll be looking to take a leg. If I have it my way, I'll be the nail in his coffin.

Q: Were you ever influenced by the legendary Bruce Lee?
Serra: I love Bruce Lee! When I was young kids were playing baseball, but I was watching *Kung Fu Theatre* with my old man. I love Bruce Lee and his movies: *Enter the Dragon*, *Game of Death*, *Return of the Dragon*. He was one of the first mixed martial artists if you ask me. He was doing arm locks in there, everything. I think it was awesome.

Q: Who is your favorite UFC fighter?
Serra: Not so much in the UFC, but Renzo Gracie for the obvious reason. He's a major influence on me in and out of the cage or ring. Other than that, Royce Gracie—who is a pioneer—and Rickson Gracie, too. I'm a fan of anybody who shows skills, anybody who steps in there deserves credit. It takes balls to step in the cage, but it's hard to stay in whether things are going your way or not. There's guys like [Antonio] Minotauro [Nogueira], Randy Couture, these guys are great champions and fighters. Chuck Liddell, even if it's not their fighting style I love I like guys that are tough. They beat a guy down and they get beat down, but they come back and go back in there for more. That's what I respect.

Q: Could you have performed better in your second outing against Georges St-Pierre?
Serra: Obviously. I look at it this way: sometimes you have a tough day at the office. Everything after you lose a fight is going to be 20/20 when you watching it on tape. Everything's, *I should've, I could've, I would've.*

I'm just going to leave it at that. He was the better man on the night and I'm not about to make excuses.

Q: Is it true that you get your training and sparring partners to 'boo' you to psych you up before a fight?
Serra: I said that in an interview as a joke. I said my trainer boos me all the time and what not—but that was just a joke. To tell you the truth, what I do is I watch a lot of Tim Sylvia fights and anytime that jerk walks out everybody boos him. So I'm like, *Hey, he can still fight so I can do it, no big deal.* I'm not a big fan of his, he's a dickhead!

Q: When you were promoting the UFC with Dana White on Fox TV, one presenter was debating with you, saying MMA is not good for kids. What are your views on this rather contentious subject?
Serra: Do I think little kids should fight in a cage? No! Do I think they should be studying martial arts or MMA? Yes! It's self-defense. I disagree with EliteXC who are trying to make a spectacle of Kimbo Slice. And I don't want to knock him. He's trying to make money and that's fine, but the promoters that are hyping up this internet sensation. Now, as a result you are going to get a bunch of moron kids with camcorders trying to be in the UFC by fighting each other in the backyard. That's not the proper way to do it. Anybody can fight anybody in the street. You should come up the right way get involved in the sport, get involved in wrestling, jiu-jitsu, boxing, Thai boxing—get involved in these kinds of matches. Then this will hone your skills and you will be ready to fight competitors, not on the street looking to make a name that way. When no-holds-barred started, it wasn't a sport, before it was a freak show. Now they are doing the right thing and it's legal—legal in thirty-three states in the US. But on the other hand, that wouldn't have been if it didn't start off in the beginning like it did.

Q: Can you recall your experiences bouncing, and how do you differentiate between street fighting and MMA?
Serra: There's a huge difference. I mean, it's easy to fight guys that don't know what they are doing—that's one thing. You can beat up

any knucklehead in the street and feel like you're superman. But when you train and you go up against the other guy who trains that's good—even if you're going into a grappling match or boxing tournament—you are fighting another skilled guy. On the other hand, you're fighting some guy on the street and sucker punch him or whatever, it's not the same thing at all. I bounced at a local bar, so once in a while you'd get a drunk to throw out or a guy who got rowdy and you'd put a choke on, but it wasn't a big deal. And it was short-lived anyway thanks to Renzo.

If there were no gloves in the UFC still, a lot of guys would get more injuries to their hands. I think it would be more of a grappling situation. Guys would get their hands busted up immediately, then it would go into a jiu-jitsu match. That's how I feel. Gloves aren't huge but they are for protection for avoiding breaking hands.

Q: If you never made it as a UFC fighter, what would you have been doing career-wise?
Serra: I might have been screwed. Just joking. Thank God MMA is my favorite sport. I don't know, man, I may have taught and taken that route. But like I said, I'm living the dream. Thank God MMA came about and I tried Brazilian jiu-jitsu. If MMA didn't come about, then I'd probably still be doing Brazilian jiu-jitsu. I would be involved in the martial arts one way or another.

Q: What is your biggest achievement so far?
Serra: Aaah. I want you to guess that one. What do you think?

Q: I think it's winning the belt.
Serra: Yes, it would have to be the belt—UFC welterweight belt. The other thing is I won the Pan-Americans and international competitions. Another thing I'm proud of is the match I won against Jeans-Jacques Machado, who was a legend in the jiu-jitsu world. But there's nothing that takes the place the fight with GSP, when I won the belt that this was the icing on the cake. If I retire tomorrow I know I was the champion.

Q: Have you experienced a change in the UFC since it has filtered into the mainstream?

Serra: Yes, you know what I've seen both worlds because I was fighting in 2001, when no one knows you, when you're walking around other than hardcore fans, once in a while. Or on the week of the fight, it kind of feels like being a celebrity because all fans are around, all taking pictures and you feel a celebrity for a week. But now you get the same thing when you go to the 7/11 store, the supermarket, the movie theatre. I'm kind of getting it all the time now, which is a positive thing, it's good. Everybody's cool, it's a nice thing. I'm not going to be the guy complaining about it.

I didn't come off *TUF*. Like I said, I fought before and after the TV show. I'm not the guy who just came on *TUF* and made my name. I was fighting before that and know what it was like before the mainstream explosion. Boxing is really a dying sport. The days of Tyson are over. It's not just as exciting. There are only so many ways to win and lose in boxing, that's why UFC has taken off. I'm just not saying that because I'm a participant, but as a fan. I was a fan before I got into it and I'll be a fan when I'm out of it. I love to fight. When I have a fight coming up, I'm excited whether it's mine or someone else's.

Q: What are your plans for the future, after you retire from competing in the Octagon?

Serra: Right now I just got back into training from my injury, which occurred in the GSP fight. I'm getting into good shape and fighting Matt Hughes hopefully soon. I'm hoping this will happen. He wants the fight and I want the fight, and I'm coming for him. There's nothing I wanted more from a fight than this fight. I'm coming for him this time and I can't wait. I think this is going to be a fight which is going to surpass my first fight with GSP as my favorite. I'm going to keep on fighting, it depends on how the body holds up but right now I feel great. I own two Brazilian jiu-jitsu schools in Long Island, New York. I want to be teaching way long after I finish fighting because I love teaching, this is what I do. That's why I couldn't talk to you earlier because I was teaching two classes. I like bringing other fighters in MMA. So I'll be a trainer, coach, and a teacher way after I finish fighting and that's going to be my life. I could just retire and teach right now, but I love to fight.

Matt Hughes

UFC Welterweight Champion/Hall of Famer

Question: Let's talk about your childhood. Did you have a normal upbringing?

Matt Hughes: I grew up on a farm with a twin brother, miles away from anybody else. I didn't have a whole lot of friends growing up; my sole friend was my twin brother. I grew up with a hard work ethic and had somebody to play with, that being my brother. When we got older that play turned into competition, so this gave me a deep sense of competition instilled in my body. Those are two of the factors why I've been successful and competitive as I am today—because of the hard work ethic and my twin brother I was always competing with.

Q: You have a pretty strong amateur wrestling background. When and how did you get involved in the sport?

Hughes: I started wrestling actually in junior high. We had wrestling in school in the P.E. period. Then we had a wrestling tournament at end of that. So it wasn't formal wrestling. But my first formal wrestling would have been freshman in high school. I did well. Then I ended up winning my State tournament in my junior and senior year. I wrestled in college and was a four-time collegiate All-time American. And when I got this in college I still wanted to compete.

Q: When did you first hear about the UFC?

Hughes: The first time I saw the UFC it was on a video tape. I forget which UFC it was, but I think it was number three or four. It was when

Royce Gracie choked out Dan Severn. That was the first time I watched a UFC. My brother and I watched that together.

Q: What was your initial reaction, and did it ever occur to you at that point that you may want to be part of this one day?
Hughes: I didn't know if I was going to be part of the UFC in the future. I did look at Royce Gracie and thought I could physically beat him. But at the time I was watching those tapes, he definitely would have killed me because I didn't know any submission holds whatsoever, or any defense to them. So he would have killed me at the time. It's just amazing, he's the first guy I really watched and I ended up fighting him twelve years later.

Q: Tell me about your early MMA fights before you ever competed in the UFC.
Hughes: I started out in a show called Extreme Challenge and my first fights were extremely easy. The first lasted 30 seconds, the second lasted 45 seconds. My wrestling was really superior to everyone else's. I took people down quick, and when I got on the ground I was too athletic for my opponents. I found them very easy. I did receive a few other offers so I continued to do the same thing. I just worked out regularly for a couple of years in a row.

Q: Did you feel you had to adapt to new training methods, and not merely rely on your wrestling, in your MMA fights?
Hughes: I always trained in a way where I was covering different types of training, to get better in every area. I had nothing much new to really learn. It's just the way I was—well rounded in all areas. When I first got into the sport of MMA, I realized you had to be as well rounded as you can be, and this will work to your benefit when you're fighting.

Q: What motivates you to put your life on the line in the Octagon?
Hughes: The reason I go in there is because I love to compete. Behind that is that I'm good at it. I seem to do what I'm good at, and also that's my living—that's what I do. I put food on the table, clothes on my kids' back by competing in the Octagon.

Q: How did you make the transition into the UFC, and tell me about the fight with Frank Trigg at UFC 45 (November 2003)?

Hughes: Making the transition into the UFC was pretty easy. The rules were a lot like the earlier MMA events I had fought in. I had faced some tough guys before I entered the UFC. So, when I did get into the UFC I definitely was ready for that organization and the competition level they had. So it was an easy transition. The only thing that was different was the fact there were cameras on you in the UFC, people are watching on pay-per-view—that's the big difference. The nerves were kind of working against me because everyone's watching. With the Frank Trigg fight, I had fought him before and beat him, so this was the second fight. One thing about Frank Trigg is that he's not shy about running his mouth. He, of course, ran his mouth before this second fight and this got under my skin. Then before the fight started, the referee got us in the center of the Octagon and he tried to kind of kiss me. And I pushed him away. It was then when the final works really started for us.

Right after the fight started, I had him up against the fence. He threw a knee, and there's no doubt he felt my cup on his knee and he knew it was a low blow. I turned away and put my hands across Frank's face and I looked to the ref, [Mario] Yamasaki, and he knew nothing about the foul. Frank continued throwing punches, got me down and had me knocked out. When I regained consciousness, I could see he was on top of me. The first thing that came into my mind was I was in a bad situation. For every move there is a counter and for every counter there is a counter. So I knew there was a way out. I took a deep breath and tried to think of ways to get out. I ended up getting out and on top of Frank and proceeded to beat him up until he tapped out.

Q: You have fought some tough fighters in your career. Which, would you say, was the toughest fight?

Hughes: My toughest fight was against BJ Penn when I fought him the second time, because he beat me the first time. That was a really stressful fight.

Q: What diet do you follow as a UFC fighter and athlete?

Hughes: It just depends on what I've got going on. Right now I'll eat whatever I want. But when I'm training for a fight I get stricter with my diet. I'll eat a lot of good carbs and protein. I try to stay away from fat. And I love fruit. I can eat fruit as a dessert, to be honest.

Q: How important is recuperation for a UFC fighter?

Hughes: I think recuperation is a big thing. You can't be in this game as long as I have been because when you are fighting you need to take time off. So you're not beating your body up constantly. I know some guys who all they do is train and the same way all year long, and they are not in the sport anymore. You just can't take the bumps and bruises all the time. I think, after a fight I always take quite a bit of time off, and that is all relevant to who else from gym is fighting. If someone like Robbie Lawler has a fight coming up, then I will get back in the gym and help him get ready for the fight.

Q: How do you see the UFC and MMA growing and getting even bigger as a sport than it already is?

Hughes: We're not covered day to day on ESPN yet, so that definitely would be great for us—everyday coverage ESPN—getting on more TV shows. The more adults see us the more chance we have gaining new fans. That can all be good for the sport. All in all I'm really happy with the progress of the sport. If you look back five or six years ago and compare it with now, you'll find it's a whole new world.

Q: You fought Georges St-Pierre at UFC 79 (December 2007), and did not perform to the best of your abilities. You actually looked out of shape. What are your comments on this fight?

Hughes: Of course I could have done things differently. The fight didn't go the way I wanted it to. And when that happens obviously there could have been some changes. But that's the way it is. And if we meet up and fight again, then I'll have to look at things the way I fought and how he fought and we'll come up with a different game plan. When you lose you have to look back at what I did well and what I shouldn't have done, and what I'm going to do the next time. Watching tapes of your opponent definitely helps. You look at tendencies at what they do and what they don't, and then you try to base your game plan on that.

Q: How did your fight with Royce Gracie at UFC 60 (May 2006) materialize? This fight broke pay-per-view records at the time.

Hughes: I don't know if it broke pay per-view box-office records and I just don't care about stuff like that. My pay check is the same whether two people pay for pay-per-view or two million. It's just not a concern of mine. With the Royce Gracie fight, Dana White called me up and said, "I've got your next opponent." And I said, "Who is it?" He said it was Royce Gracie. I asked when that's going to be. It was just that simple. Everyone thought it was a big fight but I never thought it was a big fight. I thought I would squash him like a bug just because he's been out of the sport for so long, and because of his age as well. I knew he was a one-dimensional fighter and I knew he was kind of "old school." The sport of grappling and striking on the ground is so much different than it used to be when he was competing.

Q: Rickson Gracie is more of a physical specimen. How do you think he would have fared in the UFC?

Hughes: I think Rickson would get killed in the UFC, to be honest. From what I've seen in Rickson's fights, I've never been impressed by him. I just think they've made Rickson to be some fairy tale. He's just not what the rumors say he is. I really don't think Rickson would be able to compete in the UFC.

Q: What has been the most enjoyable experience for you in your career?

Hughes: I think the most enjoyable thing that's happened in the UFC for me is the good times I've had—a lot of memories. And a lot of that has to do with my family—the people I keep next to me. So this is what I will take away from what I've done in the UFC, first and foremost.

Q: Do you think _The Ultimate Fighter_ gave the UFC and MMA in general wider exposure which otherwise may not have?
Hughes: I definitely think _TUF_ was good for the UFC. This is one of the things which put the UFC where it is today. It got fights on Spike-TV, which is big. It has drama in there, which attracted fans, and it's just been great for the UFC. Take _TUF_ out of the equation and the UFC wouldn't be where it is today.

Q: You were on the same season with Matt Serra. Were there any interesting behind-the-scenes stories?
Hughes: Actually, I don't have any interesting stories because I never talked to him. When he walked into the room, I didn't take interest in whatever he was doing. Whether he was talking, walking around, I didn't pay any attention to him, nor did I chat with him. So I really wouldn't have any interesting stories.

Q: Your book _Made in America_ made it to the _New York Times_ best-seller list, and was one of the first autobiographies of a UFC star. How did the book deal come about?
Hughes: The book came about because I had a lot of people asking me questions about my life, and how I was raised and got into the sport. Then I was approached by a company Simon & Schuster to write a book. So with those two together, I said yes. To be honest, I didn't really want to, but I wouldn't say I was talked into it. I thought it was the right thing to do. So I went ahead and did a book deal.

Q: Do you feel amateur wrestlers—after they graduate—don't have an avenue to make money unless they pursue pro wrestling? Is the UFC a good outlet for them?
Hughes: I think it's an easy crossover for a wrestler to come into this sport. I think the wrestlers have a real advantage in the fighting game in that wrestlers get to decide where the fight's going to be at. If he wants to be offensive, he can take somebody down and try to beat him down. On the other hand, if he wants to be defensive he can keep the

opponent standing and try to beat him standing. So, a wrestler gets to decide where the fights going to be at.

Q: In your opinion, how would a heavyweight boxer do in a no-rules fight? You need to be well rounded in order to prevail, yes?
Hughes: Well, it would just depend on what the matchup would be. If a heavyweight boxer comes into the UFC and fights another standup artist who doesn't have any takedowns, then maybe he'd have a chance. If that heavyweight boxer comes up against someone who has good takedowns then that boxer wouldn't really do that well. Everybody who has good hands is going to have that punchers chance, no doubt about that. But like you said, you have to be well rounded and somebody not well rounded is going to be taken weakest game and the boxer would be at a disadvantage. I really don't follow boxing, never really followed boxing as a sport. To me boxing is pretty boring, it's just two guys trying to punch each other and that's about it.

Q: Who are your favorite UFC fighters?
Hughes: I'm a big Chuck Liddell fan and Rich Franklin fan—both are personal friends of mine. I always like to watch [Thierry] Sokoudjou fight, to be honest—that's my list.

Q: You have at least one more fight left in you, who would this fight be against?
Hughes: I think I would be fighting Matt Serra because that fight has never taken place, but I don't know 100 percent when that fight will happen or anything yet. But that's who I think I would be fighting.

Q: If you were not a UFC fighter, what avenues would you have taken in life?
Hughes: If I wasn't a fighter I would probably be working on a farm, possibly my farm, doing something with my hands because I like using my hands whether its construction or some kind of electrical. It would definitely be something where I'm able to use my hands.

Q: What are your future plans, once you finish fighting?

Hughes: I want to spend more time with my family, that's why I would look into getting out of the fighting now. I have a three-year-old daughter who I don't spend much time with. That's the big reason. I do have a gym in Illinois called The Hit Squad, and we do have dormitory rooms setup so that people can train and live here.

Georges St-Pierre

UFC Welterweight and Middleweight
Champion/Hall of Famer

Question: What was it like growing up in a small rural town in Canada?

Georges St-Pierre: I was born in Quebec, in a little countryside place. I had problems at school, which is one of the reasons I started training in the martial arts. At school it was pretty bad and I had a really tough time. But I learned martial arts to defend myself and get out of trouble. It also taught me discipline. It was different living in a small place. I was lonely and by myself. I did not go to school in my own town because in a small town like ours, there was no school. So I had to go to a school in the big city nearby. I didn't have a lot of friends because I was an outsider and always by myself. So I had trouble making friends at school. That's how it was.

Q: What kind of incidents did you get into, where gang life was the norm?

St-Pierre: When I was young I had a hard time. I had a problem making friends because I had problems with older teenagers. Because of this, other kids would avoid being my friend otherwise they would be targeted, too. A bunch of teenagers, who were five years older than us, were creating problems with the other kids. There were a lot of incidents with me. One time I was coming out of school and there were three or four guys outside. I was walking with my friend and we heard noises behind us. We were going to take the bus, and I said to my friend, "They just spat on us." My friend said, "No, they didn't." I turned around, and I said to my friend, "Let's go to them." He said, "No, no. I don't want to go." My friend was small and the gang members were bigger and tall. I said, "You know what, you're never going to get respect if you don't make yourself respected." I went alone after them and hit the first guy, then I got beat up pretty bad because there were four of them. Even though I got beat up, they respected me because I came back for them. When you think about it, you realize it was stupid things which kids did at that age. I went back to fight them because of the honor and to earn respect. I had a lot of anger and pride in me when I was growing up. I didn't want to tell nobody about my problems. I had pride and a big ego, so I wouldn't tell anyone because I thought they'd say I'm like a baby, or a kid who cannot defend himself.

Q: You took up martial arts as a kid. Were you influenced by anyone in particular?
St-Pierre: I was influenced by Jean Claude Van Damme. I can't do the splits, though. I saw *Blood Sport*, which inspired me. This was a great inspiration to me. I wanted to be a karate or martial arts champion when I was young. So this was one of my goals. I started doing Kyokushin karate. But when I was a teenager, after my teacher died I came across something different. I saw my first UFC. Then I started training for MMA.

Q: You worked as a bouncer. What was the experience like working in a rather tough environment?
St-Pierre: Now my life is pretty easy—I'm a world champion—but it hasn't always been like this. There was a time in my life when I was studying in school and working three jobs at the same time. I was bouncing in a nightclub, working in a floor roofing place and for a government program for teenagers at school. At the nightclub, I was working with guys who were very big and strong. Most of them were using violence to take care of the problems, but I never did that. I always thought the best way to take care of the problem was talking. So that's what I did most of the time to sort out problems.

Q: Is it true that your dream was to become a UFC champion?

St-Pierre: When I first saw Royce Gracie fighting in the UFC, I was still a teenager. My teacher had died. I was very sad and didn't know what to do. I wanted to keep training in the martial arts, but I felt I didn't know where to go and I felt lonely and by myself. Then when I saw Royce Gracie win the Ultimate Fighting Championship, I right away knew that was what I wanted to do. I didn't know much about the sport. And in Canada nobody knew what jiu-jitsu was because it was brand new. So, I tried to take jiu-jitsu classes to learn to grapple. But nobody knew much about this art, but it was a very effective martial art. Royce Gracie is a definite inspiration for me and the pioneer of the sport. And no matter what happens now, he's always going to be a champion for me in my heart. He's somebody I look up to as an athlete.

Q: You actually had your first MMA fight at the age of sixteen, beating a twenty-five year old. Is this true?

St-Pierre: I have always been very good with my feet because of my karate training, and when I was sixteen I started to learn jiu-jitsu. So, I didn't know much on the ground, but I was very strong so I could power out of a submission from my opponent. At the time, the sport was illegal—it was a secret no-holds-barred competition with open-hand strikes on the floor. I had four amateur fights and I won all of them. I was a teenager fighting adults. This is before I was fighting professionally.

Q: You have stated in the past that you thought you were going to die when you fought Thomas Denny in a TKO Promotion. Is this true?

St-Pierre: This was the toughest fight of my career. I was sick when I fought him. I couldn't breathe. I dominated the first round with ground and pound. When I was in my corner, I told my corner men I didn't want to go back for the second round because I thought I was going to die. My corner men pushed me and I ended up beating my opponent.

Q: Finally, you made your debut at UFC 46 (January 2004). What did it feel like to be fighting in the Octagon?

St-Pierre: I was fighting in MMA matches in my own country, Canada, and I was undefeated at the time. I remember when Pete Spratt beat Robbie Lawler in a UFC bout, he was very tough and in the top rankings. Pete came to Canada to fight me and I beat him with a rear naked choke. This brought me to the attention of the UFC people, so they called my manger to offer me a fight in the UFC. It was a dream come true and the moment I had been waiting for a long time. Just to step into the Octagon for first time, it was like I had a heart attack. It was an amazing feeling.

Q: Your UFC fight record is impressive. You fought Matt Hughes a couple of times and won the welterweight title from him. What was the feeling of achieving this, and what do you think of him?

St-Pierre: Matt Hughes is the best opponent I have fought. He is a very good fighter. When Matt Hughes trains hard and he's at his best, he's very hard. He is the best fighter I have fought. It was an indescribable experience and an amazing feeling, something I had been waiting for a long time. Matt Hughes is getting old, but I think he can come back if he keeps training hard. We have a new generation coming up now who are better athletes, but I think he can still do it. I never really had problems with Matt Hughes—he was just talking to hype up the fight, but nothing personal. Actually, if I see Matt Hughes on the street in a situation and he needs help, I'll probably be the first person to stop and help him.

Q: Tell me, what went wrong in the BJ Penn fight?

St-Pierre: BJ put his finger in my eye. I don't think it was intentional; I think it was an accident. That's no problem. Stuff like that happens sometimes in a fight. I should've got on my knees and taken a few minutes out because I couldn't see anything. But I didn't because I was too much into the fight. And I learned from my mistake and next time I will know how to react from my experience. The first round was the worst because I could not see. I had to close one eye. And when you fight with one eye you're not accurate, the exchange of blows were not accurate. He had two eyes and I was fighting with one. When I came back to my corner, my corner men wiped my eye with water and after that the eye got a little better. I should be fighting him again soon. It's not scheduled yet but I think it's in January. There are a lot of people looking forward to this fight and I think we should do it. I can't wait. I'm pretty sure we are going to fight each other very soon. I can beat him.

Q: You fought Matt Serra at UFC 69 (April 2007) and lost your title to him, but you came back and beat him in the second fight. Do you think he got in a lucky punch in when he beat you?
St-Pierre: There's no such thing as a lucky punch. I didn't fight well the first time I fought him. Matt Serra was a better fighter on the night. I made many mistakes and got beat by a better man on the night. And hopefully I got a chance and went onto revenge my loss and showed that I'm better than when I performed in the first fight, when I beat Matt the second time. I had many problems outside the ring at the time, but I have no excuse. I lost the first fight because Serra was better than me. I should have won that fight but I lost and made a mistake. I lost my equilibrium from a punch and I just couldn't come back up. I'm a human being and humans make mistakes.

Q: It seems MMA is big in Canada and very much embraced. Just how popular is it up there?
St-Pierre: It wasn't really that big until the UFC came to Montreal, now it's huge. There are a lot of fans everywhere and people want to see another UFC coming in Canada as soon as possible.

Q: Any disappointments so far in your career that come to mind?
St-Pierre: My biggest disappointment was when I lost the fight to Matt Serra. Always, a loss is hard to take in, but sometimes you realize it could be a good thing. It makes you change your routine and makes you think about why you lost and makes you a better fighter.

Q: Do you feel it is important to switch on and off? Do you turn into another person when you enter the Octagon?
St-Pierre: When I go into a fight, I forget all about my problems outside

of the Octagon and leave all the distractions outside. I focus on only one thing, and that is to beat my opponent.

Q: Do you think UFC fighters are the toughest athletes in the world?
St-Pierre: Most of them are the best athletes in the world. What we do is a mixture of fighting—boxing, kickboxing, wrestling, jiu-jitsu, and judo—so we have to be very athletic. I train twice a day, six days a week. I do sprints, conditioning, boxing, wrestling, Muay Thai, Brazilian jiu-jitsu, and MMA—all mixed together. My main coach is Greg Jackson but I have different coaches in different disciplines.

Q: Why did Diego Sanchez leave the Jackson camp?
St-Pierre: He left because he has a daughter in California, that's what everybody told me. I don't think he left because I came over to Jackson's—maybe it has a little bit to do with this, but I think it's more because of his daughter. In the future there's a possibility of fighting him. He's pretty good. It depends on his next fight and my next fight.

Q: You're a big movie buff. Will we be seeing you making a transition into Hollywood, just as Randy Couture did?
St-Pierre: I think it's a possibility, but right now I'm focusing on fighting and not on doing movies. Maybe one day if I have time I will pursue that avenue.

Q: What are your plans for the future?
St-Pierre: I fought John Fitch recently. John Fitch has a lot of heart, he's like the Terminator—he never gives up and always comes back. I was happy with my performance. I will continue to fight in the sport, but I'm not one of those guys who fight because he has no choice; I fight because I love it and because there's a lot of money, too.

If I wanted to I could have done something else because I have a diploma. The morning I wake up and I'm not happy with my job, then I'm going to do something else. If I didn't fight in MMA, I could have been a professional trainer. I would like to thank my fans and also Affliction for the support they've given me.

Vitor Belfort

UFC Light-Heavyweight Champion/
UFC Heavyweight Tournament Champion

Question: Vitor, what was your childhood like?
Vitor Belfort: I grew up in Brazil. When I was really young, I was a professional volleyball player and I really liked sport. I also used to play soccer and tennis. I grew up in a neighborhood which was a tough neighborhood and it was all about survival. Fighting in the street was common and we had to defend ourselves. I started to do martial arts to protect myself. I was four years old when I started doing judo. Then when I turned thirteen, I started Brazilian jiu-jitsu, and at fourteen I started doing boxing as well. When I turned fifteen, I made a decision that I wanted to do vale tudo. In the city where I lived, there were regular robberies and street crime. I didn't want to look like a punk with people robbing me and making fun of me, so I started doing martial arts. And this really helped me. I never like violence but I like the sport of fighting. Many people in Rio de Janeiro try to take advantage of other people, so I started to do martial arts to protect myself and this helped me.

Q: Do you feel Brazil is much more dangerous than America?
Belfort: Yes. In Brazil there's more corruption—too much poverty and social problems. You will see people with the attitude like, *Why does that guy have a nice car and I don't have it?* They want to have it, too. I think there are less opportunities here in Brazil and the poverty is high, which makes Brazil more dangerous than America for sure.

Q: When did you have your first vale tudo fight?

Belfort: I used to do vale tudo in the gym where I trained, people would come to the gym and they would fight. Back in those days, it was martial arts style against martial art style—judo against jiu-jitsu, boxing against jiu-jitsu—to prove which martial art was effective. At the time, when I was fighting Carlson Gracie was my coach. We had a relationship like a father and a son. He took me under his wing. When I was eighteen years old, I fought in my first professional fight in Hawaii in the Superbrawl tournament. I beat my opponent [Jon Hess] in 17 seconds. Back in those days they didn't have weight divisions; I was 190 pounds and my opponent was 300 pounds. He was very tough and really good. I gained experience and right after this fight I went to fight in the UFC. They invited me to fight for the title in the heavyweight division. This was the time when the UFC had started doing weight classes. I fought in both the heavyweight and the light-heavyweight divisions. I fought two opponents on the same night and won the heavyweight title. I was the youngest UFC heavyweight champion ever at the age of nineteen. Nobody has broken this record to date.

Q: What did you think of Royce Gracie beating bigger opponents in the earlier UFC?

Belfort: Royce was great. He proved that jiu-jitsu was the most effective martial art in the business because if you don't know jiu-jitsu, you are going to have problems. Right now we have MMA. You can be the best boxer in the world, or the best wrestler in the world, but if you don't know jiu-jitsu you are going to be submitted and lose. I feel jiu-jitsu is one of the most effective fighting styles.

Q: What did you think of the cultural differences when you moved to America?

Belfort: The difference between the two countries is that America is the land of opportunity. In America, you have the opportunity to make it big in all sports. In Brazil, the only sport that gets you anywhere on the world stage is soccer. There aren't many opportunities for other sports. The good thing about America is that you can do anything. American people support whatever you do. I like the way they're professional and the opportunities that are available.

Q: What was your experience fighting in Japan?
Belfort: I like Pride. It was a great experience. In Japan the fans support the sport and there is a lot of respect for the fighters. The culture is different, but there are opportunities in the sport. I like it a lot. The fans there are more quiet, observant, and different. They know the difference and they understand the sport technically. The sport is developed in Japan.

Q: At UFC 46 (January 2004), you beat Randy Couture for the light-heavyweight title. What are your views on Randy, and the fights you had with him?
Belfort: For me, he's one of the best fighters in the world. He is so nice as a person, a good fighter, good human being and it was wonderful for me to fight a guy like Randy. We had a total of three fights where he beat me two times and I beat him one time. It was a good experience for me and he taught me a lesson in the first fight, which was: never underestimate a fighter. Randy is the kind of a guy when he goes in the ring, it doesn't matter if you are a better fighter than him, he's going to make sure that he's going to stick to his game plan and he's going to fight you. He's not going to back up, but he's going to go forward and after you, and stick to his game plan. Randy is a perfect example as a fighter and a coach. We are good friends and right now I'm training at his facility out of Las Vegas with his trainers. Randy has helped develop the sport of MMA.

Q: When you fought Randy, your sister had recently been kidnapped. Did this affect your mindset and performance in the fight, and leave you despondent?
Belfort: Yes, sure. Two weeks before the fight my sister disappeared, but I was so focused for the fight I wanted to be the champion of the world again. I was the champion of the heavyweight division, and at the time I was fighting in the light-heavyweight division. I got the call from the

UFC telling me I didn't have to fight if I didn't want to, but I went and fought. I won the belt. Then Randy, in the rematch at UFC 49 (August 2004), won it off me. At that time, I was very out of focus and depressed because my sister was still not found. Randy was ready and focused mentally physically and spiritually. He got the belt and he deserved it. I was really out of focus. I think my strategy for this fight was not to go after him. He caught me with an elbow and a head butt and I couldn't do anything. I got a cut and the referee stopped the fight.

We never know what could have happened if the referee didn't stop the fight. I like to think about that and see what could have happened, but at the same time I don't want to take anything away from my opponent. Randy was very ready for the fight and beat me in the fight and he deserves it. So, that's how I see it. I'm the kind of a guy I don't look back but look at the future. So I learned my lesson. In MMA anything can happen. You can never give the opportunity to your opponent; you have to make sure you have to dominate him from the beginning to the end. Randy dominated this fight and he deserved the win. [Author's note: While Brazilian officials have ruled Vitor's sister to have been murdered, the Belfort family believes she is still alive.]

Q: When you fought Tito Ortiz at UFC 51 (February 2005), you broke his nose—yet you lost via decision. Just how disappointed were you?
Belfort: This fight with Tito was a big robbery. The judges robbed me so big and everybody knows, he knows, even his brothers in his corner know who really won the fight. The judges gave the fight to him. And we had a problem. I won the fight but I'd been cheated. In the last round, I got tired and he just lay on top of me and he didn't do anything. He was just trying to buy time. I'm ready to fight him again and I'll beat him again. I got mad with the UFC. I was really disappointed with the decision. Back at the time, Tito was a big name. It was a big upset and I was very disappointed. I think Affliction are going to put the fight on because I think Tito is going to sign for Affliction soon. I think this will be a big fight for Affliction to put that on pay-per-view. We're going to make millions and millions of pay-per-views because

everybody wants to see the rematch—Vitor Belfort versus Tito Ortiz II. That would be a big fight.

Q: You demonstrated your phenomenal hand speed against Wanderlei Silva at UFC 17.5 Ultimate Brazil (October 1998). Do you think you became known for having the fastest hands in the UFC?
Belfort: Yes, I beat him. Wanderlei is a very tough fighter and this was a big fight for me. First of all, I thank God for this gift. It's a gift given to me. The other thing is, I train hard. I fought in boxing amateur fights and then fought one professional fight. I have good hands and boxing skills so I tried to compete and train in boxing for a while.

Q: How did you find the experience of fighting in Europe on the Cage Rage promotion?
Belfort: They invited me to fight in Europe. So I did it to prove myself in Europe and treat it as another challenge for me. I fought in Cage Rage and won the championship and was really happy. I was undefeated there and won the belt, but they never gave the belt to me. I was disappointed with the organization. That was totally unprofessional on their part. I just don't fight for them anymore because if they can't respect me as a fighter, they will never respect me as a person.

I don't know why they didn't give me the belt. I beat the champion. When I called them to ask where my belt was, they said, "We've shipped it out, the belt is held in customs." They always were lying to me. So, I thought these guys are lying to me and being very unprofessional. I'm not going to fight for them because you can't trust them. If you can't trust a person who is lying to you then you can never work for them. Right now, I'm very happy with Affliction. They treat me like a person.

Q: Do you feel Brazilians are some of the best MMA fighters? Do you encourage more people to get into the sport of MMA?
Belfort: Yes, this is the perfect time for Affliction. We have the best card and fighters. So now we are going to keep growing. Everybody is going

to be big. UFC is big and Affliction is going to be big. Healthy competition is all good. I think now is the time.

Q: What has been the highlight of your career, and which would you say has been your toughest fight so far?
Belfort: Every moment is good—everybody from fighting Randy Couture, Chuck Liddell and Heath Herring. Chuck is one of the biggest fighters in the UFC for sure. He's a good fighter and a very marketable fighter and he deserves it.

Q: Would you ever fight in the UFC again?
Belfort: Right now, I'm with Affliction. We have good fighters in Affliction. We are willing to fight with anybody, anybody with the belt we can challenge. We have good promoters at Affliction and it's good for the sport and fans. The UFC has a lot of fighters, too. Everything is going to depend on co-promotion. So we are going to need UFC people to start a record of us. I'm a fighting man. I want to fight the champion. I just want to put on a good fight for the fans.

Q: How many more years are you going to be fighting professionally?
Belfort: I'm thirty-one years old, young and fresh and ready to fight again. I think MMA needs new promotions coming up like Affliction. Right now, it's a good time for the new promotions competing with the UFC, which is good for the sport. I'm really proud of seeing this. The difference between the UFC now compared to when I started 1997 is there's more opportunities and money now. Back in that time, there were no rules but now the sport is more organized—bigger promotions, bigger money and is more professional than before. I have two houses. I live in Brazil and US.

Q: Have you any additional comments to add?
Belfort: I want to thank the fans and thank the Lord to give me the opportunity to keep fighting. He's the reason why I'm alive. I want to also thank all the promoters. We have a reason in life, one of the reasons in life is to live right and work hard.

BJ Penn

UFC Lightweight and Welterweight
Champion/Hall of Famer

Question: BJ, how did you get involved in martial arts?

BJ Penn: A guy named Tom Callos, who was a martial arts instructor, moved about five houses from my house in Hawaii. And he needed some people to wrestle around with and train jiu-jitsu with. He kept bugging my dad and asking him to send me to train with him, but I didn't want to go. He kept bothering me, so one day my dad said to me, "Just go down once and you won't have to go anymore." So I went down and ended up liking it. Before that I was just doing some boxing for fun with friends and people all around town all the time.

Q: How would you describe your teenage years growing up in Hawaii?

Penn: At that age, I was hanging out with friends and getting into street fights. A local street fighter named Saul, who was fighting all the time, has been an influence to me.

Q: Let's talk about your competitive career before you pursued the UFC.

Penn: I entered many jiu-jitsu tournaments—including going to Brazil—and I became a world champion in Brazilian jiu-jitsu. When I trained with Tom Callos, he introduced me to Ralph Gracie in California who became my instructor. Then I moved back to Hawaii and started training with a few instructors. Ralph was very good. I trained with a lot of different training partners. I trained with everybody from Frank Shamrock, Randy Couture, the American Kickboxing Academy, and Rigan Machado. It was awesome working with all these people. Training with guys like that really helped me learn fast. You have to see what the best people do.

Q: Can you recall when you first saw the UFC?
Penn: When I first saw the UFC, I was around thirteen or fourteen years old. I thought it was cool. It was like real fights but I wasn't really that interested in it. I liked to watch Royce Gracie. At the time, it was cool and I wanted Royce to win and would cheer for him, but I was more into boxing at the time. The Gracies definitely revolutionized the martial arts and opened the doors for MMA.

Q: How did you get involved in the UFC?
Penn: I knew Dana White before I got involved in the UFC because I trained with him one time because John Lewis introduced me to him. After that I talked to Dana and asked him if he could get me into the UFC and eventually he got me in.

Q: Do you remember your first fight in the UFC, and how did it feel to be fighting in the Octagon for the first time?
Penn: I fought George Gilbert and I was really pumped up and excited. It was kind of proving to myself that I'm a good fighter and I can fight with people who train for fighting. This was my favorite fight. To me, all my fights represent certain danger, whether it's against a kick-boxer, wrestler, or a huge person—it's all equal. A fight is a fight. I'm willing to do everything to win the fight. Twenty minutes before a fight, I think about the game plan and techniques I'm going to use.

Q: Would you say you are an all-round fighter, even though your base is Brazilian jiu-jitsu?
Penn: It's very important to be an all-round fighter in MMA. You have to be good at striking, grappling and takedowns. For self-defense jiu-jitsu is enough, but for MMA you need everything. I train as hard as I

can all year round and whenever I get tired, I take time off. I cover everything from jiu-jitsu, boxing, kickboxing, and wrestling. Conditioning also plays a huge part of my training regime. I do everything you possibly can think of from running, weights, calisthenics, bag work and so on. You need to find what the most important element you need to add to your game, as far as specific schedule, sit down and figure it out.

Q: You both beat and lost to Matt Hughes. Can you talk me through those fights?
Penn: I felt good and I was in great shape. I was strong mentally. I don't just remember coming out, but as soon as I got in the fight I knew I was confident I was going to win the fight. Everything just came together. It ended up him going to the ground and I ended up landing a good punch and choking him. It was over. I was really happy and very fulfilled. The hard journey was worth it in the end. In my rematch with him, I did get hurt during the fight. I don't really want it to be some excuse but Hughes won that day. A defeat motivates me to train harder.

Q: In 2004, you started fighting in other arenas. What was that experience like?
Penn: It was just different in terms of place and events. The whole feeling is pretty much the same—you go there and go to the arena and warm up and fight. As far as I know, they were all the same. Fighting in Hawaii was easy because of the same time zone and the same climate. I felt very comfortable. There are a lot of MMA schools in Hawaii now and MMA is the biggest sport now in Hawaii.

Q: In your opinion, how would a professional boxer do in an MMA fight?
Penn: I would think a boxer would do well in MMA, but he's got to learn wrestling and jiu-jitsu to survive. When you see the guys in MMA standing and exchanging blows, the only reason they are boxing is they have not hit the ground yet. The weaker person on the ground is going to be taken down.

Q: In your opinion, what makes the sport of MMA so profound and exciting?

Penn: I think everyone now understands it. You don't have to explain the rules to anyone because they know what's going on in the fight.

Q: How would you differentiate between an MMA fight and a street fight?

Penn: There are differences, but the main thing is they also have similarities like elements of punching, kicking each other and slamming each other down. Of course, in street fighting you can do anything you want because there are no rules or rounds. MMA and street fighting are two different things—you have two different attitudes. In a street fight you get mad—I'm sure it happens in MMA but it really is a sport with rounds. I've had my share of street fights but I'll never get in trouble anymore. When you fight in the ring or spar in MMA conditioning is important. In day-to-day self-defense, technique is important because it's not always going to be a long fight in the street.

Q: If you could change anything about the UFC, what would it be?

Penn: I would put in kicks, knees and stomps on the ground, and legalize kicking to the head of a grounded opponent.

Q: You fought outside of America in such places as Japan. How do you see the sport of MMA growing in the future?

Penn: I think it's grown. The sport is going to grow huge in Europe, the UK, and everywhere in the world. It will get bigger. Without a doubt, MMA fighters should be making more money. It will turn that way. Everybody used to watch other sports. A lot of people are now turning to reality shows and now we have shows like *Cops* and more realistic things. MMA is a realistic sport and a sport for the new generation. My experience of *The Ultimate Fighter* was that it was very busy, tough and I had a great experience just being on the TV show and seeing how it was filmed and the interaction with all of the people on the show. I had a great time and it really helped promote the UFC. I was in Afghanistan not long ago to visit the troops—the UFC sent us over. Michael Bisping was there, too. It was cool. I think the sport's grown to what it is now and it's just amazing.

Q: Do you have any comments on your victory over Sean Sherk at UFC 84 (May 2008)?

Penn: He got in and took me down. It was just a boxing match and I felt I was catching him with some good punches—and then I finally got to hit him with the knee and then caught him with a couple of punches and it was over. I met The Rock for the first time, he was in the audience. I'm a big fan of his.

Q: Sean tested positive for steroids. What are your feelings of athletes in the UFC taking these performance-enhancing drugs?

Penn: I think it's cheating and wrong. I think they're cowards. I don't think it's putting a bad reputation on the sport, but it's cheating and they shouldn't be doing it.

Q: What do you do to relax and recuperate?

Penn: Recuperation is very important. I just try to go out and have fun. Just do whatever, go anywhere, travel, beaches, different islands and try to relax myself. I try to eat the most healthy and natural food when I'm training for a fight and try to stay away from the bad food.

Q: Is there any particular fighter you would like to fight?

Penn: I will fight whichever fighter my fans want to see me fight in the biggest fight. I have ten years left in me fighting pro. Our sport will no doubt surpass boxing. I don't know about other lightweight fighters, but I want to fight the best out there and the biggest names and put on a good show. I want to try my best and become a champion. In MMA I like watching all the fighters. I'm a fan of everybody, all the good guys.

Anderson Silva

UFC Middleweight Champion/Hall of Famer

Question: Can you tell me of your experiences fighting in Japan, and what made you go to fight there?
Anderson Silva: My experiences in Japan were really good and this gave me the basis and experience to fight in other events. For me, going to fight in Japan was the natural course of my career.

Q: Which was your hardest fight in Japan?
Silva: Basically, all of my fights were pretty tough, but my toughest fight was in Shooto against Sakurai when I won the belt. Sakurai had beaten many Brazilians and had no losses in Shooto, but I was very prepared for the fight with a strong team behind me. My goal was to win that fight. It was tough, but I did my job right and accomplished my goal.

Q: You also fought in Cage Rage and became the champion. How did you find the experience fighting in Europe?
Silva: Fighting in Cage Rage was good. I had my good and bad moments, but in the end they promoted me very well. I also got used to fighting in the cage, and it gave people a chance to know me a little better and eventually lead my entry into the UFC.

Q: How did you get involved with the UFC? Was this your ultimate goal?
Silva: It was a big dream of mine to fight in the UFC. And it was a natural course of things where you evolve and end up pursuing your

dream when you train hard and do your job well. I was always a big fan of the UFC.

Q: You demonstrated awesome skills at UFC 64 (October 2006) in your fight against Rich Franklin. Can you shed some light on this ground-breaking fight?

Silva: I felt good going into the fight and for the belt. It was an honor to fight Rich Franklin. I respect him for giving me the opportunity. I was very prepared for this fight. I was very well trained for this fight and the goal was to fight for the title. I trained really hard for this the whole way, and it's what happens when you're given a chance and you come prepared. You carry out your game plan you have been training for.

Q: You demolished Franklin for the second time at UFC 77 (October 2007), with two consecutive knees. Do you think this proved you had the potential to "clean up" your division?

Silva: I trained even harder for the second fight with Rich Franklin because I knew he was in very good shape, and he had trained very hard for this fight. I was doing my job. Rich had a very bad moment when he made a mistake and I got him. The sport has evolved now to a point what it is now. People want to see a good fight and usually a good fight involves good standup knockouts. My goal is to go in and do my job, it would be great if the both of us walked out uninjured, but that's not always possible.

Q: Do you ever feel pressure, as you are undefeated so far in the UFC?

Silva: No, not at all. It's just a natural course of things. I just have to do my job well and show up to the fight, and forget about that I own the belt.

Q: What motivates you to fight in such a dangerous sport?

Silva: I fight because it's satisfying. And I know I can do a good job and go out there showing I'm one of the best. I've been training all my life, it's very natural for me.

Q: Who inspired you in MMA, and what did you do to make a living before becoming a professional fighter?

Silva: I didn't plan or even think of becoming a professional fighter, but I would always watch Carlson Gracie, Royce Gracie, Marco Ruas, and Vitor Belfort fight. So I had some Brazilian fighting idols but I didn't make that my lifelong dream, but things just happened naturally. I've always had to work. I've been an office assistant, worked in McDonalds for six years, but I always found a way to train and have been linked to the martial arts. I've been a professional fighter for a long time now, but really now the UFC has expanded and it's something completely different because the sport is huge in the media now. So it's a completely different setting for me.

Q: Did you ever get into any street fights in Brazil, as it's quite common there?

Silva: I've never had that problem in Brazil. MMA is a sport and street fighting is not. People have to know how to differentiate between the two.

Q: Can you tell me in your fight against Okami at the Rumble on the Rock promotion, and why you got disqualified?

Silva: No comment.

Q: How do you prepare for a fight?

Silva: You have to be very focused the whole way through even when you are not training for a fight. If you get your head in place and train you will always be prepared. I'm very focused and concentrating 100 percent before the fight and that's my job to go out there and do my best. After the fight, I try to get my mind off things and just relax.

Q: Michael Bisping has stated in past he would like to fight you. What do you think of him as a fighter?

Silva: He's a great fighter and he's starting to build himself up. He could be a good challenge in the future. I can't say that I would like to fight him; I want to fight the best, so if he is one of the best, who knows, one day. Michael Bisping is a great fighter, but I cannot predict the fight because you'll just have to see it if the time comes.

Q: Why are you a big fan of Spider-Man?
Silva: I relate to Spider-Man and have always done so because I think he's a super hero who's got bills to pay. So I could always relate to him and how he also has to struggle.

Q: You expressed your desire to fight top professional boxer Roy Jones Jr. Would you like to face him in the future?
Silva: Boxing and MMA are two completely different things, but MMA has its great champions as well as boxing. MMA might be in the spotlight right now because of what the UFC has done for the sport. Boxing has got to be respected because they have some great champions. I've always wanted to fight a great boxer, it's my dream to fight Roy Jones Jr. and I hope in the near future this fight will happen. The sport of MMA is growing very fast and new athletes are going to come onboard. And if they [boxers] think they can make that decision, then they probably will most likely go into MMA.

Q: How did you prepare for the James Irvin fight at *UFC Fight Night 3* (2007)?
Silva: My training is always the same no matter who my opponent is. I did the same training with a few adjustments here and there for this fight such as a wearing a weight jacket when I was training.

Q: You have planted a seed in the US by opening a state-of-the-art MMA gym in Miami, Florida. How is that venture doing?
Silva: The gym is going well. We have a professor there in charge. We are doing this to educate people in MMA and trying to get the focus on the sport. Obviously MMA in the USA is more in the media spotlight right now, and even though we've been doing it for a long time in Brazil—where it's got its heritage and is a traditional sport—it's not so much in the headlines compared to America. But it's getting more and more attention now and people are respecting it now. It can get even

bigger and that's what they're working hard at and there are chances it will.

Q: Do you plan on "cleaning out" the light-heavyweight division, which will make you an all-time great UFC fighter?
Silva: I'm trained to fight the best. Whoever the UFC puts in front of me, I'll fight. I have no plans to stay in the 205-pound division— my place is at 185 defending my title, leaving the 205 title to Lyoto [Machida].

Q: How many more years do you plan on fighting, and do you have other goals you would like to focus on after retiring?
Silva: I have maybe another two or three years, who knows. But my dream after fighting in MMA is everyone knows me by now. My proudest moment has been my first title defense because it was a tough thing to do. And I defended it successfully. It's hard to go undefeated, but that's what I'm training for. My life is moving slowly and I just have to keep training hard and fighting in the UFC and reach my goals. Other than that, I have to leave it in the hands of God and keep doing my job. I want to thank my fans and all of my trainers and anyone who's a part of my team.

Quinton "Rampage" Jackson

UFC Light-Heavyweight Champion

Question: What kind of a childhood did you have?

Quinton Jackson: My neighborhood was very rough. We were street kids always hanging out. We drank alcohol, smoked weed and cigarettes, stole stuff out of the grocery stores like street punks. This all happened when I was growing up. There were street gangs around. We would go driving in stolen cars on the other side of town. My brother would get his ass beat because he would go mess with people. And I would have to go beat their ass, and after that I would beat his ass. There were bullies who would bully my friends or my brother, and I would fight the bullies. When I was a kid I used to get into fights. People gave me a nickname "Mike Tyson" because the way I used to try to knockout my opponent on his ass. I was more of the protector of my family and friends. So, now I'm more of a fight celebrity fighting in the UFC and I have fans. I don't have a right to judge what kind of a person anyone is—or someone like Kimbo Slice, but I'm glad he's doing MMA and doing it legally. Everyone has their own choices to make, who's to say anything about anyone else. He's come into the sport now and I wish him the best. We're all the same in that we're professional fighters. I respect anyone who goes into the Octagon to fight.

Q: Am I right in saying that you originally wanted to pursue a career in professional wrestling?

Jackson: When I was a kid I watched pro wrestling a lot. I'm from Michigan, where pro wrestling was very popular. I thought I was going to be a pro wrestler, a stuntman, or a fireman.

Q: You fought and beat Chuck Liddell twice—in Japan and the UFC. Do you have any comments on your battles with the "Iceman?"

Jackson: I loved Japan. It was great. They had tough fighters in Japan and I learned a lot about fighting there. I always fought under pressure it helped me to become a better fighter. I fought really hard against Chuck Liddell. My intention was to win the whole tournament to show the world I'm the best fighter in the world. I beat Chuck and proved to the world I was the best fighter. My plan was to beat the hell out of Chuck and don't let anything stop me, and just whoop his ass. Of course, I beat him again in UFC 71 (May 2007) and proved to people the first victory wasn't a fluke. I knew I had to finish it quick. I had a small injury so I didn't want the fight to carry on for a long time. So, it worked out perfectly, thank God.

Q: Would you like to fight him again?

Jackson: I wouldn't mind fighting Chuck again, but after his last fight, I don't think he's going to fight for a while. I hope he recovers and gets back into the Octagon. He's an icon for the sport. And if he decides to fight, I'll be back to my best. It's good to see someone get knocked out in a fight, but it's bad for the fighter afterwards. Before I can even think about fighting Chuck, he needs to get back to the top form. I'll fight Chuck one more time and I'll knock him out, too.

Q: What is your friendship like with Tito Ortiz?

Jackson: Tito and I have been friends for a long time and I look up to him. I go to the Big Bear Mountain training facility to train. He's an icon for the sport. Tito has that X-factor. He's one of those guys you want to see—win or lose everybody wants to see Tito fight. If you think about it, a lot of fighters don't have that; only one percent of the fighters have that. Tito has that and I've got that—Michael Bisping's got that. You want to listen to what we have to say. I like Chuck Liddell, but everybody just want to see him fight, nothing outside that. Fans of the sport want to see him in the Octagon just fighting. But outside that it's different. But with Tito, you want to see what he's doing and what he's saying. When he's done after the fight, he has something to do or something to say, like the t-shirts he puts on after the fight.

Q: Do you watch a great deal of UFC fights?
Jackson: I don't watch it a whole lot. I'm just a weird person in my own little world. But I watch it when someone like Georges St-Pierre or Randy Couture fights. I want to see what Randy's going to do, whether he is going to knock the person out or submit him. He's an old guy but still going strong. I like to watch my friends, Michael Bisping and [Cheick] Kongo, fight. I don't watch too many of my own fights, but I'll watch them now and again. The UFC has made me more of a fan than I ever was when I was fighting in Pride, to be honest.

Q: You're a spiritual person and embraced religion. What made you go this direction?
Jackson: My mom and grandma were very spiritual. And when I was older I started to go to church. Now I'm a child of God and I try to be spiritual. God chose me to be in his Kingdom. Spiritual thinking must not be misunderstood, like some other religious people who do the wrong things to use religion for their own wrong doings. I just want people to know that I'm a child of God and I'm happy with what I am. This has made me a better person. If it doesn't then there's something wrong with you.

Q: The much talked about Forrest Griffin fight was controversial—everybody knows it. It seems Forrest did not share this view. What is your take?
Jackson: Forrest can say whatever he wants, but everyone else says it was a controversial fight. I watched the fight and I thought I won. Firstly, he just won the rounds—two and five in my eyes. You know what, the fans

think so, too. I don't care—the fight's old news—but I think a bunch of fans should do a poll on what they think. He thought he lost, too. So I don't know why he would say it's not controversial. I'll tell you what, the next time I fight Forrest I'm going to be better prepared and in a better frame of mind. And it's going to be a lot better fight for Rampage, trust me. I lost respect for Forrest because he didn't think it was a controversial fight, everyone else thinks it was. The fight could have gone either way because that's what happens in UFC, but by no means it should have been a unanimous decision.

Q: Now that you will be spending some time in the UK, what do you think of the UK scene?

Jackson: I love the UK. I'm coming out here and I can do my thing with less distractions. And it's cool. I like training with Michael Bisping and I'll train hard and get better. Michael is one of the hardest working fighters I've seen. I've had a lot of people before saying, "What are you doing joining the Wolfslair team?" And also, "What you doing with the Bisping team? You're the champion!" I'll tell you what, Michael Bisping is a good fighter and a lot of people around him are good. And I can be a lot better fighter and sparring partner by working with these guys. I've come here a couple of times before and spent some time and was very impressed at what I saw. I think it's the best team on the planet. So I'm really happy here. I think the UFC is going to grow bigger all over the world. It's the fastest growing sport in the world. Some other people may make comments and criticize the sport, but we're not talking bad about any of the other sports. We put on good full-contact fights; it's a great sport.

Antônio Rodrigo Nogueira

UFC Interim Heavyweight Champion/Hall of Famer

Question: You started martial arts training at a very young age. How and when did you get involved?

Antônio Nogueira: I stared judo at the age of five. Most of the kids in Brazil do judo to develop discipline, and it's a very common and a popular sport in Brazil. I trained for nine years. Then I did tae kwon do and some boxing. I stared doing boxing and jiu-jitsu when I was a teenager. Then in the '90s, I started MMA and moved to America.

Q: You had an accident when you were a child. Did this affect your training in any way?

Nogueira: I was eleven years old when I had a truck accident. I had a really hard time for eleven months in the hospital. I couldn't walk. I had a lot of difficulties. I was a normal kid, but I couldn't do any sport after the accident for a while because of the difficulties after the accident. But I tried to get involved and had good support from my family.

Q: How popular was MMA in Brazil at the time?

Nogueira: When I was growing up, it wasn't that popular. I did a lot of different kind of martial arts, but MMA wasn't as popular as it is today. When I was fifteen years old, I was doing a lot of boxing and judo and also started watching the first UFC back in 1993. I was a big fan of Royce Gracie and all those guys. I started training in jiu-jitsu because of Royce Gracie's style. I already had experience in boxing and judo training. That's when I thought about getting into MMA after seeing the first UFC.

Q: What were your impressions of Royce Gracie, who was a small slender-looking guy beating up bigger guys?
Nogueira: Jiu-jitsu was the more appreciated fighting system and liked by other styles. Today we have fighters who are athletes and are big, who have good technique, too. They know jiu-jitsu, wrestling, and boxing. Before it was style against style, where a jiu-jitsu guy would be fighting against a karate guy, or fighting against a boxer. This showed that jiu-jitsu was the more superior martial art. I think Royce Gracie's technique was superior to all the other guys from the different martial arts, and that's why I started studying jiu-jitsu. When I saw Royce fighting, I said to myself, *I've got to do what he's doing*, which was Brazilian jiu-jitsu which had good technique. Rickson is a good jiu-jitsu stylist, but I think his brother, Royce Gracie, is much better than him because he's fought the top fighters and he showed good jiu-jitsu. Rickson had his time and he's 48 years old now. He didn't fight in America, but he could've done that. But his brother did. That's why I became a professional fighter because I was watching his brother Royce's fights. Rickson did good in Japan but I think Royce is more well known in America.

Q: Were you ever influenced by Muhammad Ali?
Nogueira: I love Ali! He did a lot of talking but he was good in his time. He helped to stamp out racism and did a real good job. He was in a sport which he used to deliver some message to the world against racism. He did a good job and he was a great athlete. And that's why I like him. I'm a big fan of his.

Q: What do you think would happen if a heavyweight boxer competed in the UFC?

Nogueira: Boxing is a very different sport compared to MMA. If a boxer fights in the UFC, he has got to be prepared. I'll compare the UFC and MMA to boxing by giving you an example: you've got a normal surfer and, on the other hand, you've got a surfer who surfs in the big waves. Not many people can surf in the big waves and not many people can fight in the UFC—only the tough guys. I compare it this way: you have to train in karate, boxing, wrestling and it takes a long time to get to the UFC standard. There are a lot of techniques and different things to learn, it's a very tough sport, believe me. If you have been on the top in another sport, it doesn't mean you are going to be a good UFC fighter—it takes time.

Q: When did you make your MMA debut?
Nogueira: My first fight in MMA was in 1995, when I was twenty-two years old.

Q: Can you tell me about your success in Japan?
Nogueira: I started in Florida, in Orlando, then went to fight in Japan in 2000 in a competition called RINGS, which was a new tournament really growing in popularity in 2000. I had some good friends there. It was my dream to go to Japan and fight in good shows and show my technique. The Japanese love the jiu-jitsu style. So, this was a stage in my life where I loved to fight over there and had my best fights of my career there. I was the Pride champion and also King of Kings champion. I had a very good time in Japan.

Q: What is the difference between the American and Japanese fans?
Nogueira: The Japanese fans understand the jiu-jitsu style because they have a lot of judo guys fighting there who are good on the ground. So they understand the sport technically. They know the names of the techniques and positions—this is the difference. I like to fight in both countries.

Q: When you fought Fedor Emelianenko, what problems did you encounter in the fight?

Nogueira: He's very tough. He's good at wrestling—actually, he's better than me in wrestling. He threw me down and was good enough on the ground and gave me a lot of problems in the fight. Everything I tried I just could not control him. He beat me twice and one was a no contest. I hope we can fight one more time or even two more times in the future. He's the toughest guy in the world and in the list of top fighters. I hope in the future I can fight him again.

Q: Your first fight in the Octagon was against Heath Herring at UFC 73 (July 2007). How did you feel about fighting in the UFC?
Nogueira: Yes, this was a good fight and actually I had fought him a couple of times before in Pride in Japan, where he was a big name before entering the UFC. I was a new fighter coming through and he had beaten some good fighters. He was a new rising star in Japan and we had some good fights. When we fought in the UFC, I was in control of the fight. I was doing good by dominating the fight standing up, then he surprised me but he couldn't knock me out. I came back in the second round, where I pretty much dominated him, but he's hard to submit. He's one of the top fighters. I tried to beat him with my boxing and standup skills, but this strategy didn't work against him. He's tough enough.

Q: Why did you make a transition to fight in the UFC?
Nogueira: When you work in a company for a while and they start to have some financial problems, you decide to make decisions because the company may do something different. I was waiting for what was in store for me in the future with the Japanese organization. I didn't resign with Pride. And also at the time, someone asked me to come to America to make a team. In the UFC, they have big-name fighters and the sport was growing so I was keeping in tune with what was happening there. I was established in Japan as a fighter and a big name. The sport was really growing in America and they were going to pay more money. So when Dana White's offices called me, we had a conversation. And then Dana White and I had a conversation and I agreed to fight for the UFC when my contract finished in Japan. Dana gave me a good proposal so I came

over. I was happy and my family was already in South Florida. I had a lot of students there so I opened my own gym in Miami. So everything happened at the same time. I've got my family here in Florida and it's a good place to be right now.

Q: Do you think fighters must go to America to make it big? Even though no-holds-barred was big in Brazil, do you think the Gracie Brothers sooner or later had to come over to the USA to really get noticed?

Nogueira: That's right. America is the center of everything all over the world. I was big in Japan and the big main television channel in Japan was showing my fights. But if you are in America and are well known, you will be well known all over the world. People take note of anything that goes on in America because there's better promotion, more events, and because of Hollywood everybody follows what the Americans are doing. That's why I felt that when I'm in America, I will be known more all over the world. When the UFC grows more in America, then they will bring the UFC to Japan and the sport's going to grow all over the world.

Q: There are a lot of Brazilians coming through the UFC right now: Anderson Silva, Wanderlei Silva, and you, of course. Do you think more Brazilians will conquer the UFC in the future?

Nogueira: I think the Brazilians are the best in this sport because we are very traditional. Like I said, Brazil has been doing the sport for more than sixty years. We have to fight in the best place and the UFC is the biggest event in the world right now. This is why all the Brazilians are coming and looking forward to fighting in the best place.

Q: What elements of training do you incorporate when preparing for a fight?

Nogueira: I do a lot of jiu-jitsu and Muay Thai, as well as boxing. A couple of times, I train wrestling including Greco Roman, about two times a week we spar MMA-style, integrating everything. We have to train separately jiu-jitsu to get good at jiu-jitsu, boxing to get good at boxing—we can't train only in MMA sessions. You have got to have some different disciplines and two to three times a week we mix it up with hard training in MMA. I also incorporate free weight lifting to get in the best possible condition for a fight. I've been doing that a lot for twenty years now.

Q: Do you feel you are likely to dominate the UFC heavyweight division, and who would you most like to fight?
Nogueira: Whoever the UFC wants me to fight I will be ready to fight that person. I will be fighting Frank Mir soon. I'm still hungry and I have a lot of things to show. I think I'll show a lot of submissions in the UFC in my future fights. I'm ready and in good shape to defend my belt and have a couple of more years yet left in me. I had a lot of tough fights in the past including against Mirko Cro Cop and Bob Sapp—those were both tough fights.

Q: You beat Tim Sylvia to clinch the heavyweight title at UFC 81 (February 2008). What did you think of your opponent?
Nogueira: Tim was in very good shape and I couldn't put him down. He was very good it was very hard to hold him and put him down. So I had to find another way to beat him. He knocked me down in the first round. I fought his game for two rounds and when I put him in my game, we went to the ground where I finished the fight in the third round. It was a very tough match first half of the fight and at the end my technique worked.

Q: Tell me about your new venture, in which opened a new gym in Miami with Anderson Silva.
Nogueira: We opened a gym in Miami and we have coaches offering good training and fighters are coming through. It's the biggest MMA place in Miami. We have the most experienced coaches teaching there. So, we have a good wrestling coach, a good boxing coach, a good jiu-jitsu coach and it's a great place to be training in MMA. We have a mat space of about 3,000 square feet, a cage, and professional rings. We have one of the biggest MMA teams in America. We

are going to have some top fighters fighting in the UFC and at all the big events.

Q: How do you relax?
Nogueira: I like to watch movies and go to the beach in Miami. I like to spend my time in my house, too. I've got dogs and I love dogs. Sometimes when I'm not fighting, I like to go on my motorcycle. And I also like spending time with my girlfriend. I love to eat Japanese food. I've been traveling a lot and when I'm doing seminars all over the world, I like to meet different people in different countries and experience their cultures.

Sean Sherk

UFC Lightweight Champion

Question: What is your martial arts background, and who influenced you as a martial artist in the early days of your training?
Sean Sherk: When I was young I started wrestling at the age of seven. I wrestled competitively for thirteen years and I took about a year off. I started training MMA in 1994 at the Minnesota Martial Arts Academy, and have been there ever since. We trained shoot wrestling, Muay Thai, kickboxing and wrestling. My influences were the early wrestlers like Dan Gable and the early UFC wrestlers Dan Severn, Mark Coleman, and Ken Shamrock.

Q: When did you first come across the UFC?
Sherk: The first UFC I ever saw was UFC 2 (March 1994). I think this was the first to be on pay-per-view, which was with Royce Gracie and Ken Shamrock in a 16-man tournament. That pretty much drove me to go and find a gym and train. I was really fortunate that one of the phenomenal gyms was here in Minnesota, which was only 20, 30 minutes from my house. I trained with Greg Nelson back then and we would train shoot wrestling. He was also a wrestler and had a submission background in addition to having a Thai boxing background. So, he had all three arts which I started training in, and training MMA. When I showed up at his academy, I talked to him for five minutes and took a class. I knew I was in the right place as soon as I showed up, it just felt right. So, Greg Nelson had a big influence on

me. We've got tons of great fighters at the academy coming through the ranks now.

Q: How did you get involved in the UFC?
Sherk: I believe my first MMA fight was in 1999 when I fought in a smaller show. I also fought in local shows before making the transition into the UFC. I was just winning all of my fights. I think after my eleventh win, I got a phone call from Monte Cox, who at the time was a big figure in the MMA world—and he still is. He asked me if I wanted to fight in the UFC. I said, "Alright, man. That's a dream come true for me." So, like everybody else I worked myself up. My first fight was at UFC 30 (February 2001) [against Tiki Ghosn], which I won. It was a one-fight deal. So they didn't use me anymore for a while. So I went back fighting in the smaller shows until I was nineteen when I ended up signing a three-fight contract with the UFC.

Q: What was the difference between fighting in the unforgiving arena of the UFC, compared to the wrestling tournaments you were accustomed to?
Sherk: It's all a sport-based theme. That's what I love to do and the love for competition and sports that I have is ingrained in me. The difference is that in wrestling if you get beat once or twice in a season, those losses go away and you start fresh again. But with something like MMA, when you get beat, it stays on your record for life. So I think the wins and the losses are a lot more important in that aspect. And also because it's my job—I do this for a living. I always had the goal to win the UFC title. Wins and losses make a difference.

Q: On April 25, 2003, you were given a title shot against the welter-weight champion Matt Hughes. Was this a tough fight for you?
Sherk: Yes, it was a huge fight. He was regarded by many as pound-for-pound the best fighter in the world at the time. I was a huge underdog, five-one I think. Nobody really gave me a whole lot of a chance. As I've always said, I trained really hard for that fight and came out and fought. And although I ended up getting beat, I earned a lot of respect from the fans and the fighters.

Q: Can you tell me about your experiences fighting in Japan?

Sherk: Pride was probably the biggest show in the world. They were selling out the Tokyo Dome. A 20,000 arena was considered a small show. Pride was a pretty big deal and I got a two-fight deal, but the money wasn't good so we just ended up taking the one fight. I fought one of their champions over there [Ryuki] Ueyama. My goal was to go over there and show the Japanese fans and the promoters of Pride who I was, make a name for myself and become a mainstay with the show. Unfortunately, after I won the fight they chose not to sign me anymore.

Q: At one point in your career, you actually packed it all in because you said you were not getting enough fights. Is it true you went out and found a normal job?

Sherk: What happened was I got let go from the UFC after I got beat by Matt Hughes. I also stopped fighting in the small shows and went to Japan to fight in Pride where I beat one of their top guys, but they chose not to re-sign me. So I was stuck fighting in a lot of smaller organizations and could not get big fights. None of the top guys would fight me. I was a real dangerous fighter to fight in a smaller show because the money wasn't right. So I couldn't get fights and opponents. So after my kid was born, I basically said, "I can't do this anymore." So I walked away from the sport and got a normal job, flooring.

Q: Do you think that, as the sport evolves, the athletes will be paid mega-bucks?

Sherk: I hope so. I really do. I hope it changes during my time because I would like to get those paydays I deserve, too. Right now you've got a lot of big shows coming on the scene like Affliction, Elite XC, and they're all trying to compete with each other. And with competition, it drives up wages for the fighters because you've got people competing for us. I really hope the paydays get better because I don't want to go back to work in a full-time job after this.

Q: You finally got a fight for the lightweight belt at UFC 64 (October 2006), where you beat Kenny Florian. What do you have to say about that win?

Sherk: That was my first fight as a lightweight in the UFC. They basically gave me a title shot which was good. My credentials at the welterweight level have always been real good, so they gave me the shot against Kenny Florian. He is a well-rounded fighter with good jiu-jitsu and striking skills. We went out there and did our thing. I was able to pull the fight off and win the belt.

Q: What motivates you to fight and compete in the Octagon?

Sherk: I've always been a super jock. I loved wrestling, playing football, baseball, lifting weights. I was into sports my entire life, so being a professional athlete was always a dream of mine. This is a dream come true for me. Being a professional athlete and being able to make a living doing something I love is a dream come true. I can't complain.

Q: You have a unique training regime, which includes some fascinating drills such as the tire flips and gorilla drills. Can you explain what exactly these are?

Sherk: That's part of the caveman training that I do API with my conditioning coach. He comes up with different training regimes for me to do, conditioning drills, etc. If you look at a fight, you use different muscles so many different types of cardio, different type of exercises. I work with my conditioning coach a couple of times a week, and he puts me through just a bunch of different programs. No program is exactly the same, as this keeps your body guessing. The sledgehammer drill is going to work some cardio and power. A lot of boxers do this as well by chopping wood. It teaches you to use your entire body for power. The gorilla drill, that's another one where you use your body and just great for cardio. We like to end our training with this kind of stuff, and we go real hard for four-and-a-half minutes and spend 30 seconds doing gorilla drills.

Q: So far, what has been the highlight of your UFC career?

Sherk: My best moment has to be winning the belt. For me it was a dream come true. Something I worked for a very long time and everything I'd been through in MMA. It was something I didn't think would happen at one point. At one point, I actually walked away from the sport, but winning the belt was definitely the defining moment of my career.

Q: Can you shed light on your day-to-day activities?
Sherk: When I'm training for a fight basically all I do is train. I get up in the morning, eat my breakfast and hangout with my family a little bit. Then I go to the gym usually around 11:30 a.m. I work out two or three times a day depending on what the day's schedule is. Each day I do different stuff. I train six days a week for about twelve weeks before a fight. When preparing for a fight, it is physically and mentally grueling. So, when you are not training for a fight I like to get away from it and just relax and hang out with my kids, and try to do some fun stuff that I like to do. In winter time I go snowmobiling. In the summer I go paintballing on the weekends. I try to get some good activities and hangout with the family and eat normal food.

Q: Your fight with Hermes Franca at UFC 73 (July 2007) became controversial, as both fighters tested positive for performance-enhancing substances. You have always denied taking any illegal substances. Can you comment on this?
Sherk: Basically they accused me of taking Nandrolone. I had 12 milligrams in my system and the cut off limit is six. I didn't do it. So I went through the appeal process and I did everything to prove I hadn't taken anything. I had blood tests done, which is a lot more accurate for steroids because it stays in the system longer and it's easier to find in the blood. I went to the lie detector test, which I took three times and passed it all three times. My lawyer went through the whole entire testing process.

They made a lot of mistakes in the testing process. They found that there was actually carry over in the machine they were testing in. They tested everyone's sample in the same machine and they supposed to clean the machine out between tests. Three people were tested before me for steroids. When it was my turn the machine did not read zero. There were still steroids in the machine and they ran my sample anyway. I just find it kind of funny after that entire process. After it was all over with, the California commission contacted Quest Laboratories, which was the lab that ran the samples. They then reduced my sentence from a year to six months, which is pretty much saying they are not willing to overturn it. It was just a really bad situation to be in. I lost my belt to a lot of scrutiny and a lot of stuff from fans. It's all over with now and I'm ready to move on.

Q: Any comments on your loss to BJ Penn at UFC 84 (May 2008)?
Sherk: My goal was to try to exploit his cardio and make him tired. I thought I could outpoint him in the first couple of rounds on the feet, and then start shooting on him in the later rounds when he got tired. But his cardio was pretty good for that fight and the best I'd seen. He wasn't breathing really heavy; he was standing between rounds and not sitting down. So, he trained for this fight and knew I was going to try to run him out of gas so he trained hard for it. He was a better fighter that night. I've always got along with BJ until we were preparing for this fight. It's just one of those things. I don't take things personally. I know it's just a sport. I want that belt back. I can say that for sure. If he decides to stay in the 155-pound division then I want to fight him again.

Q: Any particular fighter you would like to fight in the UFC?
Sherk: Right now, for me who ever make sense I'll fight. I just fought BJ Penn, who is one of the biggest names in the sport, and I lost my belt and I want to get that belt back. I'll fight someone who is a contender who has been around for a while and someone who is a big name.

Q: How many years do you have left in fighting?
Sherk: I really don't know how many more years I have left, it depends on my body but I feel pretty good physically. Maybe I would open up a gym in the future and train fighters who can be world champs one day.

Q: What's your relationship with Brock Lesnar?

Sherk: I don't work out with him because he's too big for me to work out with. He's a physical specimen, a phenomenal athlete and he's got all the attributes of a middleweight and a heavyweight. He's going to be a force to be reckoned with. He learns really fast and he's picking this game up fast. And he's got a very strong wrestling background along with his athletic ability. He's going to be hard to deal with.

Q: Before the advent of the UFC, the general public had less respect for martial artists. How have things changed, and have the UFC fighters endeared themselves to the public?

Sherk: I think people understand the sport a lot more now because everywhere you go you see it. You read about it and see it and people are learning and understanding what the sport is all about. People understand how hard we work and how well rounded we are as athletes, and people respect that. With the growth of the sport there's more understanding. Remember that I've been fighting for nine years, before anybody knew what it was all about. Back in the early days, people didn't know even what MMA was, and I didn't tell people what I did because I didn't want to stand there for 20 minutes explaining. I didn't fight in Tough Man competitions because that's what most people thought it was. They had no idea what MMA was. People understand a lot more now because they see it a lot more.

Q: Anything you would like to add?

Sherk: I would like to thank the Minnesota Martial Arts Academy and all the guys who train with me and help me get ready for a fight. I couldn't do any of this stuff if it wasn't for those guys. Also I would like to thank all my sponsors and my loyal fans.

Brock Lesnar

UFC Heavyweight Champion

Question: Brock, how would you describe your childhood?
Brock Lesnar: I grew up on a dairy farm. My childhood was like any other kid, I suppose. Growing up on the farm, I had a lot of work to do and not enough money to pay the bills. I wanted to wrestle in the senior Olympics when I was young, but I never had any one thing I wanted to do when I grew up. I just knew I didn't want to be a farmer, though, when I grew up.

Q: How did you get into amateur wrestling, and how far did you get?
Lesnar: I got into amateur wrestling when I was five years old. My coach at the time only lived a couple of miles away from me. My parents knew him and I just started to go to wrestling classes when I was really young. I was pretty decent at it. I think when I was at 100 pounds, I won the state title. From then I wrestled in high school and I was somewhat successful, placing third a few years in a row. When I was wrestling in junior college in Bismark, North Dakota—where my family was from—I became a heavyweight champion. Then I was recruited by the University of South Dakota. And my first year there, I was the finalist in the State championships and placed second in the NCCA tournament. In my senior year, I won the heavyweight championship—that was in 2000.

Q: Growing up as a teenager, did you have any other interests in combat sports?

Lesnar: I had interest training in boxing, but the boxing gym was 50 miles from my house. I could never get there. Friends of mine actually went to boxing, but I could never afford to and never had the time to get there because of my work.

Q: Let's talk about your pro wrestling career.

Lesnar: I was recruited by the World Wrestling Entertainment who had seen me win the NCCA title, which was televised on ESPN. I enjoyed wrestling as a pro for a while, and after a while it became stale. So I wanted something new as I was very competitive and missed competing in real matches. I traveled a lot. Being on the road every day, it was all the same. Some of my memorable matches were with Kurt Angle, among others, but I enjoyed it. It was a good experience for me but after a while it became stale. It was the same thing every day. I also wanted to spend more time with my daughter.

Q: What sparked your interest to get into MMA?

Lesnar: I had interest to get into MMA many years ago, back in 1997, but I didn't really know how to get into it. I was living in California in 1997 training for the summer training for wrestling. Probably there was only one place I knew that had a gym that specifically trained for MMA fighting near me. I wanted to fulfill my college wrestling dream and pro wrestling, so I didn't pursue MMA back then. When I got out of amateur wrestling, MMA wasn't very huge at the time. I had a guaranteed contract with pro wrestling sitting on the table, so it was easy enough for me to make the decision.

Q: I hear you were inspired by Royce Gracie. How did you hear about him?

Lesnar: I watched him in the very first UFCs. He was a very petite-looking human being choking people and making them submit. This was very intriguing to me. His small size and controlling people the way he did, it was pretty remarkable. I thought it was very interesting. Royce Gracie is the very first guy who really made it interesting. He got into the Octagon with anybody—guys weighing 300 pounds—he was the pioneer of the sport. He's been around for a long time. He was fighting and still is fighting. Later he fought in the K-1 Dynamite show at the same show I made my MMA debut. This is where I met Royce for the first time.

Q: Can you describe what it felt like fighting in your first MMA fight?
Lesnar: It was an excellent feeling, it was very surreal. To me, it was a great feeling to get in the ring and be competing. Before fighting in MMA, I checked out Pat Miletich's gym and different people in Arizona and Indianapolis. Since I had been on the road for a long time when I was wrestling pro, it was really important for me to be at home, train and do what I always wanted to do—and that was to fight. For me to be able to come home every night and sleep in my own bed and train was a big factor in choosing a gym. I was going to train with Royce but we were never able to work a schedule out.

Q: What is the difference between the pro wrestling training you were accustomed to and the MMA training you do now?
Lesnar: It's not even the same. It's like amateur wrestling training is different to pro wrestling. Pro wrestling is entertainment. You have to be an athlete to be in the ring. For me, training for MMA means to train in different disciplines every day—striking, kicking, jiu-jitsu, elbows, Muay Thai. Pro wrestling training is not even comparable to MMA training. Now I train one or two times a day, five or six days a week. The whole key to training is you are then able to recover and get the maximum out of it and be ready for the next day's workout. So, it's beneficial to me. We train pretty hard. I have to listen to my body I'm not a spring chicken either. And day by day, week by week, the more we do, the more I can absorb and try to prepare myself when a fight's coming up.

Q: How do you feel about WWE wrestlers making a transition into the UFC, and who is your favorite UFC fighter?
Lesnar: Kurt [Angle] would probably, but I think that time has come and gone already. I don't see a lot of them making the transition for the

lack of amateur wrestling experience. I like watching Georges St-Pierre, but I don't have any particular favorite UFC fighters. I like watching them all as everybody brings something different to the Octagon.

Q: In your UFC debut in 2008, you fought Frank Mir and actually went in real hard and had him in trouble, until he took hold of your ankle.
Lesnar: I knew he would attempt to go for my legs. I got over excited. I spent time learning how to defend and learning every discipline. So, only lack of experience is the key word there for my loss. Someday I may have a rematch with Frank, but right now I have to focus on Heath Herring.

Q: Do you feel the money fighters make is sufficient or will this change in the future as the sport continues to grow and evolve?
Lesnar: I hope so, for the sake of fighters.

Q: Why do you think the UFC is taking over boxing and professional wrestling?
Lesnar: It's good for the sport. UFC is new and refreshing to the people and that's what people want—something new and different and the best versus the best fighting. People want to see the best in one area against the best in another area. They are able to see this when they tune in and buy the UFC pay-per-views. The sport has evolved to what it is now and it's changed a lot of different things. Hopefully I've brought WWE fans along with me into the UFC. If you look at the ratings they speak for themselves.

Q: What is your ultimate goal in the UFC?
Lesnar: I want to win the UFC heavyweight title. I appreciate everybody hanging with me. Careers come and go and can be ended very quickly. I just take one day at a time. And as for future plans, I don't believe I would go back into pro wrestling.

Michael Bisping

UFC Middleweight Champion/Hall of Famer

Question: Can you please shed some light on your childhood upbringing?

Michael Bisping: I was born in Cyprus on an army base, as my dad was in the military. We spent a couple of years there and then moved to Clitheroe, in the North West of England. We moved a little bit to various houses, as you do when you're in the army, but I can't really remember too much about that. Then we settled back in Clitheroe where I've spent most of my life. I had a pretty much normal upbringing. My parents never had too much money, but they always tried to give us the best things they could. I got involved in the martial arts at the age of nine. I always enjoyed martial arts movies, and any movies with fights such as *Rocky* films and the old '80s ninja movies, Jean Claude Van Damme and Bruce Lee movies. My brother started to go to jiu-jitsu classes. I wanted to tag along and went from there and fell in love with it. I went to school around here. I enjoyed school and did quite well in the class, but I never tried or put too much effort into my school work—that was my problem. I got fairly decent grades but could have done better. It always said in school reports: Michael could do a lot better if he tried harder. I suppose I could have done better, but I was too busy training martial arts and messing around, trying to be the class clown.

Q: Is it true you were banned from soccer because of your dirty tackles?

Bisping: I was quite rough on the football pitch. I did a lot of shoulder barges, so it used to make people mad. I started playing rugby because it suited me a lot more. I played for the Clitheroe Youth Team and moved on to the Blackburn team. I was pretty decent at football and was a bit bigger than the other kids. I was very competitive and always have been. I used to go for the ball and if I didn't get it, I would keep trying.

Q: When you started competing in martial arts, did you feel the need to go out and get a proper job in order to make a living?

Bisping: When I was younger, I used to go to a lot of amateur tournaments and the kickboxing. I used to get paid for the fights but it wasn't much. I think 250 pounds, something like that. So you can't really make a living out of that. And to be honest, at the time I didn't really look at martial arts as a way of making a living and a profession; it was more as a hobby and a way to keep fit. It was something I enjoyed and like many people did it for the passion of it. I met my girlfriend and had a couple of kids. I had a couple of kickboxing fights before I met her. Then this was not really something I would make a living from so I kind of gave up on it. We had kids and I went onto hold down a full-time job and looking after the kids. This didn't leave me much time for training, but I had done it all ever since I was a kid. So, I suppose I wasn't bored with it, but had done it for a long time and I was working various jobs.

At the age of twenty-two, I thought to myself, *What am I doing with myself? Where's my life going?* Like I said, I always did pretty well in school and considered myself intelligent, but I was working some jobs which didn't really require any qualifications or any real intelligence. I thought I could be doing something more useful in this world. So I used to think, *What could I be doing?* To be honest, I toyed around with the idea of going back to university. I used to DJ on the side on the weekends. So I thought I'd DJ on the weekend and go to university during the week and try to get decent qualifications or a degree, which is something that would get me a better job and provide a better home and more income for my family—just to generally better myself because I wasn't happy with the way I turned out.

The more I thought about it, the more I kept coming back to the martial arts. Then I thought to myself, *I've always been good at this.* So I thought I'd try to be a boxer. MMA was around but it wasn't really big as we see it today. And I didn't know too much about MMA, to be honest. So I started to be a boxer, trained in the boxing gym and had a couple of fights and won them all by TKO. I got in touch with my old jiu-jitsu instructor from years ago who was in Nottingham. He told me about MMA and that I'd be really good at it. I was doing some competitions as a kid, but I didn't know at the time but it was actually amateur MMA. A couple of guys I beat quite easily had gone on to fight in the UFC and have fairly decent careers. So this is something I started to think about. I gave up work and started training for MMA.

Q: How did you get onto *The Ultimate Fighter* series?
Bisping: I started training for MMA and I was doing really well in the UK. I won all my fights. Any belt in the UK on offer, I'd won. I also held the British kickboxing title at the time. So, I started thinking about looking overseas and fighting in larger promotions, ultimately the UFC, which was where I wanted to be. My manager Anthony at the Wolfslair gym contacted the UFC and gave me a contact in the UFC. They said they'd had their eye on me and would give me a fight in the UFC with no problem. But they thought I'd be great for *The Ultimate Fighter*. They said they had an upcoming season of *TUF*, which would feature light-heavyweights and middleweights and they were looking for an English guy. They told me they were going to have auditions in London and asked if I could attend the auditions.

In the meantime, I spoke to the executives at Spike-TV who were creating the show. I was pretty much chosen before I went to the auditions. I'd already beaten the other light-heavyweights who attended the auditions, so this made me the obvious choice really. So, I went to the audition and the process. I was told I was on the show and to keep it quiet. The next day they flew eight of us English guys out to Vegas. While we were there, we were locked in a hotel room for a week and weren't allowed to leave at all. The reason being is they didn't want us bumping into each other. There were fighters from America all over the place who were trying out for the show and didn't want people to know who was on and leaking details. It was all to do with confidentiality.

It was horrible, to say the least, to be stuck in a hotel room. They brought us three meals a day and the meals weren't very nice. If we walked out from the room and got caught, we would have blown our chance of getting on the show. So it was a case of sitting in the room and reading a book or watching the same movies over and over again. I got called into the interview room. I was there for a few minutes and cracked a silly joke. Everybody in the room laughed their heads off, and they said "Yes, you will be perfect for it. Get out of here. You need to just pass your medical test and we'll get you on the show."

Behind the scenes, there were quite a lot of stuff and heated arguments that went on when filming between the fighters, which I thought would have made it onto the show. But I suppose it had to relate to the storyline so they left them out. There were various different film crews walking around the house the whole time. They had cameras in the corners of the rooms as well but actual crews and sound guys. Every time, let's say someone's upstairs in a different room and you're sat in the kitchen, a feud starts upstairs and the crew go rushing upstairs as the production team would tell them someone's talking shit upstairs. We weren't allowed to speak to the film crew at all. If we spoke to them we could lose our job. When we all got bored, we would try to get the film crew to talk to us, but they wouldn't respond.

Q: When you won the series, did you feel you had actually "arrived" at the UFC?
Bisping: Yes, absolutely—it was weird. When Anthony from the Wolfslair gym had got in touch with the UFC, he mentioned *TUF* to me. He said, "You're going to go in there and you're going to win it." That was obviously the plan. I was going to go in there and try to win it. Having aspirations to win the thing and actually winning it are completely two different things. But that's what I went in there to do, and that was to win. That was my mindset. I wasn't going out there to make friends, but to win at any cost.

Every time I won a fight, I was very pleased and was getting just that close to it, one more fight and I'm in the final. The guy I was fighting was Josh Haynes. I was comfortable as I knew I could beat him. So I was excited about that. When I won the fight by TKO, I just collapsed on the floor, star-shaped with my arms and legs out. It was just a sheer relieve the pressure I had put on myself and pressure to win and provide for my family, everything I had done to that point, the sacrifice in choosing this career finally it paid off. I won a decent contract in the UFC, which meant my family was going to have a little bit of more money. So, I collapsed on the floor and the doctor comes up to me and says, "Are you OK?" I said, "Yes, I'm fine there's nothing wrong with me. I'm just lying on the floor, it's a sheer relief." It was a great moment.

Q: You were stripped off the Cage Rage belt. Why was that?
Bisping: I'm not sure, to be honest. I fought in Cage Rage in my third pro fight and I was supposed to fight [Renato] Babalu [Sobral], but he didn't fight because he was injured or something. So I fought Mark Epstein who was their champion and was the co-promoter's friend. I think they brought me in just to get beat up, they never expected me to go in there and win, thinking Mark Epstein would destroy me. Anyway, I went in there and I beat him by TKO in the second round. They said Mark didn't have enough time to prepare and he wasn't ready, so they set up a rematch instantly. I said, "Yes, no problem, I'll fight him again." So I fought again and this time I won by a knockout in the third round. I thought it was pretty clear that I beat him fair and square both times. I had a couple of fights with other organizations. Later I found out I'd been stripped of my title when I read it on the internet, to be honest.

I was going through the Cage Warriors forums and came across the news: Michael Bisping stripped or his Cage Rage title. So I looked at the Cage Rage website and it had the same thing on there, too. So I rang up [co-promoter] Andy Geer and asked him, "What's going on here?" He said, "Yes, we've had no choice but to strip you." I asked him why and he said it was because of management issues. "What do you mean management issues?" I asked. He said, "We can't really go into it." I told him, "I don't know what you're talking about. So is that it, I'm stripped of my title just like that?" He said, "I'm really sorry, Michael" And he put the phone down on me. That was my feud with Cage Rage. To be honest, I think they didn't want me to be the champion in the first place. They were trying to build up their own guy and wanted someone from London to have the belt so they can sell more tickets. Every time I fought in Cage Rage, I've always brought coach loads of people with me. I suppose they wanted someone from London to be the champion—I'm not sure. I fought in Cage Warriors and they were great and looked after me. I fought for them a number of times and this was a good organization to work for.

Q: You're the Ricky Hatton of MMA in the UK. How are you treated by the fans?
Bisping: The fans are amazing. It blows my mind to see I've got fans. Doesn't seem quite right with me as I feel I'm just a normal guy. A few years ago, I wouldn't even have dreamt about having this conversation. To say I've got fans, seems a bit strange and alien to me, I suppose. I'm fighting in front of big crowds and TV. They're amazing wherever I meet them. They just want to meet me, or want a picture or an autograph and have nice things to say. I always get kind messages through my website whether it's England, America or Canada.

I remember when I fought in Canada, I was walking in Montreal and a huge crowd gathered. I must have been there for three hours. If people are standing in a line or in a crowd to see me or shake my hand, I won't just walk off and say I've got to go because these people are waiting. I remember in Montreal it was a huge crowd, 350 people all gathered around. I was there for about two hours taking pictures. It was very surreal. I was with a couple of my friends and we were laughing our heads off, having a good time. They'd never seen anything like it. The fans are amazing and I feel blessed and very fortunate.

Q: Your only loss came to Rashad Evans. Do you feel you would have won, had there been no point system?
Bisping: Absolutely, if the fight was a five-round fight or there was no point system—where you carry on until someone wins—I would have

definitely won the fight. At the end of the fight, Rashad was out of gas but I was fine. He won the first round, I won the second—the third was very close. I think end of the third round he was tired. He got me down—it wasn't really a takedown but more of a scramble—and he ended up on the top. I think that's what clinched the fight for Rashad, that's why he was awarded the fight. Two judges said he won; one judge said I'd won. Looking back in hindsight, I should have pushed the pace a little more. He was tired and I was fresh. Rashad is a tough character he's undefeated, there's no shame in it and I learned a lot from that fight.

Q: Charles McCarthy fired verbal assaults your way before the fight. How did you react to this?

Bisping: He was very critical about my abilities—my entire game. Before the fight I'd done a few interviews about Charles McCarthy, and I said in my interviews that I'd never met the guy and that I had nothing against him. I had no opinion of the guy. He was an average guy and may the best man win. But he went on to do interviews with the British press. I'm not sure if he was trying to play mind games but he went onto say, basically, that I had no skills and I was the most average fighter in the UFC. And that I didn't have any ground game, wrestling and no striking and there was nothing I could really do to him. I was pretty pissed off by that, to be honest. It was very insulting. It was in the British press so a lot of people were reading about all this. So I thought I want to make an example of this guy. And I feel I did that in the fight. I completely dominated the guy. I hit him with every combination under the sun, and hit him with 25 knees effectively, dropping him in the first round. He could never continue.

Q: Regarding your relationship with mainstream media, have you got any interesting stories about your contact with them?

Bisping: On the whole, now compared to couple of years ago the media have taken more interest in covering the sport and more people are interested in the sport. The media can't deny the fact that the sport is growing and people want to know about it. Maybe at the start that wasn't the case, but they are very welcoming towards it now. They ask intelligent questions about the sport, as opposed to the start where they asked stupid questions like, "Is it dangerous?" or "Has anyone died yet?"

Now the reporters know what they're talking about. Controversial stories? I remember in the lead up to the UFC 70 (April 2007) at Manchester, in the M.E.N. Arena. I had a radio interview with BBC Manchester, a lady who presents the weather sometimes—blond hair in her mid-forties, can't remember her name. Anyway, I go in and sat in the studio and she's talking on air and I'm waiting sitting there. She says on air, "Up next, if you've ever seen the film *Fight Club*, our next guest is Michael Bisping, who fights in the UFC."

So then she turns to me she says, "Right, Michael, so you fight in the UFC." And I said, "Yes." She says, "Look at the size of you, how big are you? You must be at least 18 stone?"

I'm about 14 stone, I'm not a small guy but I'm not overly big. And she says, "You're 18 stone and covered in scars." I said, "I'm not covered in scars. I've got a few scars on my head. I banged my head as a kid but I'm not covered in scars."

She says, "This sport is for thugs, isn't it?"

I said, "No, it's not for thugs."

She says, "It's barbarians!"

I said, "It's not a sport for barbarians . . . "

She says, "Well, you look like a barbarian."

And, I said, "Really? I'll keep my thoughts on what you look like to myself, shall I?" She looked like mutton dressed as lamb. Then she started criticizing the sport saying people can die. I said to her, "Well, have you ever watched sport?"

She said, "No."

I said, "How the hell can you sit there passing judgment and talking about the sport when you've never even seen it? What are you basing these facts on, anyway?" We got into an argument on air. Basically, she didn't have a leg to stand on. She wrapped the interview and ushered me out.

After UFC 70, I went back to the hotel and we were celebrating. There was me, my girlfriend and a few of my close friends. We were sat at a table with Randy Couture, Jean Claude Van Damme, and Wayne

Rooney. It was quite surreal. I was always a fan of Van Damme when I was a kid. I was in a good mood and having a few drinks and a good laugh.

Q: What do you think of Royce Gracie, the pioneer of MMA?
Bisping: Royce Gracie, just like you said, is a pioneer of the sport and the Gracie family in general did great things for the sport. They came up with idea of the UFC. He won the early UFCs a couple of times and he's a great fighter and a legend in the sport.

Q: Your friend, the heavyweight boxer David Haye, has taken interest in MMA. Do you think he may compete in the future?
Bisping: We're quite friendly and he's a great guy. He's a fantastic great boxer and a credit to British boxing. Yes, I've read interviews where he's said himself he's planning to get into MMA eventually after he's done with boxing. I think David Haye, in boxing, will really shake up the heavyweight division and he's definitely got what it takes I think to be a UFC champion. He's like a world-class boxer with heavy hands. He already knows a bit about the wrestling and jiu-jitsu. The kind of determination and the fighting spirit he already has, combined that with Brazilian jiu-jitsu and wrestling and standup MMA game—which he already has been expanding on a little bit—yes, he's got potential to do great things in the sport. I mean, he's already doing great things in the world of boxing, a world champion and probably the best British boxer at the moment. If the guy came into MMA, then I'd say, "Watch out, all the heavyweights!"

Q: Do you feel boxers had lot more respect before than martial arts fighters until the UFC changed things?
Bisping: Yes. I suppose I can understand what you're saying. Boxing has always been televised in households all across the country. People worldwide always have had respect for boxers. It is big money and boxers are recognized as athletes. It wasn't always the case with martial arts—it is something you did as a hobby or to keep fit. I don't think martial artists were ever classed as athletes or even respected for their fighting

ability. Now the UFC—not just the UFC, which is the most dominant that everyone knows about, but MMA—has made a transition into the mainstream now. Since this happened, people realize martial artists should be taken seriously and the skills you learn whether it's Thai boxing or, Brazilian jiu-jitsu are good, and these men have got serious fighting ability. It's definitely a good thing.

Q: Who are your favorite UFC fighters?
Bisping: Right now I've got to say I love watching Anderson Silva fight. The guy's a great fighter and great to watch. He's a very dominant champion. He's got a very good style which I like to watch. Roger Huerta is good to watch. Lots of things about the UFC is they've got some great fighters. I tend to watch more strikers than a wrestler who just want to take someone down and control his opponent. I admire the skill involved and good jiu-jitsu. I love to watch great jiu-jitsu, but if someone takes someone down and lie on top of the opponent, and win with points decision, I'm not really a fan of that. I like to watch a bit of action. Not everyone gets along in this world. On the whole most of the fighters in the UFC, as a matter of fact in MMA in general, are decent guys. Me and Matt, who was on *TUF* with me, didn't get on too well, but we've kind of buried the hatched on that. We had a little fallout, its old news now, you don't hold grudges.

Q: Anderson Silva seems to be dominating everyone he fights, do you think you can triumph against him?
Bisping: I hope to fight Anderson Silva. Number one is: you have to earn the right to fight someone like Anderson Silva. He's the best in the world. You've got to earn the right which is what I'm doing right now by building myself up, working my way up to get that privilege to fight him. He's probably pound-for-pound the best fighter in the world. So if I get that chance I'll take that fight seriously. This is definitely what I want to do and achieve.

No one's really been able to test him yet, so I would like to go in there and see what I can do. I think I could test him and definitely give him a good fight. We'll have to wait and see. A lot of people think when someone goes in there up against him he just wipes them out and destroys them. I'm training really hard now. I'm not still the finished product. There are a lot of areas I want to get better at. I'm happy with my progress that I've made. After the next fight, I'm taking a trip out to Thailand again training Thai boxing. Then I'm off to Brazil to work on my jiu-jitsu. I'm willing to make the sacrifices that I've got to make to be the best I can. Hopefully when I get the chance, I'll take the advantage and beat him.

Q: How is your relationship with Dana White?
Bisping: A lot of people talk a lot of shit on the internet about him, but they don't know what they're talking about. Dana White takes good care of fighters. He really looks after me and looks after all the fighters. He always says, "If you need any advice or anything, call me at one in the morning, anytime, and I'll be there for you." And he sticks to his word. He takes care of us, he helps us out financially. The UFC is like a big family. I haven't got a bad word to say about Dana, to be honest.

Q: What would you be doing today to make a living, if you did not turn to professional fighting in the UFC?
Bisping: I don't know. I'm not sure. I did put a lot of effort being a DJ when I was younger, which I enjoyed but felt it wasn't a proper job and I wasn't going to be big. Only a few people in the world have achieved that. I always enjoyed construction work, enjoyed building things, so maybe something along these lines. This was my problem as a kid, when I left school I didn't know what I wanted to do. I was very envious of those who knew exactly what they wanted to pursue. I never did. That is why I didn't end up going to university because I didn't know what course I wanted to do.

To answer your question, I wouldn't know. When I was a kid I was a big fan of Frank Bruno. To me he was a great boxer and a great character. The future for me is just keep on training and keep fighting in the UFC. And maybe when I get towards the end of my fighting career, I'd want to open my own academy and train fighters, or maybe manage fighters when I'm done. I've got a lot of experience and I know a lot about the business now that I can offer the upcoming fighters. The UFC has changed my life utterly and completely. I'm still the same person and I always will be. I've got more money now, that's the main difference—we could afford the nice things in life. On the whole, the main thing on how it's changed my life is I was never happy doing the other jobs I did. I used to hate them, to be honest. Now I'm earning more money, but the main thing is I'm doing something I love. I'm very lucky.

I love training and I love working out. So I'm fortunate I'm able to make a living in what I love to do. I'm really passionate about my job, which reflects on my whole life. I'm not angry. I'm a happy person on the whole. So, me and my family are happy. I want to thank all the fans from the bottom of my heart for all the support I get from everyone, it truly amazes me every time. Whenever I walk out to fight in England the crowd go crazy, they're very excited and passionate, it blows my mind. Thanks for all the support and I hope I continue to entertain you with my fights.

Chuck Liddell
UFC Light-Heavyweight Champion/Hall of Famer

Question: Chuck, let's talk about your childhood when you were growing up in Santa Barbara, California.
Chuck Liddell: My mom raised us as a single-parent and did a great job. Growing up, I loved sports. I played football, baseball, and wrestled at San Marcos High School. We lived with my grandparents and I loved it. My pops taught me everything I know about loyalty and honor. I had a great family. My grandfather and grandmother helped us, it was really good.

Q: How far did you get in wrestling?
Liddell: I got into wrestling when my high school football coach asked me if I wanted to wrestle. It was great I did pretty well. My junior and senior year, I finished in the top five at the CIF tournament. I ended up wrestling at Cal Poly in college—all four years. I was a decent wrestler.

Q: Were you studying any martial arts or boxing at the time?
Liddell: When I was twelve, I was watching *Kung Fu Theatre*, actually. I got interested in martial arts and started karate at twelve. By chance I signed up at Koei-Kan Karate-Do. It was run by Jack Sabat and that style of karate was perfect for me. It was still about discipline and concentration, but was combative and I have always liked that. I was a gym rat. I couldn't get enough sparring. After college, my college buddy

introduced me to a gym that taught Muay Thai boxing. And from there I started MMA.

Q: Can you tell me about some of your experiences working in bars, and your unique hairstyle that has become your trademark?

Liddell: Actually, I was going to a concert with my friends and had my hair shaved really short. My friends were shaving their heads, and I said, "There's no way I'm shaving my whole head!" So I cut it differently and I kind of liked the reaction I got. I worked for a while as a bartender and bouncer. There were instances of me having to break up fights and the boss was cool, we did a good job. There were very few incidents where I had to throw people out. We didn't have much trouble—we could get them out peacefully by talking to them. I had a really good time.

Q: When did you first hear about and see the UFC?

Liddell: I saw the first UFC with my friends and thought it was great. We checked it out and I became interested from day one. It was real fighting and it put together two things I loved. I figured I might be able to make a living at it. It turned out to be true.

Q: How did you pursue your dream of competing in the UFC?

Liddell: I had competed in Division-I wrestling, karate, and kickboxing. This guy who promoted kickboxing shows, who knew I could wrestle, asked if I wanted to fight [UFC] and to send in a tape. UFC 17 (1998) was the first one I fought in. I fought Noe Hernandez and won by decision. A friend of mine called me up and said, "You guys should get a manager. He's good and he'll be good for you." So, Dana White became my manager and it just all worked out well. I used to spar with Tito [Ortiz] when I had a fight coming up.

Q: What feelings do you encounter when stepping into the Octagon? Do you feel fear, and feel as if you're putting your life on the line?

Liddell: No. I get excited walking out no matter what. I love having the crowd and love that roar when I walk out. When they close the cage it's just about me and the other guy.

Q: Let's talk about some of your most memorable fights with Tito Ortiz, and would you fight him again?

Liddell: It was fun. I finally could show people that I could beat him like I always said I could—and it was good to shut him up. But he is always going to be one of those that run his mouth. I don't like that kind of thing. He talks a lot, a lot of times he's not willing to fight some guys. You have to fight anyone and not try to dodge anyone or pick or chose fighters you want to fight. I've already had the fight and beat him so I don't know why anybody would want to see the fight again. But if he came about and he came on from a winning streak and give the people and media a reasonable fight then yes, sure.

Q: What about fighting Randy Couture?

Liddell: I lost the first one and it was great to avenge in the second one. And the third one was to prove it wasn't a fluke that I beat him. He is a great champion. When I fought him the second time, I knew I had him because he looked tired for the first couple of minutes. It definitely helped beating him. I've always fought the toughest fighters I can get. I try to fight all the tough fighters and not dodge anybody that wants to fight me.

Q: You are one of the few non-grapplers to really do well in the UFC, when nearly all the champs tend to have a very strong grappling base. What is your opinion on this?

Liddell: I am a striker with a strong wrestling base. I am very hard to take down, but I have always been really good at taking people down. That was usually my strategy in college: take the guy down.

Q: Can you highlight your training routine before a fight?

Liddell: I train twice or three times a day, five days a week. I have a great team at The Pit. They know how to get me ready for a fight. We work on everything, from wrestling, striking, and conditioning, and I train hard. I don't party before I have a fight coming up. Actually, I have a hard time as I go out, but I drink water hanging out with my friends when I'm at home and with my camp. When I'm at home and not out and about two or three weeks before the fight, I'm asleep at ten at night. When I'm out I'm out till two or three in the morning.

Q: You went on to fight in Japan for the Pride organization. Can you tell us about any of your fights, and the experiences there?
Liddell: I wasn't there long, but it was good.

Q: Your epic fight with Wanderlei Silva was a great victory, which once again proved your ability to beat the best MMA fighters. What was it like to fight this exceptionally all-round tough opponent?
Liddell: It was a fight that I had waited a long time for. I would have liked the knockout, but it was still sweet. It was a great fight for the fans.

Q: Kimbo Slice is making a name in the MMA world. Do you think the promoters are trying to hype up a street brawler?
Liddell: He's not very well trained. The hype of him is from his record from his You Tube fights on the streets. He's just not good. The people he's fought are not very good. There's nothing impressive. He's not fought anyone impressive. He's training with Bass (Rutten) right now who is working him. If they want to hype him up then let them. He's doing the right thing trying to learn to be a cage fighter and working on it.

Q: Your book *Iceman* hit the *New York Times* bestseller list. Can you shed some light on why the fans are intrigued about MMA?
Liddell: It is a great sport and more people are realizing how many things it brings together. It isn't just boxing or wrestling. In MMA fighting is real. The training is tough. These days young kids are training in MMA and they are going to do amazing things.

Q: Do you feel the UFC and its fighters have, at last, been embraced by the fans and respected the way boxing has been for decades?
Liddell: By fans, yes. I think it's more exciting and more things can happen in a fight, many ways to win and may different ways to lose—it

makes it a much more exciting fight. I like boxing but it's not the same for me. Our sport includes boxing but a lot more things you have to learn—boxing is limited. Doing interviews I try to explain to people and fans what the sport is all about, and do autograph signing and get out and talk to fans. I like the sport. I love the sport and what I do and make sure I'll be still doing it. I think it's been a great reaction from the fans.

Q: What are your plans for the future?
Liddell: To fight. I plan to fight as long as I can and my body holds up. I love fighting and I have plenty of fight left in me. I think I have about two to four years left and I hope in this time I'll be doing the same thing. I'll keep on fighting as long as my body will let me. I'm not complaining. I'm making the kind of money that we'd never had made otherwise. Dana has helped the sport grow and few might have turned against him because he's making so much money. He takes care of the fighters as far as I know. I like to spend time with my kids and spend some time seeing business side of it.

Randy Couture

UFC Light-Heavyweight and
Heavyweight Champion/Hall of Famer

Question: Randy, when did you get involved in amateur wrestling?
Randy Couture: I started in grade school. My best friend's brother was
wrestling. We went to one of the tournaments where they happened to have
a novice division, I think. I got my first broken nose competing in that tournament. My opponent put me in a headlock and I didn't know what a headlock was back then. I went through several stages. I obviously wrestled in
school and won state championships in high school. And I wrestled for the
United States Army, which I joined in 1982, and a couple of other championships and then the world championships. I was also a three-time Olympic
team alternate from 1988 to 1996. I then wrestled at the Oklahoma State
University for four years. I was an All-American three-time runner up in
Division One. I started winning national titles in Greco-Roman wrestling.
I ended up winning four national titles with the Pan-American teams and
competed in world championships representing the United States.

Q: When did you first come across the UFC?
Couture: One of the athletes I coached brought a UFC tape down and
we put it in the VCR and started watching it. One of the guys I went
to college with named Don Frye was fighting in the competition. I was
immediately intrigued by the sport and sent in an application. And the
UFC rang up about six months later, with me finally getting the chance
to compete at UFC 13 (May 1997).

Q: What did you think of Royce Gracie, who was dominating bigger and stronger opponents?

Couture: I didn't really tune into Brazilian jiu-jitsu and Royce Gracie until after my first UFC fight. I entered the UFC 13, after that I got a lot of background and studied it more. I entered as a wrestler first time. And then realized I needed to learn a lot of stuff and started looking at Royce Gracie, and other jiu-jitsu practitioners, and what they were doing and what their strengths were. Wrestlers started studying striking from boxing—Muay Thai and these boxing drills integrated into the wrestling background they had.

Q: How did it feel fighting in the UFC for the first time, and was it a lot different to what you were accustomed to as a competitor?

Couture: It was a lot different from what I was used to, the crowd was loud. Walking out there was pretty overwhelming. There were a lot of things on my mind, you go out and compete and try not to be over-whelmed by the whole thing.

Q: Can you talk about your most memorable fights? Would you say this was against Chuck Liddell or Tito Ortiz?

Couture: I've probably had a few during my career, but probably the first memorable fight for me was my third UFC fight [at UFC 15 (October 1997)] against Vitor Belfort who was pretty much untouchable at the time. This was a pretty memorable fight for me. The toughest fight I've been in is the Pedro Rizzo fight. I fought for five rounds and, to date, this is the toughest fight I've ever had.

Q: Can you shed some light on your training sessions before preparing for a fight?

Couture: I like to peak ten weeks before a fight. I study tapes of my opponent and decide what we think his strengths and weaknesses are and try to watch out for them. We get a game plan together—a lot of striking, sprint work, conditioning, and I like doing a lot of sprint train-ing, also lots of plyometrics. This topped with a couple of days a week real hard sparring where my partners try to wear me down—this is done with multiple partners. Other times, sparring and striking in different situations, worst case scenario training by putting myself in a potential worst position from where your opponent can put me in and I have to find a way to survive neutralize it, and try to win the fight. All-in-all a well-rounded approach.

Q: How much of a part does mental preparation play?
Couture: I can't speak for the other fighters, but certainly visualization, controlling the voices in the head telling you that you are afraid, keeping your anger in control and you know what you need to do, which are the mental skills that I try to practice. A lot of it is visualization exercises and application exercises during the training cycle, so you see what people are trying to do. I think it's a big piece. A lot of the guys who don't have a strong set of punching skills can take advantage of other gifts they have such as mental attributes and approach.

Q: What would you say to the critics who labeled the UFC "human cockfighting?"
Couture: I think it's antiquated thinking like this. They need to look at our track record. This statement is coming from a very uneducated perspective, from those who think it's just a blood sport and a bunch of thugs. Many fighters come from very respected and talented backgrounds. In this sport it requires a lot of training and sacrifices. They need to tune in and come and look at what's really going on.

Q: UFC is making a mark in the mainstream. What are your opinions on UFC versus boxing?
Couture: Not just UFC but the sport of MMA—UFC is only part of it. And to put the sport in a position where it can be more mainstream, there is still a long away to go. I haven't seen anything that big sponsorship wise in MMA, but one show is going on one of the major networks in the United States but no major corporate sponsorships for the athletes. It's come a long way and the pay-per-view is doing very well now, but there is a long way to go in comparison to boxing—there are some

differences. Everybody wants to compare it to boxing; boxing has its base and UFC and MMA has one as well.

Q: Why do you think boxers have been considered as the toughest men on the planet, while Olympic amateur wrestlers never got the same level of respect and financial rewards as them?

Couture: Well, it's like comparing apples to oranges. Wrestlers don't have a professional outlet for the sport. Professional wrestling, as everybody knows, is entertainment, it's not a real sport. Boxing, both at amateur and professional level, is a sport, and MMA is a sport. Olympic and amateur wrestling has no real outlet. You can see more and more Olympic wrestlers making a transition into professional MMA. I don't think you can say that the heavyweight champion of the world in boxing is the toughest guy on the planet anymore. That used to be the case, but not anymore. In an open fight, in a free fight, where you're not looking at rules, where you're not talking about boxing rules, it's a completely different game. Boxers don't have experience in no-rules type of fights, whereas mixed martial artists do.

Q: You are one of the few guys fighting in your forties. What keeps you going?

Couture: What keeps me going is I'm very passionate about the sport. It's what I love to do, and as long as I'm still capable of doing it, I don't see why I should do anything else. And I'm getting paid for it . . . I'll keep training.

Q: How do you see the future of the fastest growing sport in the world?

Couture: I think it's going to continue to grow. The last generation before this was the boxing generation. Last generation wanted to watch the superstars in boxing, but this generation wants to see mixed martial artists.

Q: Am I right in saying you made a transition into Hollywood? Tell me more about the *Scorpion King* movie.

Couture: It's the prequel to the *Scorpion King*. The Rock is not in the movie but it's the Rock's character as a boy growing up. Rock wasn't actually involved in the movie. I'm the main bad guy in the movie and it was a lot of fun to work on it. It was really great shooting in South Africa. We were there for six weeks with Universal Pictures. The director of the film was Russell Mulcahy, who worked on such films as *Resident Evil.* He was great to work with. I think you'll like the movie.

Q: Presently what projects are you working on?
Couture: I'm waiting on a couple of projects, a possible two-hour pilot, a popular action drama and a couple of other movie project offers. The autobiography is basically experiences in my life. I hope it's positive. We're all given a lot of challenges in life and adversity and find a way to be successful. I have a passion in what I do and I'm very happy that the book came out. I hope people like it.

Q: Why did you leave the UFC for a while, before making a return?
Couture: It was never anything to do with any other organizations. Basically it was a phase in my career where I had to make the decision to fight, and that made the right sense to me—like fighting Fedor [Emelianenko] who is the best heavyweight in the world. I would love to compete again but the UFC, unfortunately, can't make that fight happen.

Q: Should the UFC be paying the fighters more money than they currently are?
Couture: Yes, not just in the UFC but mixed martial artists in general should be getting paid better across the board in other organizations. The top boxers are making $20 million, $40 million for a fight. On the other hand, the top mixed martial artist in the UFC makes $500,000 per fight. As one of the top fighters, I'm certainly not complaining. The money I've made in the sport has been a great way to earn and make a living. But, at the same time, compared to other professional sports, it's paying low level compared to other professional athletes.

Q: Anything you would like to add?
Couture: People can check out the training we provide at Xtreme Couture. I hope to be fighting hopefully at the end of the year, where

and when I don't know yet. I'm at the point of my career where I have to take fights that are right. And for me Fedor, who is one of the two best heavyweights in the world, is the guy I would like to compete against, but unfortunately the UFC can't make that fight happen.

Dan Henderson

UFC Middleweight Tournament Champion/Hall of Famer

Question: Dan, let me transport you back to UFC 17 (1998), when you won the UFC title in 1998. What was the difference back then compared to much later when you fought in the Octagon—until you retired in 2016—as the sport garnered a huge following? You beat Carlos Newton, who broke your jaw, to be crowned champion.

Dan Henderson: It seemed like a pretty big deal back then, even though there weren't as many people in the arena like it is today. I was excited to do it and it was different. There were lots of different disciplines and we were trying to learn—nobody knew everything back then and people were not well rounded. It was more about who can learn everything faster. It was toward end of the fight—two, three minutes left in the fight—it was a punch which didn't daze me or anything and it didn't hurt, but I did notice something was a little bit weird. I took him down after that and my jaw kind of shifted a little bit. I thought to myself, *That's not right.* And after the fight it got swollen. So I went to the doctor and it was broken.

Q: Let me transport you back to UFC 100 (July 2009), which was a momentous event. Can you tell me about your rivalry with Mike Bisping, who was very vocal, but you have a polar opposite persona?

Henderson: I mean, I just typically don't like to talk shit too much, and he does. And leading up to it, I was just waiting for the chance to be able to punch him and hurt him, try to shut his mouth a little bit, knowing that I was capable of. I thought it was, for sure, a pretty good matchup between me and him. I was just waiting for my chance to be able to do that.

Q: What goes through your mind in the dressing room prior to making that walk to the Octagon? What kind of emotions gripped you before you walked out to face Bisping?

Henderson: I'm pretty relaxed. Sometime I take a nap when I get there. I focus on my game plan and know what the game plan is. And I'm visualizing a little bit. Typically I'm pretty much relaxed. I grew up wrestling and competing all my life. I made two Olympic teams prior to that. As far as competing and being on a big stage, I've been there before. I learned being relaxed is a lot better than being nervous about things. And at the same time, I was very excited to go out there and finally punch him in the face. So, that's kind of what went through my head. And as I start warming up, it's game on.

Q: The famous demolishing flying elbow you hit Bisping with while he lay on the ground knocked out. Was that icing on the cake?

Henderson: I mean, I punched him and my whole arm kind of slid across his face. I mean, I didn't just do it because it was him; I would've done that to anybody, but it made a better story because he had a bigger mouth and I went to shut it up.

Q: Dan, you fought some big names in your career—Rashad Evans, Vitor Belfort, Lyoto Machida, Daniel Cormier, Mike Bisping, etc. What would you say was the most memorable fight?

Henderson: Wander Lei was pretty much memorable. Cormier fought me exactly how I thought he was going to fight me. I didn't think he was going to stand up and trade punches with me—he and I didn't. I just didn't get my takedowns as well as I was planning on, or hoping to. I planned on being taken down because I knew he would, but I didn't get up as well as I thought I would be able to. He's pretty heavy and controlling on top—being a good wrestler like that—it makes it tougher for me to try to neutralize him when the guy just wants to take you down. He did a good job in executing his game plan.

Q: Fedor at one time was regarded as the best heavyweight in MMA, and even the best fighter in the sport. You fought and beat him at Strikeforce (2011). What do you remember when fighting this giant of a man?

Henderson: I was pretty relaxed going into that fight, even though a lot of other people around me were a little bit more nervous than my other fights. I was capable of hurting him and controlling him with my wrestling. He came out trying to knock my head off right away. I didn't expect him to be quite so aggressive when the bell went. I reacted to it. I caught him with a very good left hook right at the beginning of the fight and kind of backed him up. I think that's when he figured out that the little guy can hit pretty hard, too.

Q: How do you research your opponents, and what did you do to accumulate data on Fedor before locking horns with him?

Henderson: I had been fighting alongside him in PRIDE and then watching him in Strikeforce as well. I watched him for many years so I had a pretty good idea of what he was good at and what he was capable of. I obviously watched a lot of his fights previously I didn't want to be in front of him and trade punches. I wasn't afraid of doing that, but that's pretty much his strength—his power and his quickness for a big guy. I didn't want to fall right into his strength. I was planning on getting into his clinch, wear him out, making him tired and then try to finish him on the ground or in the clinch. It ended up us trading punches in the open a little bit. He knocked me on my butt, but my wrestling pretty much ended up winning the fight.

Q: He never fought in the UFC, but was regarded as being the best. Does it make a difference, and did he kind of miss out in terms of greater exposure as, let's say, the best UFC champion receives?

Henderson: Yes and no. I think during that time there were more countries that were watching PRIDE than the UFC around the world. A lot of people were able to watch PRIDE back then, it was pretty well known around the world. As the UFC started becoming big and once they purchased PRIDE and Strikeforce, that's probably when he should have come over to the UFC. And he probably would've been much better known than he is now or was then for sure. But I think PRIDE was well known around the world, but definitely not in the US as the UFC was. To answer your question, during that time when he was the best, I think he was the biggest fighter in PRIDE then. He really did miss out toward end of his career by not moving to the UFC.

Q: What has been the best experience in your career, or life?
Henderson: Having my kids aside, which is of course a big thing for me—I love my kids and my wife—as far as the sport goes, I don't know. I guess making two Olympic Games. Then when I beat Wanderlei when I won the second belt in PRIDE was a big one, too.

Q: What would you say to people who are oblivious to the sacrifice an MMA/UFC fighter has to endure, both physically and mentally?
Henderson: Obviously if you want to do something right and be the best in, it's going to take a lot of sacrifices. MMA is one of the more demanding sports physically on your body, the more preparation you put into it the easier they are. Wrestling is very similar in that regard. I grew up wrestling since I was five years old. I have been accustomed to that my whole life. As far as people not knowing what sacrifices we make, I think a lot of people understand that there are a lot of sacrifices, but they don't understand the extent of these—not being able to go and do certain things because you have to train and you can't jeopardize not training, and not doing other things that others have no problem doing. It's a huge tool physically and mentally, you have to be willing to sacrifice a lot of things to be able to be the best at MMA and to get better yourself.

Q: Anything you can share pertaining to fighting Mauricio Ruas at
***UFC Fight Night 38* (2014)?**
Henderson: I wasn't hoping it to be that type of fight, but it ended up being a pretty tough fight. And I like him and respected him as a person and a fighter, it was definitely a big challenge for me. I already had fought him before. It was a very good experience for me.

Q: At UFC 204 (October 2016), you fought Mike Bisping in the rematch—I was actually ringside, as a member of the media. You were the oldest person to fight for a belt, at age forty-six. How did the rematch materialize?

Henderson: I was already under contract with the UFC I was debating on when I was going to retire. I had fought in LA, which was somewhat unexpected because I was supposed to fight six weeks earlier in Florida against Lyoto Machida, but he tested positive. So they put me on the LA card against Hector Lombard. And Luke Rockhold was supposed to fight Chris Weidman at the main event, but Weidman got hurt so Bisping replaced him. And I think because Bisping getting a knockout against Luke Rockhold and I had knocked out Hector Lombard on the same card, a lot of the fans were asking for a rematch. I think it was in the interest of the UFC to make the fight happen. If it wasn't good for the UFC, then it probably wasn't going to happen. Dana took care of me pretty well. I had a good relationship with him. He was the boss and made all the decisions.

Q: You hit Mike with an H-bomb, which you became notorious for.

Henderson: I was hoping to knock him out again, but I knew it would be hard compared to the first time I had fought him. And because he had knocked out Luke Rockhold, I definitely was going to respect his hands, but he honestly didn't hit me with anything hard. I knew he will be moving around and I wanted to pick my shots a little better—and I did—and knocked him down in the first round, and in the second round almost had finished him. But when I followed up on the ground I barely missed. He was able to recover. One of the reasons I was retiring was I just wasn't recovering as fast as I used to, the fights got a little tougher. I felt like I still finished strong in the fourth and fifth rounds. I know I took him down in one of those rounds. I felt I did fairly well. I did enough, especially with the two different knockdowns, to win the fight—especially he hadn't damaged or hurt me at all. By the look of him, you could tell I had damaged him quite a bit. And since then they really put a bigger emphasis on damage when they judge fights and aggression, especially knockdowns. I didn't get any of the rounds

I knocked him down, which nowadays it's different. It's unfortunate that I never got the decision, especially being my retirement fight. I should've walked away with the belt that day.

Q: Do you feel it influenced the judges decisions the fact you were retiring and Mike was on his home territory? It could've gone either way, I think.

Henderson: I mean, I don't know. I'd like not to think like that, but obviously I feel no matter where the fight was, if it was on a playground or on a street in front of all your friends, one guy looked like him and the other guy looked like me, there's no question that everybody there would—including your friends—know you beat him up. For some reason, that wasn't the case that night. I felt like I had beaten him up. Basically, just bashed him in and at the same time he did nothing. I've been in some fights where I have been beat up a little bit, given more than I have taken, but I really didn't take anything in this fight as far as hard strikes. Unfortunately it didn't go my way. It would've been nice to retire with the belt. To answer your question, yes, that might have been something to do with the decision, but I'll never know.

Q: Being a wrestler, did you find it onerous to adjust to striking when you had made the transition to MMA, as some fighters are fear-inducing strikers who have a propensity to trade shots? You hit hard, as I witnessed firsthand in the arena that day.

Henderson: Yeah, I do. I guess I didn't hit him [Bisping] hard enough that night. I did hit hard, but as far as striking goes it was more about learning how to do it right and setup my striking with my wrestling and things like that. I think it wasn't that hard to learn. Being a wrestler my whole life, I was used to being able to learn body movements and the techniques pretty quickly. It was more about spending time and learning. The biggest thing, especially coaching other people—wrestlers also—is if guys are ready to get punched or not. That's the biggest problem with some of these wrestlers in MMA—they're mentally afraid of getting punched. There's a mindset you've got to have. I wasn't afraid. Obviously I don't want to get hit, but I wasn't afraid of taking punches, either. So, that's the biggest key I think. In my career I was pretty solid. And physically and technically my whole life it was a pretty easy transition for me.

Q: Lastly, can you talk me through your training camp for UFC 204, and whether you had to focus on anything specific?
Henderson: I don't think he was a bigger threat in any way out of the ordinary, I should say, than most of my other fights. He wasn't especially great at submissions or anything like that for me to focus on. The thing I was going to focus on in my training camp was making sure my cardio was going to be able to push five rounds. I know he's always in pretty good shape and has good cardio. That was my biggest concern. I did get tired a little bit in the fourth round, but I felt like I was strong, took him down in the fifth round and felt like I controlled him without taking a whole lot of damage. I think I hit him more than he did.

Carlos Condit

UFC Welterweight Champion

Question: You fought Dan Hardy at UFC 120 (October 2010) in London, and are the only fighter to beat him by knockout. What do you remember about this fight?
Carlos Condit: At the time, Dan had just come off the title against Georges St-Pierre. Dan was basically the number-one contender in the division and he had an impressive record. He was a dangerous striker. I was excited about the fight. I felt confident, but I was also nervous to fight a guy as dangerous as Dan. That fight could not have gotten better for me. I felt everything just came together that night. So, the outcome went obviously my way. I put on a performance. Like I said, I was very nervous. I had somewhat made a name for myself but Dan was more well known. And I was fighting in his country, his backyard, basically hostile territory. I had a lot of people telling me that I was going to get knocked out.

Q: Speaking of Georges St-Pierre, a fighter you faced at UFC 154 (November 2012). Was this for the welterweight championship belt?
Condit: Yes, interim belt. GSP is a guy I look up to and almost idolized for a long time. And standing across the Octagon from him was surreal. It was like a dream. My camp for that fight was interesting because my coach had actually coached him and so he took a step back. So I had some different people in my corner for that fight. I'm a realist when it comes to my opponents. I build them up in my head

as spectacular as everybody else does. So, I think that's a double-edged sword. There is a reason why GSP is at where he's at, the great champion that he is. When it comes down to it, I believe in myself. I believe I can rise up and put on a fantastic performance and beat anybody on any given night. It's just executing when it comes down to it.

Q: In the third round you kicked him in the head, which has since become a talked-about moment. Can you tell me more about that?
Condit: Pretty much at that point of the fight I was being taken to the ground on my back, I knew I needed to get creative and pull something out of the bag. The combination was a similar pattern what I had been working with my striking coach. I got overexcited after I dropped him and I tried to go for the finish but gassed myself out. It's a moment that people will remember.

Q: You were going to fight George St-Pierre at UFC 137 (October 2011), but it got cancelled. Why did this fight not materialize?
Condit: Yes. It was a series of events. He was supposed to fight Nick Diaz who was coming from Strikeforce. And Nick didn't show up at the press conference and so they gave me a title shot. Then Georges got hurt and so me and Nick ended up fighting. Nick is basically a guy I had watched fighting I was a fan. I was excited to get the opportunity to test myself against him. Then I was waiting for GSP to come back after he recovered from the injury. It was a sequence of events interesting for title fight. I talked to GSP a little bit after the fight. Him and I we're familiar with each other. He trained in New Mexico for a while.

Q: Do you feel GSP is the GOAT? A lot of views are floating around, but I feel it's not easy to really pick one champion and stamp the GOAT on him.
Condit: I think Jon Jones is the GOAT. What he did, how he handled his opponents that he fought, especially in the earlier title runs, I don't think that can be matched.

Q: Back in the days, in the UFC, there were no weight divisions. What's your view on that? Should they bring an open-weight division?

Condit: I think from a pure martial arts and fighting standpoint, it's very interesting to watch guys of different sizes because in the real world, you don't step on the scale before you fight—it doesn't matter who's big, who's the other guy. As far as sport weight classes are necessary part of keeping things organized. There are two different schools of thought. I think it's interesting I was a fan back in the days, too. It was interesting to watch. Where you do see open weights is in Brazilian jiu-jitsu tournaments, where you can see a tiny guys against big guys.

Q: You took off almost two years from the sport. How did you spend your time?

Condit: I took a couple of breaks in the last five years. The more recent break was after I lost to Mike Chiesa. I tried to get a fight for a while and the UFC wasn't scheduling me. Then finally they scheduled a fight for me against Court McGee. After a year I had fought Chiesa, and I went out to get an eye exam before the fight to pass my medical. I had a detached retina, which I had to get fixed, so that put me almost another year out before fighting McGee. Then I came back training then finally fought last October with him.

Q: Do you get recognized when you're out and about?

Condit: Oh, yeah. Albuquerque is not a huge place. Fighting here is very popular. So I'm recognizable.

Q: Your favorite fighter? Favorite food? Favorite all-time film? Favorite music or musician?

Condit: Favorite fighter right now is tough, let's see, I like Max Holloway because I love his attitude and his ferocity, and he has skills, but his ferocity is second to none. Favorite food is, I'm pretty simple I go for a good steak. But that's a hard choice because I love a lot of things. Film is *Fight Club*. Music is I love Chris Connell.

Q: When you fight, are your close family members too nervous to watch?

Condit: My mom will go to the fights, but when it's my turn to fight she doesn't watch me. She's there but she doesn't watch. And certain members of my family get pretty nervous watching me.

Q: Your fight with Matt Brown took place in January 2021, at *UFC on ABC*. How were you feeling going into that battle?

Condit: I felt great. Last two fights I felt really motivated and trained at the camp well and switched up my team a little bit. And the results speak for themselves. I had two unanimous decision wins against guys who are very tough veterans. He's a guy I respect a lot in the sport and we were scheduled to fight before but he got injured while training so we finally made this happen, especially during Covid when everything that could derail the fight. I was scheduled to fight Chris Lyle several times it was a fight that the fans wanted to see. Chris was a super exciting fighter and brought a lot of intensity, we were scheduled to fight twice, or maybe it was three times. I got hurt once or twice, he got hurt, so it never came to fruition. As far as getting fights in the UFC, usually the UFC contact through my management. I think one or two fights have been started on social media, that's how me and Michael Chiesa got scheduled.

Q: Can you share the most interesting thing, or bizarre incident, of your career?

Condit: There's been quite a bit. I was able to travel quite a bit, including meeting the troops in Kuwait and Afghanistan. That was interesting and an experience. I'm excited to continue climb back on the ladder. I'm currently working on a contract with the UFC. I feel great. I'm looking forward to putting on a performance for the fans.

CHAPTER THREE:

NEW ERA CHAMPIONS

Lyoto Machida

UFC Light-Heavyweight Champion

Question: Let me transport you back when you fought Randy Couture at UFC 129 (April 2011) in Canada. At the time, this broke the UFC attendance record when over 55,000 packed into the Rogers Centre. What can you tell me about the fight?

Lyoto Machida: For me it was a very special moment in my career because since I was eighteen years old, I had been watching Randy Couture fight and he was one of my favorite fighters. Not just because he was a champion, but the weight he carried outside, how he behaved outside of the cage. He was my idol. The best thing I can do when fighting him is to give my 100 percent, put all my energy into the fight. Not to diminish him in front of people, but to give him an honor that I gave my 100 percent. That's what I did and it was an honor to fight him, one of the best.

Q: You worked with Steven Seagal. What did you guys discuss and train in, and what advice did he give you for this fight?

Machida: Steven Seagal is my friend. He went to my fight and we saw each other in the week of the fight. He just mentioned the crane kick. He said, "Lyoto, maybe if you do a front kick it will be a great scenario for you because Randy Couture is a wrestler." Steven Seagal is a visionary. Sometimes he can foresee the movement of a fight. Also coincidently my father had mentioned the same kick to me two months before this. The great crane kick was trained by my father originally. Steven Seagal just randomly mentioned it and he had this vision. He visually made me believe even more that the kick will be more effective in that situation.

Q: Some fans have come to appreciate the efficiency of Shotokan karate—and traditional martial arts for that matter—in the Octagon. You proved that someone can come from a traditional background and prevail. Can you shed light on this? What are your sentiments?

Machida: It's important to understand that karate and all the martial arts are effective in MMA if you train the right way, and if you adapt for the real situation that you are going to face. It's also very important to understand that I'm not here to give the wrong illusion to people: that if you train just regular karate, just regular other martial art, you're going to be ready for MMA combat. No. That's not true. You've got to adapt to the sport like I did with my father and my brothers. I went back to the roots of karate training a lot. So the techniques that are not allowed anymore in competitions of karate and other martial arts, we put everything together for MMA. It's so important to understand this. Even with Brazilian jiu-jitsu, if you train as a sport it's not going to be effective in MMA—you have to adapt. It's so important to measure all this because some people don't understand that they need to adapt in order to be effective, to be able to use the art properly in martial arts.

Q: Jon Jones fight at UFC 140 (December 2011), who is one of the greatest. Am I right in saying this was your first submission lost, and that you refused to tap?

Machida: Jon Jones is a champion. It's hard to describe in words how good he is. He has dominated for over ten years. It's very rare to see somebody who does that. My fight against him was very tough. Especially in the beginning, I think, I had the upper hand, because I could control the distance and hit him a couple of times, which he felt a lot. He said to me in the press conference right after the fight that he felt my punch. But as a champion he could turn everything around, which he did in the second round and he got the victory. I have no complain about that, but I just want to say it was well deserved for him because he could change everything.

Q: He's now in the heavyweight division. Do you feel he can prevail in this division and dominate like he did in the light-heavyweight division?

Machida: Actually, I don't like to foresee any future situation—especially when it comes to other fighters—but I can say that as a champion Jon Jones can be in any division and if he keeps devoted to his training, he can have success without a doubt. But you never know how he's doing in training, so that's why I don't like to foresee the future. But I will say I think he has a lot of qualities to prevail in the heavyweight division, it depends on him. It's very difficult to predict when you don't know the inside of a fighter in terms of what's going on in their career at any given time. We are all human beings and we change sometimes. We never know our minds, we never know what's going on at the time, what kind of training the other person is doing. He's a true champion and has been for many years, but we never know what's in the future.

Q: You trained at the Gracie Academy in Los Angeles, but now train in Florida.

Machida: I have a good relationship with Rener Gracie and his brother—the academy in LA is run by them. They are my friends. We always trained together, more before because I used to live in LA. Since I'm in Florida now I'm not training there anymore, but as soon as I go there I always try to visit them. They not only teach about technique, but they have a lot of other things to share with a lot of people.

Q: Do you have any hobbies beyond martial arts? How do you relax?

Machida: I like to be with my family at home because when I'm at the training camp, I don't have the time available most of the time. So when I'm home I like to read a lot of books. I like to watch other sports and play with my kids. I'm a very simple guy. I don't have any luxury habits like cars, stuff like that. Most of the time I like to be calm, I like to meditate and I like nature, which is so good for me it makes me feel satisfied in life.

Q: You lived in Los Angeles and could be seen walking around Beverly Hills, where it's common to bump into the paparazzi. How do you personally handle fame?

Machida: I just moved to Florida. Fame for me is just part of my job and it's part of the journey. I really like to be among my fans, but we all know that you are going to be left by yourself one day. Everything is going to pass one day, you've got to be ready for the ordinary life, a life when you don't have fans because one day nobody is going to remember me since there will be new generation of fans. But to be honest, I don't mind to think about that. I understand that times go on and you just need to understand that your time is going to pass—it is part of life.

Q: The USADA suspended you in 2016, and you weren't happy with their decision. You were banned for eighteen months, but you felt it was unfair.

Machida: Actually it's something that is already in the past. Of course at that moment it was really sad because of that situation, but we always have something to learn from in our life. Maybe I had to learn something from that situation because I consider myself innocent, but even then I was punished. I adapt myself and I served the eighteen-month ban. It's the past and there's no reason to delve on the past. For me I try to lead my life in that sense I try to live in the moment. It was something in the past that was damaging for me. But even then I overcame all the odds that were put in front of me. As I said, if it doesn't kill you, it makes you stronger. That's the concept I like to believe in. Just live in the present moment because you never know if you're going to be alive tomorrow. If I look back I probably would feel depressed. If I look too much to the future I get anxiety. So I try to live in the moment and give my best.

Q: At UFC 224 (May 2018), you beat Vitor Belfort in Brazil. Anything you'd like to share about that event?

Machida: There is no real important story about that fight but the training camp was really hard. Vitor is one of the best. His name is in history books. I had the chance to claim that victory that day. As I said, one day you win, another day you lose, but I'm focused on my next step. The fight was amazing.

Q: Is there a difference between fighting in the UFC and Bellator?
Machida: No, pretty much the same. We go inside the cage and it's pretty much the same. Bellator is growing a lot. I consider Bellator one of the best. They are very serious when it comes to the fighters—they take so much care of us. They're so good. I just want to say thank you to all the crew at Bellator. The UFC is the same. UFC is great too. It's the biggest.

Anthony Pettis

UFC Lightweight Champion

Question: You became the UFC lightweight champion at UFC 164 (August 2013), beating Benson Henderson. Can you relive this moment with me?

Anthony Pettis: Yes, going back to that day, fighting for the belt—not only for the belt but fighting in front of my hometown of Milwaukee, Wisconsin—was just a crazy moment in my life. I was ready. During that run I was always on point ready to fight. The opportunity came up and I capitalized on it. I went in there and I got a pretty much flawless victory with a first-round arm bar with no damage taken. It was one of those moments in my career that was unforgettable. It was a surreal moment because I remember going into that arena as a kid, sitting there in the higher seats because my family didn't really have a lot of money, but now going in there to see my name lit up on the billboard was a crazy moment, honestly. It was one of those moments I always remember because of the history I have with this arena.

Q: What was floating through your mind when they wrapped the belt around your waist?

Pettis: The first thought I had was, *I'm the best in the mother F in world*—that's what I said out loud. It took a while to sink in—even weeks after the fight. It seemed like having that belt in my house, just all the emotions that comes with the training camp, it all finally came to fruition. My whole career I was trying to become a champion and that moment finally came. It was just a surreal moment in my career everything was finally clicking perfectly.

Q: When you were growing up and before pursuing MMA, did you ever contemplate pursuing any other sport, or have interest in?
Pettis: I started with tae kwon do, which was my main background. When I was young I spent a lot of time training in this art. I also played basketball, which was my second sport.

Q: You've opened up your own MMA management company recently. Please tell me more about this venture.
Pettis: Yes. I just setup my management company end of last year in 2020, but January 2021 is when we really started. We have a great roster, about 55 guys from all different levels. The goal of the management company is to give back to these kids, and a lot of them are adults who want to pursue this as a career. So I'm making this opportunity happen for them a lot smoother than what I had to do when I was coming up. I had to find a gym. I had to find someone to promote me. With my Showtime Entertainment Group, we have a training center, we have the management, and we have the opportunity to find the sponsorships. Not only that, but I'm kind of creating a "family" with this venture. I want this team to be more like a family as opposed to a competition zone. All the guys I'm choosing come from a traditional martial arts background. We all have a certain fighting style and I can help them go to the gym and develop.

Q: A lot of professional athletes, when they retire, become bankrupt because they don't invest their money wisely. How do you see your business side develop, as you're still actively fighting?
Pettis: Right now I own two gyms. I own an MMA gym and a barber shop. As far as business goes, I'm pretty diversified. I can invest. I think as far as MMA goes, this is my first venture into that world and I'm really enjoying it. I do coach. I help out but it's not a career in coaching. I am in this position and I have a great team behind me. I'm not in a position to lead someone's career as a coach as it's a totally different

mindset. A lot of these guys that I'm managing are training with me. They grew up training with me. I want to make sure I'm representing them to the best of my ability. I'm giving them the opportunities that they deserve.

Q: You mentioned that when you started fighting you had to contend to finding a gym and management. How do you feel the management side in the MMA world has evolved?
Pettis: I think it's definitely changed a lot from when I was starting out. When I won the belt I didn't have a publicist, but I had a manager that did very well for me. I think the disconnect is that they don't know the fight world. They do well making money, producing and getting the opportunities, but as far as what it takes to stay on top to be a champion, and the balance between how many sponsors you should be getting, obligations outside your training, no one was taking care of that. I kind of had to take care of that on my own. I had to make some mistakes. I made a lot of mistakes in my career. I know what to look for fighters to stay on top. Once you're not winning, no one cares. Sponsors are not coming, appearances aren't coming. So the main objective for a fighter is to win and win as long as they can. I've been doing the sport for thirteen years, which is crazy because it's a long time. I've been blessed I've been in this position for so long. I saw all the changes. I saw when the UFC was sold, when WEC merged. I understand most phases of the game and I made a lot of connections. I feel where I'm at my career, the opportunities I have and the connections I have for younger fighters, I'm leading from the front line. I'm still actively fighting they can see how it should look on the highest levels.

Q: UFC pay packets were meager, but now the top champions are making millions per fight. Nevertheless, some fighters feel they deserve more. What are your thoughts?
Pettis: I think it's kind of like that in most sports—the money has to come from somewhere. UFC is still a new company. I mean, it's only twenty-seven years old. To see how much it's gone up from when I first was fighting to right now, the pay is definitely way up. But it still is

hard to make a living as a profession for some low-end fighters. For my younger brother it was my goal to make sure he was established, to make sure he was making good money. That's how the management side kind of started. I was looking at it from the perspective of my younger brother's career, helping him make the right decisions—where he's at, and be able to do at his age in his career level. I think everybody feels they should make more money, but in UFC it's like a queue, as Dana says, "If you're winning the fights, you're popular and you want to see more money, you'll make more money." And I was in that position. I made great money with the UFC. I had great sponsorships. I was on the cover of Wheaties box. I had the highest pie in the UFC. I also have been at the lowest low, losing a couple of fights in a row. I know how that felt. There's difference when you're winning and when you're losing. So, I think the fighters that are a mediocre mid-level fighters—not in skill levels, but how many numbers they're selling and how many people want to watch them—that's the kind of the disconnect with the payments structure. The guys that are popular definitely are taken care of. Guys who are mid-level are like, "Hey, we should be making more money." And I get it. I think they've been working all their lives and been putting their bodies on the line every time they go in a fight for entertainment of millions. So I can see both sides of the story. I was in a position where I was making millions of dollars to show up and fight, and I was also in a position working my way up to that position.

Q: Can you shed light on the negotiation process of a UFC contract?
Pettis: It's weird because most managers are only part of the negotiation when the first fight contract is signed. Most of them are not in a position to negotiate. They're kind of happy with numbers the UFC gives them. UFC does a good job of that in that they control the market that way. So the managers that are dealing with younger fighters, their objective is to get them into the UFC. Unless they're superstars and they have a following, managers get them their first contract but don't negotiate per se. UFC isn't there to negotiate; they offer the new kid an opportunity to blow up, which is fair. Once you get your first contract, based on what you've done in the first several fights, second

contract is when the negotiations start. A lot of these younger fighters don't realize that there are no negotiations on the other side—there is no going back and forth of how much the UFC is going to pay. With other organizations—Bellator and ONE—there are opportunities to negotiate. But everybody wants to be a fighter now. When I was coming up there weren't that many people in the gym. There weren't 200 guys trying to become fighters. There were merely ten of us. And it was an easier market to navigate through. Now my fight class has 50 to 60 guys—and there are 150 guys—who want to become fighters. It's definitely a different market now.

Q: Tony Ferguson, who is an unusual character with a propensity for peculiar behavior, fought you at UFC 229 (October 2018) in Las Vegas. What can you tell me about the fight press conference?
Pettis: They offered me that fight on a four-week notice. It was kind of a last-minute fight. He came out of a knee surgery. It was horrible for me during that time coming from 145 pounds when I fought Max Holloway, because my body was just holding on. Everything I ate changed by cutting that weight. So it was tough for me. Tony Ferguson, he's a great guy, honestly. I'm a fan of his fighting style. I didn't know what to expect because he was coming off with a weird personality. He was saying all sorts of things. I don't know what he was doing, but he shook my hand he was very respectful. It was a great fight. That's one of the fights that I wish I can go back and fight again. I didn't want to rush in. I threw a bomb and I broke my hand. Unfortunate things happen in the fight game. For me, that's still one of my favorite fights. I had fun out there and I showed I was a warrior. It's one of the fights I'll look back on and be proud of.

Q: Do you think he puts that weird persona on, or is it really him?
Pettis: I think it's probably naturally him because when he was trying to sell his other fights, he was talking trash and he was acting a little funky and a little weird. But my fight, he wasn't really talking trash. He wasn't really trying to sell the fight like that. He was still acting little pretty weird. It's kind of his personality. He's a guy who's involved in martial arts and trains hard, but doesn't necessarily have the best people skills.

Q: If a UFC fighter gets injured, do they have something to fall back on if they're out of action for several months, or even an entire year or two?

Pettis: You better have some money saved up if you break your hand or leg. If it happens in the training camp or the fight itself, then you're covered because you're insured. The insurance covers it. The UFC pays for it. You just have to pay your deductible. As far as payment goes, you don't get paid unless you fight. So if you're taking a year off due to an injury, you better have enough money saved for that year or you're going to be in a bad situation. I've had hand injuries where I had to take off six to eight months off. I had a knee injury that I had to take out a year for. And during that year, the only payments you receive are what you have coming from other streams of income. For me I have my gyms, my barber shop, so I was OK and I could focus my attention on these. But for a lot of fighters this is all they do, their only income is from fighting. So they're in a bad spot when they can't fight for a year, and they rush back in to take another fight when they're not necessarily ready. And that's when you see a lot of fighters take a downturn on their career.

Q: What's the best advice you ever received about fighting, or life in general?

Pettis: This year 2020 I started exploring the mental health of sport, getting a sport psychologist's understanding of that process. I've had so much growth as a person, as a father, just understanding things. It's hard to say in one sentence, but basically it's given me an understanding that thoughts are just thoughts and emotions are just emotions. How do I separate myself from making a decision right after I feel an emotion or have a thought? Because especially in the sport world, you're fighting somebody where you, let's say, have a bad first round—my last fight is a prime example. My first round was bad. You have to separate yourself from the emotions you have—the bad first round and the thoughts that come from that. And you go out there and produce what you do. And for a lot of fighters, in their career the window is so short they only have the opportunity to explore that mindset, mental side of the game, and get like the basic rule of the engagement when they're battling themselves. That's the toughest fight. When you're fighting someone you both are prepared, but then you just change in your own head the thoughts, they can take over you and take you out of the Octagon into a totally different place. When the 15 minutes are over, you think to yourself, *Shit, what happened!?* I wasn't understanding this early on in my career in terms of what was going on in my head. It was pulling me from the Octagon, pulling me away from what was going on that moment in the fight. So, focus on being in the present moment, understanding how to get myself back to that moment no matter what thoughts or feeling filter into my head.

Q: You triumphed against Alex Morono at *UFC Fight Night*, a fight which took place in December 2020 in Las Vegas. Before the bout you actually expressed openly how dangerous your opponent is, which is a bit uncommon in the sport.

Pettis: Alex Morono was a last-minute fight as well. I was trying to stay busy in 2020, and Alex had two fights. I think Leon Edwards got Covid so that opened up a spot for me to be on that card. I was the only one that said yes really quick. The UFC gave me a couple of different names. I offered several names to fight, but they declined. Morono was like, "Yeah, I'll fight him." I knew who he was but I hadn't studied his game. Once I started studying his game, I knew he was a dangerous guy. He was one of the tough dudes. He is kind of new into MMA, but guys who are new to the sport have a lot more to give because they haven't taken the damage, or have had bad experiences in the Octagon. When they are fighting me, no matter who they are, they're the best version of themselves because it means a lot to their careers because of my name and stature in the sport. So, we knew we were in for a dangerous fight. Biggest thing in my camp was to stay in the presence. I'm in there fighting and now my thoughts aren't somewhere else other than the Octagon. No one can beat me I don't think. It's when I get frustrated my thoughts start leaving my body making decisions based on emotions and not the game plan. But that was our game plan for that fight. And the first round I had a little hiccup—I slipped. He got punches in. I lost that first round. I was upset with myself, but I pulled myself together and took my time with my attack. And then I outworked him and out-classed him in the striking department, in the wrestling department, pretty much every aspects I outclassed him. That was my performance.

Q: What would you say affects your mindset and performance when your mind is clouded with winning, or losing? I mean, how do people around you affect your performance because of the pressure? After all, two warriors walk into the Octagon; one wins and one has got to lose.

Pettis: Once you go in there and you're determined, you're so focused on winning-losing that you lose the ability to navigate through the hard times like in your training camps. And I've been there. Thoughts can overtake you where you're thinking, *My fist hurts.* In most training camps something happens. None of us really go in there 100 percent free of injury. So, in the actual fight the guy might have crazy energy in the first round, but your energy is everything's based on thoughts swirling in your head, *I've got to win this fight.* If you don't make the right decisions and the smart decisions, then you're performing out of not really instinct but emotion. You're thinking, *Maybe this is going to happen,* and you start thinking of A, B, and C. Before you know it, the whole fight is over while you're too distracted worrying about winning the fight. It's the deep stuff I'm talking about. It's detaching yourself from the win or lose mentality, and instead being in control and focusing on doing in the present moment. When I do my training camp, I can't control whether I win or lose, but I can control the kind of training session I have and the vision. So once I change my mindset, my perspective based on that performance, like how my workout connects to me mentally, my skill level will jump up like crazy.

From 2020, I had an amazing role as a professional and not just a fighter. I started learning and experimenting with other martial arts. It was getting back to that phase, it was a mental block. I was thinking about my losses where I was basing my next move on that, saying to myself, *How do I win this fight?* That's not necessarily the best way forward—the best way is to be in the present and take your time, fully work out, and the results will show. So, I take it day by day now.

Eddie Alvarez

UFC Lightweight Champion

Question: What prompted you to pursue MMA?
Eddie Alvarez: I grew up in a very bad neighborhood in Philadelphia. I grew up in north Philadelphia and fighting was very popular there. I grew up having a lot of street fights and I wrestled in high school. When I got out of wrestling in high school I didn't go to college. MMA was still not mainstream at the time. And I was getting into a lot of street fights and not doing much. I wasn't going to school, I wasn't competing. I was just working a regular job and I decided to take a path. I used to fight when I was young in the street because I was afraid. I needed to fight to prove myself because mostly deep down I was afraid. And now I fight because I choose to. Now I don't feel I have to prove anything.

Q: UFC 205 (November 2016) at Madison Square Garden was a historical moment for the UFC. How did your fight with Conor McGregor materialize?
Alvarez: It was back and forth—it was very difficult to materialize because there were a lot of unknown things all up in the air. They didn't really announce it till five weeks before the fight. So, it was difficult because I didn't know whether we were going to fight or whether we were not going to fight. Then finally five or six weeks before the fight, they finally agreed and announced it. So, there was a little bit of difficulty for that fight to happen in the first place.

Q: You once said to me that a fight with Conor McGregor doesn't start in the Octagon, but the fight starts with him way before leading up to fight night.

Alvarez: He was this flashy showman type, which definitely is not my style, not what I do. I'm from an old-school fighting style where we just kind of show up and fight each other. But I think the sport kind of needed that at the time. There was stagnancy and the UFC needed a showman, someone who would bring eyeballs to the UFC, and he was good at doing that. He brought a better balance. A lot of fighters, including Conor, brought legitimacy to the sport of martial arts, but you also need entertainment and a lot of fighters don't have that. Conor is Conor and he helped with that. I was shocked to see a lot of the local people supporting him. I'm from Philadelphia. I'm not from New York. And I started my career in Atlantic City. Between New York, New Jersey, and Philadelphia, I had a good following, but it was shocking to see local people kind of pulling for Conor. He did such a good job in the sport promoting himself that there was a lot of local people, even people in my hometown, who were pulling for Conor and on his bandwagon. That was kind of shocking to see. I had a lot of fun with the whole lead up with that much attention, that much excitement. That was a great lead up. I never really take anything too personal. I don't get too wrapped up what's said before the fight or make it personal. I understand that we, as fighters, have a disagreement which is usually that I can beat them or they disagree and feel they can beat me. So we get into the Octagon to figure that out. We're probably going to have that disagreement and we're never going to agree with each other. We want to know who is right.

Q: How did the fight get sanctioned in New York because it was, as I said, a monumental achievement, as MMA competitions were banned in that state?

Alvarez: I think the UFC spent some money lobbying. They used a lot of UFC fighters such as Chris Weidman and Frankie Edgar. They used a lot of influential athletes and fighters to help lobby to get the bill passed so New York would accept the sport. It took a little bit of time but it made it happen.

Q: At UFC 211 (May 2017), you fought Dustin Poirier who, of course, beat Conor McGregor in a rematch later in 2021.

Alvarez: I remember being in the fight with Dustin, and he was doing a good job keeping me at a good range. I felt I had to pull it into a war. I thought I could do a better job, and close the distance and made it a fist fight instead of a tactical distance fight. We did that we got into a little bit of a war and I hurt him. I went into the finish but got a little reckless. When you're in there, fist fighting, you're not necessarily thinking—you're just reacting. I remember I hurt him with a left hook I think, caught him open, then I think he was playing halfway up halfway down, and I hit him with a knee and he was falling. And I hit him with a knee and knocked him out but it was an illegal shot. There was a lot of controversy behind this fight.

Q: What is the best advice that your coach gave you?

Alvarez: Me and Mark Henry are friends. He's part of my team and he's my coach, and so is one of my other good friends Ricardo Almeida. I think the biggest thing my coaches tell me is, even in the wake of a lot of adversity, and maybe even when I'm losing, they constantly remind me what I'm capable of and push me forward. I think sometimes in fighting the lows are so low, the highs are so high, if you don't have the people close to you who keep reminding you what you're capable of and how powerful you can be, it's very difficult to move forward. I think the constant encouragement, the constant vote of confidence they let me know that I'm capable of more than what I think I am.

Q: How does pay-per-view in the UFC work in terms of figures, a fighter's share?

Alvarez: You get the share of the pay-per-view when you are the champion. If you're not a champion, you don't have a belt around your waist, then you don't get the share in pay-per-view bonuses. Only the champion gets to do that. That's sort of how pay-per-view works in the UFC. As the pay-per-view buys sell more, it gets higher in terms of you may get a higher rate per buy. Between certain numbers you'll get more, so let's say you get x amount of dollars per pay-per-view and the numbers go beyond a certain level then your share per sale increases too. That's typically how it works.

Q: Were you surprised at the value of the UFC when Zuffa sold it to WME agency for a staggering $7 billion?
Alvarez: I've been incredibly shocked to see how it's come along, yes. I never expected the sport to get this big ever in my lifetime. If I ever joined other promotions, I wanted to win world titles in multiple organizations all over the world. And I've done that. Every time I joined a promotion I've become the champion. I wanted to do this with every organization, not just the smaller ones but the larger ones as well. I'm still doing that. Just becoming the champion all over the world fighting the best guys in the world, also being able to make millions of dollars and support my family when I'm done fighting that was a goal of mine. It wasn't just to fight to become a champion but to make it worthwhile for my family. So when I'm done, we can live a comfortable life.

Q: What are you doing these days?
Alvarez: I fight for ONE Championship now, which is based in Singapore. I should be ready for a title shot soon. Hopefully I'll be the first fighter in history to win every single major world title in every major MMA promotion. Some fighters get paid a lot more now fighting for other major promotions and not fighting for the UFC. You can make a lot of money outside of the UFC today than you ever could.

Q: Any particular life lessons you've learned along the way?
Alvarez: Since I was younger I have owned a real estate company that I started when I was around twenty-five years old. I invest in stocks and I invest in real estate. I have a bar restaurant, and I enjoy investing—it's a big part of my life and something I enjoy outside of fighting. I think your career is a marathon and not a sprint—you shouldn't try to rush anything. Certain moments, certain things come and are overwhelming. Whether you're overwhelmed with sadness or losing, you should take a deep breath and relax, these feelings are only temporarily and they go away. Work hard and keep moving forward. Sometimes things in our

minds become greater than what they really are, and if we make quick decisions in those situations sometimes it can change the course of a lot of things. So, I think taking a step back, taking a deep breath and having gratitude of what you need to do and work hard and everything you want will become a reality.

Q: Any particular fighter you'd like to fight? Does a rematch with Conor McGregor invoke your interest?

Alvarez: Yes, that would be nice to be able to have a rematch with Conor or I think the only other fight I'd be aspired to would probably be the Khabib [Nurmagomedov] fight—that would be the only other fight that I'd really want. I think to be able to fight him what they call pound-for-pound GOAT that would be something. I think he's a tough opponent for anyone. He will probably stay retired I think. I don't think there's anything that would draw him back into the sport.

I have a lot of respect for Conor because it's very difficult to be the fighter that you have to be when you have a hundred million dollars in the bank. Being a fighter happen to deal with a lot of "nos" and a lot of rejections, a lot of adversity. And having a hundred million dollars in your bank doesn't bring you any "nos," you don't really have to deal with a lot of adversity anymore, your life changes. So, to voluntarily put yourself in the face of adversity even when you don't have to, and make it a challenge during that moment, I have a high regard and respect for that. It's easy to fight when you have to, but it's not easy to fight when you don't have to. Right now in my career I want to make history in the sport, and I want to make this which will be really difficult to ever replicate. I think winning a belt in every single major promotion is going to be something that's never going to be replicated for a very long time. And I need to stay disciplined and diligent and continue to do what I'm doing so I can do that. And there's not long to go when I can achieve that.

Junior Dos Santos
UFC Heavyweight Champion

Question: Crossover fights have become the norm in combat sports. You wanted to fight in a boxing match with heavyweight boxing champion Anthony Joshua. It's interesting that you actually trained alongside Joshua. Can you tell me more?

Junior Dos Santos: I was there for the Olympics, and he came to Brazil to do some promotion. And I was commentating for the Olympics in Brazil. He was doing some promotional work for Under Armour. We both did a little training together on the beach. That was very cool. He was sharing with me some of his knowledge and we were having a good time together. I enjoyed being there with him and to get to know him. It was a good experience for me, especially because I kind of admire a lot of people in the boxing world and he is a great champion. It was great to have had that time with him.

Q: Joshua recently lost to Usyk. Do you feel he is going to come back stronger—like he did against Andy Ruiz—and be on top again?

Dos Santos: Of course everyone wants to win all the time, but sometimes you find yourself in some difficult challenges and it's normal. I don't think that lost takes anything away from him. I think he's going to comeback a lot stronger, for sure. Winning is the result of good work, good mentality, good state of spirit, many things need to be combined to get a good win, especially on that level of boxing. So, he was always fighting at the highest level and Usyk won the fight against him because he did a good job. But I think Joshua is going to come back stronger and it's going to be interesting to see the rematch.

Q: Speaking of boxing, you have been widely acknowledged by the experts and critics to have the best boxing skills in the UFC. Lately there have been MMA fighters pursuing boxing, such as Vitor Belfort, Tito Ortiz, Anderson Silva, and Tyrone Woodley. You are the perfect specimen to be challenging a top boxer.

Dos Santos: Well, boxing is having a great time right now—it's coming strong. And, like you said, I was always known as a boxing guy in the MMA world. I was always there to knock my opponents out using boxing skills against them and I always did that very well. I had something in my heart that said that one day I would endeavour to fight in a boxing match, but it never happened because I was in the UFC and things were working well for me and I was having a good career. And I didn't just want to step away from that career and have a boxing match, no way! But right now, God knows what he does, I have a lot of faith and I believe things are happening and I will have this chance now to box with boxers. I'm looking forward to boxing. I have a lot of boxing skills, and now I'm especially focusing on pure boxing because before I had to train Muay Thai, jiu-jitsu, wrestling, everything. Now it's only boxing. So I'm going to get even better. Vitor Belfort fought Evander Holyfield, but the thing is, one thing that is important for me is that I'm not merely stepping in the boxing world to make big fights like some of these guys are doing right now to just fight retired guys, or guys who are coming in from the MMA world; I'm stepping into the boxing world to be a challenge for the big names, to become a champion one day. I have a firm belief. I always work so hard in what I'm dedicated to. It's not going to be any different about having a boxing career like I did MMA career—to one day reach the highest point level to be the heavyweight champion of the world for one of the big major organizations, to be fighting maybe Usyk, Tyson Fury, Anthony Joshua, or Deontay Wilder—any one of these guys. I know I've got to build it. I will build it and I'll get there. Of course it's hard for some people to just accept that or just believe that. They can doubt me. But people in general, a lot of people will believe me, will support me. But the majority will doubt me, and they have that right to doubt me. I have a right to believe in myself and make it happen.

Q: Can you comment on Tommy Fury fighting YouTube personality Jake Paul, which has now been cancelled? What do you think about Jake Paul? Should a top boxer or MMA fighter derail the Paul train now?

Dos Santos: Jake Paul and his brother Logan came from nothing, but they're making a lot of money. People want to see it. I see that it's interesting. Jake Paul has fought two MMA guys, one of them was Tyrone Woodley who was a champion in UFC—he was known for having good hands—and Jake Paul won. He's making a lot of noise. It's OK to do it. Now he was fighting Tyson Fury's brother. I think Logan Paul was supposed to fight Anderson Silva. I would like to see that as well. That would be a good fight. When the Logan brothers were challenging MMA guys, they would have never fought me because I'm not like any other MMA fighters; I'm a striking guy as I have boxing skills so they would never fight me. So, I gave them an option. I said to them that we could do ten rounds in a boxing match and I would fight both of them, one each round—so five rounds each guy—where they would switch each round. If one of them gets knocked out early, then the other guy would have to handle it for the rest of the rounds. That's what I told them, but of course they didn't give much attention to that because they know they're not stupid. That original proposal I brought to their attention, I still want to do it today! I would fight both of them the same night.

Q: You fought UFC heavyweight champion Stipe Miocic on more than two occasions, who was also acknowledged as the baddest man on the planet.

Dos Santos: I fought him in 2014. I had an injury because I had torn something, but I was still able to move very well actually. It was a very hard fight we were going against each other very hard. We hurt each other a lot, but at the end of the fight I got the win. It was the toughest fight of my career. Like I said, I had the injury and right after the fight I went back to Brazil and had the surgery. I respect him a lot. I think he's a great fighter and a great human being. He's a great representative of our sport.

Q: Do you feel talent and genetics are vital, or can a fighter, a person, become a professional fighter?

Dos Santos There is a very good phrase that I like: the hard work beats talent when talent doesn't work hard. That's very true. Even if you have good genetics and you have got a lot of skills and you're very good at what you do, but if you don't work hard on the highest level to be who you want to be, to be the champion you want to be, you're not going to be successful. So, genetics help a lot, to have a lot of talent at doing things, but you have to work very hard. You've got to be in shape to go in the ring or the cage and give one hundred percent of yourself. If you're not ready, not in good shape to show the skill and the talent, then you're going to fail.

Q: What was one of the most amazing things when you were fighting in the UFC?

Dos Santos: I think it was life changing. To be in the UFC and to have the results I achieved. I come from a very poor family in a small place, and then I was fighting in the biggest MMA organization in the world. So, for me the power of the media and the exposure you have in the UFC, it's great. There are so many things that impressed me, from how big the UFC was and how things were working. I remember to this day when I had my debut UFC fight. After I knocked my opponent out I was walking out of the cage and one of the UFC organization members looked at me, and he said, "Welcome aboard." I never forgot that phrase. I will never forget what he said to me because it was so amazing, it was so important and I was so nervous because I was fighting in the biggest organization in the world against a guy who was contender for the title at the time. I beat him and for me it was so amazing.

Jan Blachowicz

UFC Light-Heavyweight Champion

Question: Growing up in Poland, you were influenced by action movies from the age of nine, which was a prelude to studying martial arts. Is that true?

Jan Blachowicz: Everybody my age was. We watched *Blood Sport*, *Enter the Dragon*, and we just wanted to be like Jean Claude Van Damme and Bruce Lee. It was the beginning.

Q: Prior to signing up for the UFC, you fought in MMA in Poland. How was MMA perceived in Poland when you started fighting? Did the sport draw the public's ire?

Blachowicz: Everything in the beginning was small—we had small events and one was a bigger event. My first pro fight was in 2007. Before that I was fighting in amateur fights. I signed a contract with KSW in 2007. In the beginning nobody understood the sport in Poland—everyone thought it was just something where two bad (non-skilled and brutal) people are fighting inside the ring. And they would see fighters kick the head, and when they were on the ground the fighter is punching his opponent in the face. The audience knew that it was a tough sport. After a couple of years, people started to understand the sport better and understood that it's a beautiful [technical] sport. Right now people love MMA in Poland and it's a very big sport. When I won the UFC belt and I came back to Poland, first a lot of people came to visit me at the airport. I couldn't believe it. They were singing songs. It was an amazing dream. I went to my hometown, which is a small city on the border of Czech Republic. More than a thousand people came to visit me there in the city center. I think right now I'm kind of a national treasure—that's how I feel. People were in joy and I'm proud of that because I literally made the whole country come to me when I came back with the UFC belt. People came to see me by driving six hours in the car just to take one photo and shake my hand. It's an amazing feeling when people from a different part of Poland come to visit me. I just want to say thank you to all the fans for supporting me and I hope I'm going to continue my journey.

Q: You signed with the UFC in January 2014. Was it a hurdle in achieving this, as I'm sure there are so many fighters around the world who want to be fighting in the world's most prestigious battleground?

Blachowicz: What I remember is—and it's a really nice story—when I signed with the UFC I had an injury. I had a knee operation when I did my medical. I started training again. I was the KSW champion at the time, which is a big organization in Poland so the UFC knew who I was. They knew I was really good. They gave me the chance to fight in the best organization in the world. I had been fighting my whole life and this was a dream come true. I think basically because I was the KSW champion the UFC signed a contract with me.

Q: In March 2018, you fought in London Jimmy Manuwa at *UFC Fight Night*. Can you shed light on what it's like for a UFC fighter to be on the road, traveling abroad?

Blachowicz: It's only a two-hour flight to London from Poland. A lot of Polish people are living in England—a lot of my fans are there also. I like London and England also. I feel great over there. We found some really good restaurants. I'm a fan of Harry Potter so we went to the film studio and checked out the train from the films. I enjoyed a lot of things in England. I love the city. It was very nice when I beat Jimmy. The whole arena was quiet for a moment. It was a very nice feeling. He had beaten me on my ground before and now I beat him on his ground.

So it's one-one now. When I traveled to London—because it's only a two-hour flight—I didn't plan on being there two weeks before the fight to adjust to the climate there. But, only one week before the fight, we trained at the hotel. The UFC arranged everything what we need, so it wasn't a problem to train. I had my training partners, sparring partners, my coaches with me. So I had my whole team with me at the hotel. If it's in Brazil, for example, then I have to be there three weeks before the fight because I have to adjust to the climate and the timing difference.

Q: At UFC 239 (July 2019) in Las Vegas, you beat Luke Rockhold. What did you think of your opponent prior to fighting him?
Blachowicz: I knew he was very good at grappling. He was very good in jiu-jitsu and has really good standup skills—he's southpaw. And everybody told me he's very strong. But people forget that even though he may be strong, I am stronger. So I wasn't afraid of him. My coaches and I watched his fights together. We examined his moves and his mistakes. We knew what we had to do to win against Luke Rockhold. He tried to take me down constantly. He wanted to put me on the ground and finish me on the ground via a submission or ground and pound. But in the first round he caught me. I thought to myself, *OK, maybe he's strong, but not stronger than me. I just have to defend his takedowns.* After the first round finished, I kicked him in the head and knocked him down. I knew that this was the beginning of the end because I realized that when he went to his corner his legs were weak. So I said to myself, *OK, I'm going to hit him on that spot now for maybe two, three minutes and it will be all over.* He tried to take me down again in the second round. I finished him with punches.

Q: Talking of coaches, what advice did your coach impart to you?
Blachowicz: I have up to five coaches. I have a standup coach, jiu-jitsu coach, wrestling coach, conditioning coach, and a head coach— the most important one who connects everything and makes a game plan against an opponent. So, everybody gives advice in what should be done, what to expect and what I'm required to do. Also, what my opponent is capable of doing and what I need to watch out for. So, before a

fight all five coaches do their research and they tell me what to do, what to look out for and what I have to do on fight night. They scream at me in the corner on fight night, "Put your hands up!" and "Now is your time to use your jab! Use your kick!" We work really well together.

Q: UFC 253 (September 2020) was the monumental fight for you against Dominick Reyes, as you were crowned the UFC light-heavyweight champion. Not every fighter gets a title shot. How did you work yourself up?
Blachowicz: I deserved the title shot because I had a good winning streak. I beat a lot of good guys. I had my good manager who spoke to the UFC matchmakers and they had to give me the title shot I believed. Inside the Octagon I proved myself. They had no choice I believe.

Q: Winning the belt has put you on a bigger platform with both the UFC and the fans alike.
Blachowicz: I believe I'm going to keep the belt till end of my career. I don't know how many more years I'm going to fight, maybe three or four years more. I believe I will keep the belt right till the end when my career ends. I believe I can and that nobody can take it away from me.

Q: You broke Dominick's nose in the fight. Fighters get injured in the Octagon, of course. During the fight, did he realize his nose was broken or was it after the fight?
Blachowicz: I think he knew because his nose was badly broken—it wasn't just a minor injury. I think he said to himself, *OK, this is the end.* He felt if he didn't survive this round he wouldn't make it to the third round. That was in my head. I was also thinking in my head that now I have to be careful because he's going to put everything he's got against me as he only had maybe one minute left. That this was his one chance to try to knock me out. So this is something I had to be aware of in that moment. But I knew he was hurt, with the broken nose, and so I thought I'll finish him in this round and it will be all over very soon. A few seconds later, I beat him on the ground with punches.

Q: On that note, let's talk about aggression. So you're saying he went into top gear? How does a fighter control the aggression in a fight—as you're under emotional stress—knowing it can have an adverse effect?

Blachowicz: You need to control your emotions every time, not just in the fight—before the fight, but also in the fight. Because if you don't control this, like you said, you can make mistakes and lose the fight. So you need to know when to release the aggression and unload everything on your opponent, and say to yourself, *OK, now.* This is something you have to learn. It's something you work out in your head, mental training, to control your emotions. Everybody is a little bit different. I tell you this but someone might tell you something completely different. I'm telling you how I think, my way is good.

Q: Jon Jones left the light-heavyweight division. You have been vocal about fighting him.

Blachowicz: After I beat Cory Anderson he promised me that I'm going to be next for him. What does he do? He goes into the heavyweight division. So maybe in the future I can also go into the heavyweight division so I can catch him there. Right now I'm staying in 205. I hope I am a longtime champion of this division.

Q: You have a fight coming up with Israel Adesanya, who is undefeated. He's a skinny fighter, but very good. Can you say with certitude that you are going to be able to handle him?

Blachowicz: He will be defeated soon. He is skinny. He's really good with amazing striking skills. He has weird striking—you've got all types of striking styles. He's also tall and has a reach. It's going to be a good fight I think, which fans are going to like and talk about for a long time. I like fighting standup. He also likes fighting standup. So I think it's going to be a standup battle like my previous fights. If I'm going to have a chance for a takedown, I will take him down because if I take him down my ground game is going to be much better than his. And in standup, we will see because it's 50/50. But on the ground if I take him down then it's going to be my territory. But as I said, I like to fight standup and I'm able to control the opponent by kicks and by using my fists. This is the short way game plan.

Q: As a professional UFC fighter, certain qualities are imperative—power, speed, endurance. How would you discern between power and speed?

Blachowicz: Every fighter uses different skills. Someone is very quick, someone is very strong, and then you have fighters who are strong and quick. I think I'm very strong and I have very good timing. I 'read' the fighter and know what to do in the fight. A lot of the times fighters in a fight don't know what to do when things go wrong; I know what to do. I always have a plan B, plan C, and I know how to use my skills in a fight.

Q: Can you tell me one of the most compelling stories while fighting in the UFC, and what would you say is the most important thing in your career? I mean, some fight for the belt, while others do it for the money or prestige, etc.

Blachowicz: Right now, what can I tell you? I don't know what to say. I will keep this a secret. You have to connect everything—money, the belt, this is the best job for me because I love to do this and don't have to. It's a pleasure to fight and it's something I love to do. So, if I connect all these elements they are important—not only the money, not only the belt.

Q: World's strongest man Mariusz Pudzianowski from Poland has been fighting in MMA. What can you tell me about him as a fighter, the distinction between his earlier fights and present-day performance?

Blachowicz: When he was training he trained in our gym with us. When he started MMA he was only strong, but right now he knows how to use his power. He knows how to move on the ground. He knows how to move in standup. He's got pretty good wrestling. So, right now he has trained MMA for more than ten years. Now he's a much better fighter than he was in the beginning. In the beginning his cardio was weak, but now it's pretty good.

Alexander Volkanovski

UFC Featherweight Champion

Question: Alexander, before pursuing MMA you actually played rugby. How and why did you make the transition at the age of twenty-two?

Alexander Volkanovski: Yeah. I played rugby league, which is a popular sport in Australia, during most of my teens till I was twenty-two. I played with my friends. It's something I was pretty good at. I was pretty handy playing in the front row forward—one of the big boys in the frontline—where you take the ball up. So, that was my position. Then I decided to do MMA and it's all fallen in place for me. Now I fight in the featherweight division. I went from 97 kg (215lb) playing rugby league to fighting at 66 kg (145lb) in the UFC. It's a crazy transition but a good one because rugby is a tough sport. You have to be, I wouldn't say "rough," but it's a very physical sport and made me who I am. Again, I'm used to these big boys because that's the position I played, and the featherweights in the UFC are tiny compared to what I was used to.

Q: Your first pro fight in MMA was in 2012. Can you tell me the initial feeling of entering the cage back then? Not everyone training MMA competes and experiences the brutality that a competitor experiences.

Volkanovski: It's definitely different. You transition from a team sport to being the only one in the cage where it's all up to you. If you make a mistake, that's on you—no one to back you up. It's pretty confronting, you

know, and my first time the emotions were like a rollercoaster. I was thinking, *What am I doing?* And the next minute you're pumping yourself up.
Like I said, it's a crazy rollercoaster of emotion. It's definitely different to
a team sport, that's why I love MMA. I'm competing by myself, which is
something that I love about the sport. It's all on you the fact if you put in
the work, you benefit from that. If you don't put in the work, it's on you.
If you lose or make a mistake, you don't let anyone else down but yourself.

**Q: Despite Australia's low population, which is only 25 million—
USA has 360 million and the UK 70 million—why has there been
surge of interest in UFC in Australia? It holds the world attendance
record over 56,000 in Sydney. Your first four UFC fights were in
Australia and New Zealand.**
Volkanovski: I think the fighters play a part. It's always been very big
and grown very fast. We've got champions and very high-level fighters, very competitive athletes doing really well in the UFC. And as the
fighters were fighting the sport was gaining more and more following.
We have Robert Whitaker who's a champion—and I'm a champion. So,
Australia was always going to be big. I guess the Australians love their
boxing and they love their contact sports—and the rugby, too. I think
the UFC was always going to be a hit in Australia. And the fact that we
have UFC champions here, it's definitely helped to grow the sport here.
I fought in the arena in Australia in my first UFC fight. It was a great
opportunity to do this and good to have the locals in attendance—the
whole arena was packed and as I was walking out I was feeling the buzz
and the energy from the crowd. As I'm walking out, I usually try to hold
it in because I don't want the emotions to fly. Once the fight is over, I
really got to soak in that Ozzie crowd. It was unbelievable just to soak
all that up. The crowd was incredible. It means a lot to be competing in
front of a home crowd. I'm hoping we can do all that again soon.

**Q: When you were young, did you often get involved in street
altercations?**
Volkanovski: Yes. Again, being young I guess living in a town where
rugby league was big—some say our area was rough sort of a town—I

was never the type of guy who went around starting the fights or anything like that. I've always been against that. But I'll be lying if I said I didn't get involved and to defend myself. I wouldn't say I had a chip on my shoulder, but I guess you can say I had a bit of a reputation. The fights would come to you and I wasn't the type to back down. So, it's not something I like to talk and brag about, because I like to keep the fighting in the Octagon. Being young and silly and with a lot of people and kids around, we used to get into street fights. I've always known how to handle myself, that's why I started MMA—I felt I was pretty good. It's funny that a lot of trouble would find me before I started training in MMA, but as soon as I started training in MMA and fighting professionally—and obviously I got a reputation of being an MMA fighter—a lot of people always ask me, "Do people ever try to test themselves with you?" But I've never had that. Never had anyone try that because they feel I'm a UFC fighter and want to find out how I would do. I think a lot of people expect that to happen, but I've never had that problem of people trying to confront me since I've been a UFC fighter. I don't know what it is, whether it's because it's a whole another level that no one wants to mess with or just, again, the respect, or whatever it is. It's funny. When we were younger, yeah, trouble would find me and, let's just say, I had to teach them a lesson. Now, we [UFC fighters] try to do our best to avoid that type of confrontation outside the Octagon.

Q: You beat Jose Aldo at UFC 237 (May 2019) in Rio de Janeiro. Can you tell me the great significance of having this bout manifest into a reality?

Volkanovski: I had fought in America before, but Rio was the first time I had ever been to Brazil. It was the first time for me to be sort of competing at an odd time. I was scheduled to fight at one in the morning so I tried to adjust not only to the weather, but sleep schedule. I tried to keep myself awake one or two in the morning and then go to sleep. So I was sleeping at odd times. My body clock was awake ready to fight come fight time one in the morning. So I had to make sure I was sleeping right by adjusting the sleeping routine. It was definitely different. And obviously knowing that I'm going to Rio to fight a hometown hero—a local hero—it was a crazy experience. But it was something that needed to be done. That fight is what got me the number-one contender spot, so I knew it had to be done. That's the type of fighter I am. I've got to do it and I'm not going to find the easy path. I felt this is going to lead me to the title. I thought I'll fight him when not many people would fight him in his hometown. The crowd was screaming, "You're going to die!" The whole arena was screaming like that, but I was mentally prepared for that ready to go.

Q: At UFC 245 (December 2019) in Las Vegas, you dethroned Max Holloway to clinch the UFC featherweight championship belt. Tell me about that moment.

Volkanovski: The first fight with Max was a big fight. People thought in the featherweight division he was untouchable. But we knew that we had the skill—and we had him figured out. When you're at that level, we knew the little things he was going to do and what he does well, and we need to nullify that. We knew what we do well and just play our game. I was able to shut him down and make him fight my fight. The game plan was good, not just the exchange, but every time there was an exchange I'd always get the upper hand. I always ended up finishing him with the last punch. Just things like that. It was a chess battle in there, but it was something that I had control in the whole fight, and we knew it. It was a messy fight, a fight for the title and a great opportunity, but it was just another fight for me. At that stage of the fight, I was as normal as I ever was. I showed my composure and stuck to my game plan. As I say, after all that, once I get the belt wrapped around my waist, I then soak up the energy and take it all in. It was just another fight against the champion, that's the type of mindset I have. I won't let occasions sort of derail me. I won't react differently or won't let these emotions take me in the wrong direction purely because of the status of a fight or that I'm the top person in the division. It's my job—it's what I need to do. I take a real professional route to success and this showed at that fight.

Q: Tell me about the second fight between you two, at UFC 251 (July 2020). Would I be right in saying you both agreed to a rematch at the post-fight press conference of the first fight?

Volkanovski: Dana White pretty much wanted to give him the rematch straight away. Pretty much before I went to the press conference, he was like, *Let's do the rematch.* At the time, I was like, *If we want to do rematch, let's do it, whatever.* It's funny that some fighters don't get immediate rematches but Max did. Great things were happening in our division and the UFC wanted to give him that rematch. At the end of the day, I thought I will fight, no worries. I will go out and do it again. Obviously I won again. Now they want another rematch. Max is getting treated to all these rematches it's like he's a spoilt grandchild who gets whatever he wants, rematch after rematch. Not many people are given these opportunities, but "Grandpa" Dana likes to spoil him. Anyway, I've got two on Holloway, but I've got Brian Ortega next. Whether further down the track Max Holloway rematch happens or not, we'll see. Right now I've got Ortega on my mind. That's it. July was a close fight—very competitive. Obviously Max made some adjustments after his first defeat, that shows you what kind of a fighter he is—great fighter. I made adjustments, too, and I got the job done.

Q: You have been vocal about fighting Conor McGregor to solidify your position as the GOAT in the featherweight division. Would you go up to lightweight division to fight him?
Volkanovski: Yeah. I've already taken out the GOATs of my division. They say Jose Aldo was a GOAT, and then Max Holloway—I beat both of them, one twice. Fighting Conor, who is another featherweight champion, would make sense because so I'll have taken out all the featherweight champions worthy of GOAT. That's definitely a fight I'd like to have not only because of the money fight, but to get the status. It will be a great opportunity to do that. But right now I don't think Conor can make it to 145 pounds, so I've got my eye on the featherweight division. I've got my eye on Ortega. Then I've got my eye on the next contender, whoever is after that. The year 2021 is going to be a year I'm going to have a few big fights. Then I'll solidify myself as the GOAT end of the year, and then opportunities like Conor McGregor in the lightweight division will come.

Daniel Cormier

UFC Heavyweight and Light-Heavyweight Champion

Question: Daniel, you recently retired from the Octagon in 2020, but continue to work as an analyst for the UFC. You get to witness behind-the-scenes situations. Can you share any interesting anecdotes?

Daniel Cormier: I think as an analyst, one of the guys who has been on both sides of the coin, from going in there as an athlete to broadcasting side of things, seeing the difference, especially for me the difference in between the way I feel in terms of the nerves and the anxiety, it's insane to be going into an event as a fighter. Then as being a broadcaster, the comfort you have almost feels going into the fight without having to be the one there to actually fight, it's been fantastic. I love my job. I love what I do. I'm very lucky. I think Max Holloway's fight against Calvin Kattar I watched as an analyst recently was all-on fight and absurd. Just to watch him throw seven hundred strikes in that fight and do what he supposed to do in the way he did it, that was absurd to watch. It was great to see Max put everything together.

Q: You've got a great relationship with Khabib Nurmagomedov. His fight against Conor McGregor will forever be perceived as an all-time classic. Tell me about being around Khabib, the vibe.

Cormier: There are ton of things that go on in the gym every day. It's a family in our gym, we enjoy it. We love to kind of give it as we take it. It's fantastic. I love being part of AKA (American Kickboxing Academy) and be part of the team I've been in. But just watching Khabib and those guys every day come into San Jose, you see the camaraderie those guys bring from Russia into San Jose. And you can only be in awe of and appreciate the relationship these guys have for each other. It was a great fight. We were happy the way it played out between him and Conor. He implemented the game plan that he had ahead of him and got the victory. It was a tough fight. Conor showed why he was special for so long, but vast majority of the time Khabib knows what he does. Khabib is the best fighter in the world. He dominates guys, world-class fighters, in ways that nobody else can do. It was very exciting for me, as his friend, to see him get success on that level.

Q: Khabib is currently undefeated. It seems like he wasn't given a chance to capture the belt until late, maybe he should've been given a chance earlier on, but maybe UFC was fearful he would defeat their golden boy Conor McGregor—the cash cow. Do you feel some people underestimated him before that fight in certain respects?
Cormier: I don't think that. I don't think anybody had underestimated him. I think you know it takes time to get to that title fight. It was a time for him to build himself into the fighter that he became. By the time he got to his title shot, he was ready. Do I think he would've been a champion had he fought earlier [for the title]? Yes. But by the time he got the belt he was complete. He was the fighter that you guys know and love then, there was no doubt he could get the job done then. He was a totally different person when he beat Al Aqunita, to beat Conor, to beat Poirier, and beat Gaethje. So, the timing was what it was. It was always a matter of when Khabib got the opportunity to fight for the belt that he'd become the UFC lightweight champion.

Q: Can or should Khabib, who is by some placed on a pedestal, come back, or would this depend on the right fighter to face him?
Cormier: I think it would have to be the right man. To be honest with you, it just doesn't feel like he wants to fight anymore. We just kind of have to let him go through the process of what he wants to do. If he decides he wants to, he can come back into the title fight, which will be

his. As long as he's around, he can be involved. He doesn't have to rush. He can take his time and do what he wants to do. And if he ever wants to fight, let's just see what happens.

Q: Do you feel Conor McGregor was merely putting on his persona when he fought Khabib, but the latter took it seriously?

Cormier: No. The whole thing was, there was a build-up to the Khabib-Conor fight and it was too much. Conor went too far. You can build a fight but you can also go way too far. I believe everything that happened after the fight was because of the things said by Conor in the build-up. Those are the types of things that you say that are never forgotten the moment the fight ends. When you attack religion, family, all those things, it's taking it too far. I do believe that there was a time for McGregor when everything was just build-up, because he said it in the fight in the Octagon to Khabib. He said, "Its only business." This was when they were breaking at the fence at one point in the fight. For these guys, it's not. For some people it's not. Khabib is so devout to his religion, you're attacking him and it's absolutely uncalled for. It was too much. Khabib taught him a lesson, That might be the case. I think there's a balance where Conor can still be himself but not have to go to extreme. Certain things are awful—you don't talk about a man's religion and his family, that's not good.

Q: You had some epic fights during your career. Stipe Miocic, the current UFC heavyweight champion, you defeated and then lost twice. And you fought Jon Jones twice, considered by many the GOAT. Tell me about Stipe when you faced him.

Cormier: When I fought Stipe the first time, I had the opportunity to do something special. When you're the champ in light-heavyweight class then go up to heavyweight division, you understand what you stand. You understand that you're on something special. I was very aware of this. I was excited about it, just knew then that if I can accomplish this it will forever leave me in the history of the MMA in what I would accomplish. I went out there and got the job done. Every time with the game plan the coach gave me advice. Bob Cook, Xavier Mendez, and

Rick Sanchez are all my coaches. They develop a game plan for me to fight and for this fight it was: be fast, punch when you fighting out of the clinch—it was just "be yourself." We really came up with a great idea of how to approach this fight.

Q: In your two rematches—UFC 241 (August 2019) and exactly a year later, at UFC 252 (August 2020)—you suffered defeats. He's a fighter who is, by and large, undefeatable so these battles were definitely challenging for you.
Cormier: He got better. From fight one to fight two to fight three. And he constantly just worked to get better and I found him much tougher by the end of the fights. I saw a lot of different things from him that went into second fight and then also the third fight. Hands up to all of his coaches and him, they developed a great game plan that allowed him to win these fights. They weren't easy fights. Stipe had to go through a lot in order to win those fights. He showed why he's the champion and the greatest heavyweight champion the UFC has ever seen.

Q: What would you say is the greatest life lesson you've learned?
Cormier: To live in the moment. Live in the opportunity you have because the reality is, it can be fast—one day you're here, the next day you're about to retire. So, it's just like make sure you're living in the moment what you supposed to live in, in those times, in those opportunities, and don't look at the future too much. Because if you look at the future, keep chasing it, next thing you know you're at the end of the line, you never really enjoy the process. So enjoy the process.

Q: Is traveling a hurdle for you?
Cormier: I don't mind the travel. It is what it is, but it comes with the job. I know what I have to do in order to prevail into where I need to be and provide for my family.

Q: The two Jon Jones fights were epic. In terms of rivalries, do you feel literally 90 percent of the rival fighters actually have respect for each other and the disdain they show is merely a

stunt? I mean, other than Khabib and McGregor, which was as real as it can get.

Cormier: It's the same attitude afterward; rivalries don't just die. In real situations like this they don't just die. Just because the fight's over it doesn't mean that we are just OK. In a lot of incidents like that, some of them are for show to make money, but not all of them are. All the stuff that went into the Jon Jones fight before we got into the Octagon was not the best. The ugliness of that rivalry, but we made a ton of money. But it was a bad time to be in those fights, have all this bad blood between the two of us was terrible, but the fights were fun. I enjoyed the preparation. I loved the fact the fights were so big. And it is what it is. I think I finally managed to put all those issues to bed. So, I'm lucky that not many fighters go on to a second career [as a UFC analyst]. The UFC does really well on pay-per-view that's why becoming the champion is so important.

When you become the champion, you become a partner and you have to be lucky to be part of that—if you want to try to be part of that pie. I was lucky. In my second fight with Jon Jones, there were no surprises—he didn't surprise me. I think the guy's a fantastic fighter, he always has been. He won the fight—that was a surprise to me, considering we've seen the guy win fights his entire career. It was a good fight and I was lucky to be on that stage and fight him, to be able to compete at the level I competed at. It also gave us both the chance to win. I thought the fight started really good. I felt I was on track in what I wanted him to do, but when you're fighting and it's between two great fighters, something isn't guaranteed. It can be great for you at the start but eventually you can get derailed. The entire time what happened to me in the fight, it can happen to Jon Jones as it can take one shot to win the fight.

Q: In sports and the UFC, performance enhancing drugs are not uncommon for some athletes to resort to. Jon Jones was banned because of this. The belt was reinstated to you after he tested positive. What are your sentiments on this issue, and how can we tackle it moving forward?

Cormier: That's cheating! The best thing you can do is keep USADA (United States Anti-Doping Agency).

Q: What was the monumental achievement in your storied career?

Cormier: Winning all those championships. That was the best time, heavyweight and the light-heavyweight championship. I'm one of a few people who have held two division titles at the same time in the UFC. I was the only one to hold the light heavyweight and heavyweight at the same time—no one's done that before. I've held two belts simultaneously, and Conor held two belts at same time in two different divisions. I'm not surprised that the UFC has become huge when you've got a guy like Dana White who is so determined to make this product what it is today. I'm not surprised by anything besides us [fighters]. There are a lot of times when you will have a star in the UFC and he walks away and everybody talks about him saying, "UFC's done! It's over!" And a new guy shows up, or a new girl shows up, it's about building this company into a worldwide organization that has every aspect of fighting of the word. I think Dana has lead the charge he just won't allow it to fail. It just continues to get bigger and bigger it's because everybody love watching a good fight. The stars are built, stars come, stars go, main events come, main events go, but the UFC continues to really make its mark on the sports world.

Q: Have you met Mike Tyson and, in your view, would he have triumphed in the Octagon?

Cormier: I have. He had power, right. I believe he was such a fantastic athlete he would've been fine. I think Mike Tyson could've done anything he set his mind to. So there was potential. He would have to learn [grappling] and he would have to really focus on all aspects of fighting. You just can't just do this half-assed. You've got to be completely committed to it. So, he could have prevailed but he would have to be full on training.

Petr Yan

UFC Bantamweight Champion

Question: Growing up as a kid and teenager, did you go to MMA shows and watch the UFC? If so, what inspired you about the sport? Your older brother, who was training in boxing, refused to take you to a boxing gym? Can you shed some light on that as well?
Petr Yan: When I was kid, I never watched MMA, because I was doing boxing and was 100 percent focused and interested only in boxing at that time. Because my brother refused to take me to boxing class with him, I had to secretly follow him to the gym and sign up for the class by myself. After two weeks of training, I won my first competition. And only after that he admitted that I'm his brother to the coach.

Q: Can you tell me more about your childhood?
Yan: Yeah, when I was a kid and studied in school, of course, I had some fights. I think every boy went through it and had situations like that. It's not a big deal, that's how our character was tempered, that's how boys become men. Because we moved a lot, every time in the new school classmates were trying to pick on the new guy, so I had to fight with them and defend myself.

Q: You started fighting professionally in Russia in MMA from 2013, until you signed for the UFC five years later. Can you tell me about the MMA scene there at the time?
Yan: At that time, MMA was just starting to grow as a sport in the

country. There were a lot of amateur tournaments that I took part in and gained some experience, after that I started fighting professionally. I realized it's something that I like, because in MMA you can mix different martial arts styles and it's a sport where I could make a name for myself. It was something new and really motivated me.

Q: As far as MMA clubs and fighters in Russia, what is the caliber compared to, let's say, in the USA?

Yan: Right now, in Russia, there's a lot of fight clubs, many young people training martial arts. And you can say that MMA is arguably the number-one sport in the country. In every region, MMA classes are packed. That's why I believe Russia has very strong fighters, and in near future every major MMA organization will have more champions and contenders from Russia. Judo and sambo are very popular in Russia. Judo is an Olympic discipline, sambo is a national martial art, also Greco-Roman and freestyle wrestling are very popular in Russia, too. As you know, we have many world and Olympic champions in these sports.

Q: Compared to other sports, how would you say MMA and the UFC has grown in popularity now in Russia?

Yan: Since the UFC arrived in Russia MMA has started to become more popular in my country. Many new gyms and promotions have opened up. Like I said, I believe MMA is the number-one combat sport in the country and it's still growing. Everyone knows about MMA, UFC, and martial arts right now.

Q: You have a degree in physical culture and sport. Eastern Europeans seem to gravitate toward physical exercise, weight lifting, and grappling sports. Is this somewhat part of the culture?

Yan: Yes. I was studying in a physical culture university for five years and I specialized in youth boxing coaching. Russians love not only combat, but all different kinds of sports. You can say it's a big part of culture here. Almost every guy involved in different kinds of physical activity.

Q: In September 2018, you beat Jin Soo Son in Moscow at *UFC Fight Night*. Can you tell me about the atmosphere in the arena?

Yan: It was the first historical UFC event in Russia, and I was lucky to be part of that big event. I fought a very good opponent and we won "Fight of the Night" bonus, and I believe I made myself known on a large scale. Atmosphere was amazing the stadium was packed with more than 20,000 fans. And when you fight in your own homeland and the whole crowd supports you, it feels amazing.

Q: You beat Urijah Faber at UFC 245 (December 2019) in Las Vegas. Can you share your thoughts pertaining to this fight?

Yan: At UFC 245, I fought Faber who I won with a head kick KO. In that fight I was in my control the whole time. I had great preparation. I was confident and ready. It was my first time in UFC when I didn't have any injuries before the fight. I knew that Urijah is an experienced fighter and may surprise me, so I couldn't underestimate him and take it easy. You can say that this fight happened on my field for most of the time, striking technique is what I focus on for a very long time, so this contest went in my favor.

Q You've been vocal, claiming Henry Cejudo has ducked you. Why do you think this is?

Yan: Henry Cejudo was talking a lot, but when our division got filled with many dangerous contenders who can give him many problems, he decided to run away. And after he left, he is still talking about how he could beat everyone. But everyone knows if the fighter truly believed he could dominate everyone in his division, he wouldn't retire but he would've proved it with his actions and not twitter posts. He is "triple clown" is all I can say about him.

Q: At UFC 251 (July 2020), you beat Jose Aldo to win the vacant bantamweight championship belt. Can you please talk me through the fight? What trouble did you give him, and vice versa?

Yan: I didn't need better motivation than fighting for the belt. Also, two weeks before the fight, my second son was born, and it gave me an even bigger boost. I wanted to prove to everyone in the world that I deserve to win this belt. We used to train with Aldo before when I was younger and he was better than me in some aspects, but I knew that now I have become more experienced, stronger and versatile so I believed in my win. Jose Aldo gave me some problems in the fight, he is a tough guy—you all know that he is made of steel. He finished many people and has knockout power in his hands and legs. That's why this fight was very hard, we were going toe-to-toe and, in the end, I found keys to defeat him and finished the fight to win the championship.

Q: Dana White said the referee, Leon Roberts, should've stopped the fight earlier, because you spent round five ground and pounding Jose. Can you give me your opinion if the fight should have stopped earlier or not?

Yan: Yes, you can make a point that the fight should've been stopped one minute earlier, but at least right now there are new questions: who was the winner in that fight? And Jose's last fight showed that he didn't receive damage that affected him in the long term. I believe people should talk more about the fight itself, not the stoppage.

Q: What's the best decision you've ever made as far as your life or in relation to your fight career?

Yan: The best decision I made is when I decided to switch from boxing to MMA. It resulted in me becoming UFC world champion and most importantly that martial arts became a very big and important part of my life.

CHAPTER FOUR:
NEW ERA WOMEN CHAMPIONS

Holly Holm

UFC Women's Bantamweight Champion

Question: We know you have a boxing background. How difficult was it to make the transition into MMA?

Holly Holm: I actually boxed at a kickboxing and MMA gym when I trained. So I was around MMA. I would spar with them. I had a fight coming up and one of my colleagues was fighting, who was my sparring partner, and she said you have size and that I should do MMA. I just wanted to make sure I was really passionate about it and not just kind of curious. Over time, I got really drawn to it that I thought, *Yeah, I want to try this out.* It's one of those things I kept on thinking more and more about and was passionate about.

Q: Let's broach a subject what many considered controversial, pertaining to women fighting in the UFC. Women have been embraced by many now, which is a good sign.

Holm: I felt it would get there eventually no matter what. I had confidence in that. I know there are women in the UFC and other organizations. The thing is women are very passionate. So, when you're passionate about something, I know that you put the hard work into it. They're passionate about MMA and training very hard and people like watching them So, I know it was just a matter of time women were going to be headlining fights and be on top, the more they took to do it. I also think that I don't mind earning my way up. I don't mind working hard and earning my shot. I work hard as well. I think that women are just so motivated and being emotional creatures that we are, I think in fighting you have to have emotion. You have to have that thing that you want to win and do well. We are in there becoming superstars and people actually want to see us fight.

Q: At UFC 193 (November 2015), when you dethroned Ronda Rousey in Melbourne, it broke the arena attendance record when over 56,000 people attended. What can you tell me about pre-fight, in terms of your perception of your adversary—who was a huge name and essentially considered unbeatable?

Holm: One thing about her that I saw was she was so good at her specific skills set. I just felt like one thing that makes such a person so difficult is no matter what you do they're so good at it. So, she has her arm-bars and judo throws perfected. That's the scariest even though her opponents know that it's coming, she was always getting away with it. And then on the other hand, I guess it's more of a simple game plan because you know what your opponent is good at. Sometimes a fighter is a real scrappy fighter and they've got submissions, chokes, arm-bars and they've got knockouts, those people are kind of hard to train for. Only because it's hard to have a real straight simple game plan. Against Ronda you better be ready for what she's good at, but at least you know what you should be training for.

Q: Any compelling behind-the-scenes anecdotes you can share with me leading up to that fight?

Holm: Right before the fight, every time I was training when I would run I would picture her in my head, like her coming in and being aggressive—she's an aggressive fighter. And I would picture countering her. I would picture kind of doing my thing and staying focused. The closer I got to the fight, I knew I was ready. I think the more I felt ready the more that she realized I wasn't just coming in to participate; I was coming in there with every intention of winning. A lot of these girls that fought her, they just wanted to see how far they could maybe make it in the fight. There were women out there going in there with no expectations to win. And if you don't walk in there with every intention of winning, you won't. If you don't think you can do it, how are you going to win? So, the more close I got to the fight the more I was zeroing in on it and staying focused. I think she definitely realized that. The day before the fight, we had a face-off and I could kind of feel the energy. I could tell she was a little on a different type of energy than normal. I told my coach, "I think she knows she's in for a real fight this time." And that I'm not just assuming she'll beat me already. That I'm going for the gold. And we were talking about this. The very next day at the weigh-ins, she got right in my face, which was very fun, by the way. Some may have felt it was very disrespectful of her and that I was mad at her, but no. When you're close to a fight and you're ready to go, it's fun. It was real. It's happening. It's right in front of my face. That moment, I actually loved it. I wasn't mad at all. I was ready to go right in. I felt alive. After the weigh-ins, I told my coach that. He said, "Holly, you're going to do it. I just know it." I knew that as an emotional person there are two things. Some people who are really emotional or fight out of fear, fight really well. Then some get emotional but their emotions get the better of them. They can't control that fire. I knew that if I stayed focused, and what I needed to do during all this, when the fight starts I knew she was going to be emotional—she will want to come at me and she will fight with emotion, but I made sure I won't get wrapped in it. That's what I did and the fight kind of panned out the way I wanted it to.

Q: You broke Ronda down in the Octagon. Were there any surprises or drastic measures taken?

Holm: For the fight I think we trained correctly. Sometimes for a fight you train a certain way, and you get into the fight and nothing is happening the way you pictured it. So you have to change your game plan right there in the middle of the fight. For this fight everything kind of panned out how we thought it was going to go. It was right on our game plan. She comes in very hard and aggressive. We felt I had to be ready for that. So I had to act quickly when she did that because there is just no time to feel her out or move around slowly. I knew she was going to come in right away. So I was ready for it. My coach told me a few days before the fight when I was training. Mike Winkeljohn and Greg

Jackson helped me so much who were my main coaches for this fight. Also my wrestling coach, Israel Martinez, and my grappling coach from Gracie Barra were Rafael and Roberto. I even trained with a judo coach. I had all the help in the world. Greg did a lot of arm-wraps with me, showing me if you do this she's going to do that. A lot of clinch work. Everybody was talking about arm-bar defense. Yes, we worked on that, but we were more focused on not getting into that situation to begin with. Why wait to get there and then try to prevent it? Let's just try to prevent it before that even happens. So, that was a lot of our skill sets. A lot of her adversaries before that were kind of working on the arm-bar defenses, but we were working on not getting into that position.

When I fought Christy Martin in boxing it was play—seven years before this fight. She was swinging and I was getting under her punches. And I was literally just watching her throw the end of a punch. I would slip under and angle. I had it timed so well. I remember this and Mike was holding the pads for me one day, and he said, "Holly, you're going to have your timing so well there's going to be a Christy Martin moment again. You're going to be defending her punches she's going to be swinging." I remember in the fight when Ronda came real hard at me, she tried throwing that real hard hook and I slipped under. I knew I've got the timing right and just stayed focused, and thought we're doing what we're supposed to be doing.

Q: Why do you think Ronda Rousey stood out from the rest of the female fighters and became the number-one star in the sport?
Holm: I think she wasn't afraid to do things—she was confident. She wasn't afraid to take charge from the get-go. She was headlining cards from the get-go. A lot of females had never been there. Some people can't handle that pressure. She didn't mind it. She liked the attention and she did well with it. She liked being in that spotlight—a lot of people don't do well with it. She wasn't afraid to go in there and be the first girl to headline a card in the UFC, take charge of it and own it. And not just believed in it but she acted upon it. She was winning. She was showing everybody they need to watch her: why she had the opportunity, why she was the first girl in the UFC, why she was this

icon, why she was such a sought out fighter people loved to watch her. She was selling out cards. She was beating everybody quickly. It started to become a thing where people started to think, *How long do you think this will actually last?* People were already assuming she was going to win. I respect that about her that she took it on full force and owned it.

A lot of people can't just go in there and believe there's something special and make something happen. So, it became a thing people wanted to watch her. I watched her. I thought, *I wonder if I would get in there one day in a position to be fighting her.* I started MMA at age thirty. I didn't really know if we would end up fighting each other when I first started MMA. She had this confidence about her, whether you loved her, hated her, it didn't matter. She's done a lot for the sport because it's brought a lot of attention to women's MMA. However, in there had to be other people, too. I think she inspired some women. Other women thought, *I could do that, why can't I do it?* Then they started to train harder, and the more you see yourself capable you think you can do this, too. So, a lot of girls in MMA that are coming up are getting better and better because they saw that, and it's a possibility to fight on the biggest stage.

Q: At UFC 196 (March 2016) in Las Vegas, you faced off against Meisha Tate. What can you share with me about that fight?
Holm: There was so much going on in my life—a lot of things before the fight and after the fight. I honestly just remember that after the [Ronda] fight, I said I'm not going to be a one-hit wonder. I'm not going in there just to win the belt and lose it, then just walk away. I know that I was winning the fight till she finished me. I told myself we need more mat time. I wish I could have that fight back, that's for sure. But a lot of these experiences are part of the journey no matter what. And I've learned from it. I think it's also shown people no matter what, I learned more from losing that fight because I knew I still needed to learn more on the ground. I still feel that way today. I still want to learn even more on my feet. I feel after this fight, I needed to dig deep and I'm not going to quit but keep going. I know there's going to be criticism, but it doesn't matter because this is my life and I am going to live it how I

want to. I'm going to do what my passions are. I'm going to get better and move forward.

Q: What's life like as a female UFC fighter?
Holm: For me, I have always had a lot of support in what I do from my family, friends and fans. I was married, but I'm divorced now. There were certainly different challenges when I was married. There's definitely a life outside of fighting you're going to have to deal with. I guess I was just kind of focused. There is a personal life outside of professional life no matter what you're doing, be it working in an office, you could be running a multi-million dollar company or a small family business or be a fighter. It's all the same and we need to balance it. I think every person in life has to learn to balance personal and professional life. If you're so obsessed with one or the other, you can get anywhere professionally. On the other side, you can get so focused on your professional life you are missing out on so many things in your personal life. So, it is something I always try to keep a balance on. I listen to myself—if I need to put more time in my personal life or in training. That can be one goal or it can be daily goals. Sometimes I get up I'm ready to train, but for a minute I think I need to slow down a little, take a deep breath and not overdo it. Sometimes when my emotions get too high, there's always going to be a way to get through it, always going to be a tomorrow. Things might feel like life can feel so hard sometimes, and no matter what we are going to have to make it through. Just to take the moment and day of the time to live, that has helped me a lot. Not think about the end all the time. You cannot think so much of the future that you're letting go what's happening right now.

Q: At UFC 246 (January 2020) against Raquel Pennington, were there any complications surrounding this fight that some may be unaware of?
Holm: My first fight in the UFC was with her, so this was going to be my first rematch in MMA. I had never had a rematch. She's a very tough fighter, very scrappy. Our first fight was a split decision. I really felt it shouldn't have been, but I felt I can make it clear the second time round.

I thought she would be coming into the fight with more emotion as she wanted to avenge her loss. It was my job not to let her do that. Then about four weeks before my fight, my father had a really bad stroke. So at my training camp, I was spending nights in the hospital and spending the days in training. It was a very challenging time, but I knew my dad would want me to pursue my dreams. So it made it easy at least training for the fight. I felt I needed to go in there with a mentality that I have learned much since the first time I fought her. I would focus on training at the camp, but when I was with my dad I would focus on him. For this fight I felt lonely in the training camp. I was definitely on my own I was in a situation I wasn't familiar with. I felt like this is something I have to do and make it through. When I got to the fight I felt ready and focused. I had all these things going on outside but I also had a feeling of fire in me. Last thing I needed was a loss. So I said I'm going to make it happen and win the fight. I'm going to win very clearly, which I did.

A lot of people have a lot of emotions and opinions of that fight and think it wasn't that exciting—I didn't fight much, they were expecting a slugfest because that's Raquel's style because she's very aggressive. From our side, I went in there thinking I'm going to make a wild fight look very clean and clear. I didn't want this to be a wild fight where at the end of it people would think, *Who do you think won?* I wanted to show people it was clear I was the winner and no questions about it. And I was able to do that. End of the fight I wish I had done more, but that's just the case a lot of the times. Every fight you think you can improve. I also know that I shut down her game in every aspect. It wasn't the most exciting fight, but definitely I was able to control her at her own game. Usually in a clinch there are a lot of scrambles, she comes from a wrestling background than me in MMA.

Q: Later the same year, in Abu Dhabi, you triumphed over Irene Aldana in what served as the headliner. Abu Dhabi has hosted the UFC numerous times now. What was the experience like for you there?
Holm: Well, I knew whatever they had planned there it was going to be a very professional experience. Dana White has been able to travel to all these countries and be very successful. I feel it was a very different type

of fight experience—we were in a bubble we couldn't leave the bubble and go out. We stayed in the hotel, which was a very nice hotel. The people were very kind, the service was very good and we were very well taken care of. There's part of the beach you could go to, but that was all there was because every single business open outside of where we were staying wasn't normal—that's to keep everyone safe and nobody was going to get sick with the Pandemic going on. It was definitely an experience of its own. We had to leave on Wednesday the week prior to the fight, and you leave on a Tuesday week of the fight. So it made one fight weekender into two weeks. Going overseas and you're in a bubble was fine for me because I don't really do a lot anyway other than with my team and focus. It definitely was a very different experience in my life. I wish the situation wasn't like this with the Pandemic going on, but I'm so thankful to fight when so many can't even work.

Q: How do you perceive the future?
Holm: I love that I have been able to have this career. I just turned thirty-nine and a lot of people have been telling me I need to retire. Then after my last fight, everybody said you're becoming . . . I'm still learning so much and getting so much better. I know I still have a lot to show people. I'm so passionate about it I'm going to keep going. It's what I want to do, it's my passion and I keep striding. I keep working toward being the number one. I don't want to sell myself short. Like I said, I don't just want to participate; I want to go back and win. When I was twenty I had my first pro boxing fight. I thought I'm not going to fight past my late twenties that I don't want to get to thirty and still be fighting. Then at thirty I thought, *I can't believe I told myself that.* I started a whole new career when I started MMA fighting at thirty. I said I'll do this for five years, but at thirty-five I was like, *There's no way I'm retiring.* Here I am at thirty-nine. Obviously I still love this and it's who I'm meant to be. Yes, I don't have as much time left now. I still have some time, but definitely not twenty more years. I want to make the best of it, the most of it and don't waste my time, keep training every day, keep getting better and keep following my dreams. Hopefully along the way, if I aspire someone that maybe they're wondering if they can do it also, and they go out there and own it.

Cris Cyborg

UFC Women's Featherweight Champion

Question: What invoked your interest in pursuing and competing in the brutal sport of MMA?

Cris Cyborg: I was a high-level handball player in Brazil. I started training after one of my handball coaches recruited me to the gym. I have never looked at the competition as something brutal. To me it is always an athletic challenge between me and the person I am facing. I train hard and treat my body like a professional athlete. I like the fact fighting is a team sport because it takes a group of people to get you prepared to fight, but I also love that it is individual and it is on me to give my best performance.

Q: What was your family and friends' reactions when you revealed your career path?

Cyborg: My family has always been very supportive. My mom, of course, does not like to watch the fights and gets very nervous, but they have always been supportive of my passions.

Q: Any advice you were given?

Cyborg: I've always had the example of hard work when I first started training in Brazil with the Chute Boxe Academy. It was guys like Wanderlei Silva, Murilo "Ninja Shogun" Rua, and so many others that showed me how hard you have to train to become a world champion.

Q: You beat Holly Holm at UFC 219 (December 2017). She has a strong boxing background, of course. What strategy and game plan did you have going into this fight?

Cyborg: I am a complete fighter—we trained for everything. I felt confident in my standup and felt I won that fight four rounds to one that night.

Q: What trouble did she give you—if she did—and how would you sum up your performance in the fight?

Cyborg: I think it was a great performance and one that fans who enjoy striking can watch for many years. Holly Holm was a 13-time world champion in boxing and the first to ever become a boxing and UFC champion. And I think I showed my fans that my striking is world class.

Q: At UFC 232 (December 2018) against Amanda Nunes, you lost your featherweight belt. You were facing a strong and probably the most dangerous female fighter. Anything significant you can reveal going into this fight?

Cyborg: Everything happens for a reason. I feel I handled myself well in defeat and used the experience to motivate me to improve. They had relocated the event the week of the fight, and I was in the middle of changing management, and I really just went into the competition with too much emotion. The loss made me a better fighter. You can see in my three victories since then I've been more composed, and my strikes landed have become more accurate.

Q: Did she surprise you in any way in the fight, and do you think you surprised her?

Cyborg: No. I think she prepared for that fight and capitalized on it.

Q: Amanda is widely acknowledged as the greatest female MMA fighter of all-time. You are also perceived as being the GOAT. What is your opinion?

Cyborg: You will never hear me say I am the GOAT. I think this is something for the fans to talk about. I have been a world champion for fifteen years, and I feel blessed that fans still remember my fights in Strikeforce, Invicta FC, my time as champion in the UFC, and fans are still watching me defend my Grand Slam Championship with Bellator MMA. There have been so many women in MMA that had amazing careers that fans just never really got an opportunity to see compete. I think the legacy I leave in the sport will always be how my performances and exciting fights inside the cage helped create opportunities for other female athletes to get a chance to showcase their own abilities. I have been in this sport long enough to hear people call me the best, say Ronda was the best, or that Nunes is the best. And I'll probably still be in this sport when people start calling Shevchenko or Zhang Weili the GOAT because when you are a promoter, you always need the next GOAT—that becomes your job which is why I don't really worry about that. For me I want people to remember me, I would say, much rather about my legacy about the changes I made in the sport and the example it left for other women, hopefully inspiring them to continue to evolve the sport.

Q: You have expressed interest in fighting Amanda again in a UFC vs. Bellator matchup.
Cyborg: I am really happy in Bellator. I love the culture of the company. Scott Coker is really taking care of me and it feels like family. I think if Amanda really wants to know what her true market value is, then she should try and fight out her contract to become a free agent like I was able to do in 2020. That is the only way you are really going to know what your value is when you are able to test the market as a free agent. We have already seen Bellator MMA send fighters to RIZIN in Japan. And if that is a fight they want to give the fans, all Dana would have to do is call Scott Coker.

Q: Would you say women MMA fighters are as popular as men now?
Cyborg: I think there are several examples of where the female fighters are even more popular than the men. Women's MMA has proven itself as a ratings success on Network, Cable, Digital, PPV—it has been a success on every platform.

Q: At UFC 240 (July 2019), you beat Felicia Spencer. Do you have anything to share pertaining to this bout?

Cyborg: Felicia Spencer is such a tremendous athlete with a ton of heart. We only fought three rounds, but I set a record for significant strikes landed. I actually landed more significant strikes in three rounds than Amanda Nunes did when she fought her for five rounds. I will always remember how tough Felicia was.

Q: You were cut during this fight. Do you remember what advice your corner gave you in between those rounds?

Cyborg: Blood is just red sweat!

Q: Would you say you've always been competitive as a person, and can you share any anecdote in relation to your passion for winning and bettering yourself as a fighter and human being?

Cyborg: I believe my faith and belief in Jesus Christ as my guiding light has always helped me find passion for life and living.

Q: Why do you think the UFC decided not to renew your contract?

Cyborg: I think they knew I fought the final fight of my contract and was just about to become an unrestricted free agent able to negotiate on the open market. And that I was highly unlikely to sign a multi-fight agreement with the lack of commitment the promotion had shown in developing contenders in the 145-pound featherweight division. I think by that point it was pretty clear that all the top 145-pounders in the world—outside of Amanda—had signed with Bellator MMA, and I had already experienced how one fighter doesn't make a division. The UFC featherweight belt has been defended once in two years, and I'm at a point in my career where I wasn't willing to commit to a promotion not invested in creating the 145-pound division by bringing in the top girls in the world at that weight class to compete.

Q: At Bellator 238 (January 2020), you were crowned the featherweight champion after beating Julia Budd. Do you feel other women

fighters have a hard time breaking you down, both physically and mentally?

Cyborg: Julia Budd went eight years undefeated before that loss and has only been defeated by myself, Ronda Rousey, and Amanda Nunes. She is a true combat sports legend and it was an honor to fight someone with her pedigree. I train hard and am always ready to give 100 percent.

Q: Finally, what's the best *and* worst part of fighting in MMA?

Cyborg: The entire journey of being a fighter is so unique that it would be hard to pick the best and worst part of the experience. I think for me, even if I didn't make any money I still would have chosen MMA because all of the experiences I've encountered along the way are really priceless in reality.

Joanna Jedrzejczyk

UFC Women's Straw-Weight Champion

Question: Did you compete in kickboxing before embarking on your MMA journey?

Joanna Jedrzejczyk: Yes, at age sixteen I started when I joined the Muay Thai team. I didn't know that I was going to be a professional athlete. I loved it when I was doing it because it wasn't about my aggression, or goal of beating up people; it was all about being my own self and I realized that I love to shine. And when I had my first sparring session after two months of training, I felt I was different. I felt I was doing much more than my colleagues, my team mates, because I wasn't stressing. I wasn't nervous. For me every sparring session or every competition was a big challenge. But it changed to further achievement as I triumphed as I started winning major trophies. Then I used to train in Thailand and also in Holland with Ernesto Hoost. Actually, I started winning major trophies under Ernesto Hoost. So it felt good. That's my early background.

Q: When you were growing up as a teenager, did you have health issues?

Jedrzejczyk: Yes. When I was younger I was playing basketball. I was playing different sports in school. And when I was stretching I felt something in my body, so I had to stop when I was playing basketball. But it was a small issue. I had to stop playing but my MMA career is something which would be something bigger later. I stopped training for a bit and put on weight a little bit, that's why I actually started training martial arts because I wanted to lose some weight. And I did.

Q: Let's talk about some of your experiences with the UFC. You made your debut in 2014 with the organization. What enticed you to try this hardcore sport and pursue a perilous journey?

Jedrzejczyk: Actually, the popularity of the sport at that time. I was a multiple Thai boxing champion—European and world—but I was not making money. And I was training at my gym, which was a typical MMA gym, but I was the only one competing in Muay Thai, and I was scared of MMA. The cauliflower ears, the arm bars, all the submissions, I didn't like it. And my body was changing because MMA is a different sport than Muay Thai, because with the latter you burn more calories but in MMA you have to be somewhat muscular to do the wrestling and Brazilian jiu-jitsu. I didn't like MMA because to me it was too brutal. But somehow I adapted very fast. For me it's always a sport, always a competition. One day I said to myself, *Why not? I will go and try Brazilian jiu-jitsu.* My standup was good but I had to learn everything from the beginning. I remember how I got very frustrated, got submitted 20 times each training session, but one day I was like, *Hey, girl, if you want to make the transition, you have to learn the basics. OK, you're multiple Muay Thai boxing champion, but you're white belt Brazilian jiu-jitsu. So, get your ass over to the gym and train and be patient.* So, from twenty submissions a session it went to less.

I was able to roll with the guys and win. Eventually I was on a same level, it was great and I really fell in love with Brazilian jiu-jitsu. It wasn't easy, you know. It's not easy to learn separate arts—wrestling, Brazilian jiu-jitsu, Muay Thai, boxing. The most difficult thing in MMA is putting everything all together—you may be good at striking but you have to be ready for the takedown or somehow able to roll on the ground, too. That was the difficult part. I picked it up fast. I knew I was talented, but talent is not enough, it's also the hard work—something I always had. It was my big dream to fight the best which is why I'm here right now.

Q: You were one of the coaches on *The Ultimate Fighter* in 2016. What was the most intriguing thing for you filming the show?

Jedrzejczyk: The people. I'm always interested in people—and people made me. I love people. It was amazing. I had the opportunity to be in touch with the team, teach them, but also learn from them. It was the most important thing. So, I saw Vegas from a different angle. I love this city. It was a really great experience. It's really hard work. The only problem was Claudia Gadelha, we didn't connect with each other very well, but other than that it was a great experience. It's been a while back but when we finished shooting, my coach came to me, and he said, "You know what, I'm curious how they will show you in this program." Because they can show you as great dedicated coach and friend with the people or they can show you as a rude person like they did with me against Claudia Gadelha. I was the champ at the time so all eyes were on me. They never showed how Claudia always provoked me. I don't care about that, I know who I am. But they showed the worst parts instead of the second [fair] way. But that's fine with me. Other than that it was a great experience.

Q: What is your ultimate goal as an ambitious professional athlete?

Jedrzejczyk: To always be my best. When I was the champ or before I step into the Octagon, I always tell myself, *Girl, you've been working hard, it's just the cherry on the top. Go and shine it doesn't matter whether you win, just go in there and do your best.* I released my second autobiography just now, and my goal always has been to reveal the truth, real drama not the fake. Of course I was always hungry about winning, winning, winning, but after I lost it was painful somehow. Other than that it was a great experience. I'm enjoying my life more and more. Always deliver the best and show people that no matter how hard you fall, you can pick yourself up and win another battle in your life.

Q: At UFC 248 (March 2020), when you fought Weili Zhang—a fight widely perceived as the best female fight in UFC history. What emotions were going through your head as you battled it out with your adversary in what was an absolutely brutal epic battle?

Jedrzejczyk: You know what, I was pushing myself. I was talking to myself in the Octagon, *What can you do better? How can you be faster and stronger? Pick your punches.* Then I was saying, *You're doing your best, you're in the best shape ever.* Even if I lost, I felt I won much more than only the belt. I didn't win the belt but I felt like I had won much more. I knew it was a very close fight. I knew that it was a big fight and lot of going back-and-forth exchanges, and she wouldn't give up! That's why we put on one hell of a show. A fight is a fight. We did the best fight of the year, because we both had been working so hard before the fight in the gym. Because of the amount of the work we put in the gym every day. My friends told me that I'm very disciplined and very focused, but after this fight they said, "JJ, you were so focused on this fight." And that showed. I was very focused and disciplined, every single day I was chasing my dreams. Everything we do there's a risk. In life, too, honestly. I've been in the [martial arts] business the last seventeen years. I've always thought that I don't want to have scars on my face, a broken nose, etc. I broke my hand two times while fighting it was because of the wrong weight. But this fight I finished with a broken hand. The fight with Zhang I realized and questioned myself, *What if this time she's going to damage my brain?* I don't want that to happen. I want to be a business woman. I want to do so many things in my life. Somehow I will do it. The weight class has a big impact, everything has an impact. But if you hurt your hand, you've taken the risk and you just carry on because people don't know that we take risks to be successful not only through good choices but bad choices. My choice was to be the best athlete in the world, the baddest woman on the planet, but there are so many consequences. It is what it is and I love it. This is who I am. I will continue to do this.

Q: You've stated that you're a very busy individual. Being an international athlete you have commitments. Can you shed some light on your typical day or routine?

Jedrzejczyk: If I'm fighting in the States, I go there and train for the fight and stay there. I'm enjoying life. People only want to see me fighting, but I'm a very hungry person in life. I'm living my best life right now. The thing is, if I train I train eight to thirteen times a week if I'm preparing for my fight, three months. Last week I was home for one day only. Because this is how I do business. I do TV, I do movies, and I love it. People say to me, "Oh, focus on just one thing otherwise you're never going to succeed." Yes, I will succeed because I'm hungry. I know what's important and who's important in my life. Some people like to complain and say, "She's doing too much!" No, it's not too much. Maybe for you it's too much, you're lazy. We have different ambitions. Every schedule if I have sponsorship obligations, or media obligations, I try to adjust the schedule. First of all, I'm an athlete and I'm always going to be an athlete. I adjust the schedule but training is the most important element. But after that anything else comes. Every single fighter or athlete, they want to spend their time in whatever way they want to, but I love to work. I like to learn and I like to evolve. That's why I'm hungry. I love life.

Q: What's the salient message or lesson for you as far as career and life is concerned?

Jedrzejczyk: The fact I made it from nothing. People now see me with money, they see me everywhere. But ten years ago I used to work in my parents grocery store, making like 200 Polish money, which is like $50 a week. I can't say I was broke, because I'm rich because of the friends I have. But now I wear my stuff, I drive my fancy cars, but it doesn't matter, because I'm rich because of the family I have. I'm rich because I let my dreams come true. It's not about just training. It's all about putting in the work. It's not about willing to work but putting it into action. This is my success. Becoming the UFC champion was one of the biggest dreams of my life.

Q: How did you celebrate when you became the UFC champion?

Jedrzejczyk: You know what, for me it's never enough. I want more and more. I'm not that content after I win something. I understand it's a job, you go out there and do your best and try to win. But I was very happy that I was able to win something that I really like. We all have to act in our life. It's a role. If I'm a partner to my boyfriend, if I'm a businesswoman, if I'm a daughter, a sister, I'm a role model to people. We all have roles, it's not like fake role acting in the movies—it's a real role. We have to give our best in everything we do in our lives. It's not like I meet my boyfriend today and tomorrow when I meet my friends and I'm acting different with them. OK, my boyfriend is here and my friends are here. A lot of people should understand that we all have roles and we should give our best. Because very often if people climb the mountain, or the business, or they are CEO of a company, or they become a champion they forget something because they're like, *I'm the world champion.* No, you still might be a messed up partner, or a bad mother.

We should do our best in everything we do in our lives. And it's possible. Soon I'm releasing my movie on HBO. They have been following me for the last three years or so. This will be in seventeen countries. So you will learn about who Joanna is. I'm not this only violent person in the Octagon. I'm a very emotional person. It doesn't matter what color your skin is, what religion you believe in, your culture, what city you're from, big or small, your age or gender, we all have a right to live our best every single day.

ACKNOWLEDGMENTS

A HUGE THANK you to the staff of *Martial Arts Illustrated* and *Impact: The Global Action Movie Magazine*: Moira, Martin, Neal, John, Roy, and especially editor Bob Sykes for giving me the opportunity and embracing me earlier on my writing career. The fifteen years working relationship was fun. To all my editors at the magazines and national newspapers whose help and support have contributed to my success in my professional writing career. This includes the newspapers *The Sun, Sunday Times, Sunday Mirror, Daily Mirror, Sunday Express, Daily Star Sunday, Daily Mail, The Independent*, and the magazines *Men's Fitness, Muscle & Fitness, MMA Uncaged*, and *Fighters Only*. Also, I would like to thank the personalities I have interviewed over the years from the sports and entertainment worlds—you are an integral part of the reason behind my success.

I would like to thank my long-time personal friends Diana Lee Inosanto; Royce Gracie; Rasheda Ali; Ron Balicki; Bob Sykes; Ronnie Green; Lance Lewis; Seyfi Shevket; Joe Egan and Peter Consterdine for their countless years of support and encouragement.

I would also like to thank Muhammad Ali's brother, Rahaman Ali, for collaborating on the memoir/biography on his late famous brother—we made history. I would also like to thank my agent, Charlie Brotherstone.

I would like to thank my friends in the industry, both in the USA and United Kingdom, who have enriched my life and supported me.

I must mention some of those who have influenced me as a writer. Some of my earliest influences, first and foremost, have been Bruce Lee biographer John Little. Considered to be one of the world's foremost authorities on martial arts master and action film star, he was selected by the Lee family to review the entirety of Lee's personal notes, sketches and reading annotations and compile books on the late icon including the philosophies of Lee. He inspired me profoundly, which culminated in me being selected by Muhammad Ali's closest family member to collaborate on the definitive biography on the greatest sportsman. Other inspirations of mine include bestselling author Geoff Thompson, who had an indelible influence on me as a writer—both as a magazine and newspaper journalist and an author. I would like to mention Davis Miller—a Bruce Lee and Muhammad Ali biographer—and Matthew Polly—another Bruce Lee biographer—who both had some influence on me in later years. When I was a lot younger, the Canadian bodybuilding writer Robert Kennedy and publisher Joe Weider inspired me and planted somewhat a seed as part of the overall jigsaw.

I would like to thank so many of the UFC champions and fighters who I had the opportunity to interview. Last but not least, a special thank you to my editor Jason Katzman at Skyhorse Publishing in New York. Thank you for believing in me and this book project. Your passion for the subject matter—the sport of MMA and UFC—is clearly apparent.

ABOUT THE AUTHOR

FIAZ RAFIQ is a sports and entertainment professional writer and author. For fifteen years, he was a chief columnist for a bestselling magazine *Martial Arts Illustrated*. He's also a former contributor to numerous magazines, including *MMA Uncaged, Fighters Only, Muscle & Fitness, Men's Fitness*, and *Impact: The Global Action Movie Magazine*. He is a contributing writer for half a dozen prominent national newspapers, including *The Sun*, and has interviewed some of the greatest UFC, boxing, and bodybuilding champions in history, as well as countless Hollywood actors, producers, directors, and showbiz personalities.

Fiaz has written several acclaimed biographies, including *Muhammad Ali: The Life of a Legend, Bruce Lee: The Life of a Legend*, and *Arnold Schwarzenegger: The Life of a Legend*. He also co-authored *My Brother, Muhammad Ali: The Definitive Biography* (with Ali's brother, Rahaman Ali), which was a *Sunday Times* Book of the Year that has been published in seven languages. He's written his acclaimed journalist memoir *To the Top: Enter the Octagon, the Ring, and Entertainment* (a.k.a. *Fighting Against the Odds: An Insider's Life in UFC, Boxing, and Entertainment*), and *Champions of the Octagon: One-on-One withe MMA and UFC Greats*, is his sixth book. Additionally, he was the publisher of UFC legend Randy Couture's *New York Times* bestselling autobiography, *Becoming the Natural*, and also *The Last Round*. Bruce Lee historian, he contributed to the authorized documentary *How Bruce Lee Changed the World*.